A Drink
at the
Bar

'Great success can often find itself the marching companion of personal torment. Graham's insightful and amusing memoirs are tempered with the reality that mastering the court room proved easier than mastering his addiction. Life is a bumpy journey, and this fantastically told story is one full of colour and optimism.' **Sir Charles Walker KBE MP**

'A brilliant combination of the professional and the personal. Intelligent and often wickedly funny about the law. Insightful and moving about the personal struggle behind the glittering facade. Wit and wisdom in equal measure.' **Patricia Hewitt, former Secretary of State for Health**

'*A Drink at the Bar* could equally be called The Tale of Two QCs. On the one hand it is the fascinating memoir of a hugely gifted QC who rose to the very pinnacle of his profession whilst on the other hand it is the candid story of a QC at the top of his game struggling to overcome inner turmoil from the twin afflictions of alcoholism and clinical depression. Author Graham Boal's excellent descriptions of how the entire criminal justice system works and his personal involvement in many of the high-profile cases of the time are an instructive and riveting read whilst his breathtakingly honest, often funny, self-deprecating and disarmingly humble accounts of how he confronted his demons are at times deeply moving.' **Charlie Mortimer, author of *Lucky Lupin* and *Dear Lupin***

'This is a remarkable story of two lives – the successful professional barrister and the private life consumed by alcohol dependence and the resulting disintegration of his personal life. It is written in an engaging and open way that I hope will encourage others to seek help early and also serve to break down the stigma of this pernicious disease.' **Professor Sir Ian Gilmore, Director, Liverpool Centre for Alcohol Research and Chairman, Alcohol Health Alliance UK**

'As Graham Boal himself acknowledges, lawyers' and judges' memoirs have a habit of being either dull or self-serving or both, and pompous to boot. This is none of those things. It is an important addition to the debate around alcohol and depression. The more that we normalise these issues the better. Graham's account captures not merely the horrors of depression and a descent into alcoholism but also shows the additional damage to people's lives done by the stigma and taboo that for too long have surrounded them. That stigma is weakening and this book will weaken it further.' **Alastair Campbell, journalist, author, strategist and broadcaster**

A Drink
at the
Bar

A Memoir of Crime, Justice
and Overcoming Personal Demons

GRAHAM BOAL QC

Quiller

Published in the UK in 2021
by Quiller, an imprint of Quiller Publishing Ltd

British Library Cataloguing-in-Publication Data
A catalogue record for this book is available from the British Library

ISBN 978 1 84689 3452

Jacket design by Guy Callaby
Edited by Kirsty Ennever

Printed in Great Britain by Bell and Bain Ltd, Glasgow

Quiller

An imprint of Quiller Publishing Ltd
Wykey House, Wykey, Shrewsbury, SY4 1JA
Tel: 01939 261616
Email: info@quillerbooks.com
Website: www.quillerpublishing.com

DEDICATION

This memoir is dedicated to my grandchildren,
Matilda and Xander, and to the service users of WDP

'Life begins on the other side of despair . . .'
JEAN-PAUL SARTRE

Contents

Introduction

It never occurred to me that I would write a book for publication, particularly after discovering, over twenty years after the event, that one of the first two items on my Google page still concerns a speech I made in 1999, which caused much offence, and the terms of which I greatly regret. Although I adhere to the point I was clumsily trying to make, the way in which I made it was, as I saw immediately afterwards, highly unfortunate. Thus I assumed that anything I wrote thereafter for public consumption, other than in the course of my job, would be met with the same afterword that I saw in the press every time a case I was trying was reported: namely, 'Judge Boal is the judge who...', as in a Bateman cartoon.

I was encouraged to write this book when a friend of a friend suggested that the story of a barrister and judge who was simultaneously grappling with, and then recovering from, alcoholism and depression, might be of interest to those who were also struggling to hold down a similarly responsible job whilst trying to cope with an addictive condition and/or clinical depression.

This is an account of the life of a barrister who was, or became, an alcoholic depressive: or, perhaps more accurately, the story of a now-recovering alcoholic depressive who was a barrister and then a judge.

My story may have started on the day the Casablanca Conference ended. That was 24th January 1943, and precisely nine months later

I was born. My parents were not in Casablanca, but perhaps they were celebrating. My father, who died when I was fourteen, was described to me as a party animal, but what that phrase meant in the 1940s and 1950s is open to interpretation.

The Casablanca Conference was the summit (although that description had not then been invented) between Churchill and Roosevelt, to discuss the next phase of World War II. It was announced at the end of their discussions that the sole objective was the unconditional surrender of Nazi Germany, and that there would be no negotiated peace. The conference was the result of what had come to be accepted as a turning point in the war and followed the victory at the Battle of El Alamein three months earlier.

Both my parents were in the Royal Navy. My father was by then a Surgeon Captain, and my mother was a First Officer in the WRNS. So had they decided that it was now safe to bring a child into the world? I will never know, but it makes sense.

What a different world it was then. I can look back on a life lived as part of the luckiest generation ever born. Until the outbreak of Covid-19 in 2020, I have lived my life in a country which has enjoyed almost uninterrupted peace; almost uninterrupted, and increasing, economic prosperity; and the prospect of living about twice as long as a man born a century ago. If ever what Cecil Rhodes said about being born an Englishman– 'remember that you are an Englishman, and have consequently won first prize in the lottery of life' – applied to anyone, it applied to me.

The purpose of this memoir is to try to investigate how those two aspects of my life, practice at the Bar and alcoholism and depression, may have inter-related, and to see if what I describe may strike a chord with others, both within and without my profession, in the hope that it might help someone, somewhere deal better with what life throws at him or her. In so doing, I need to try to assess whether I took full advantage of my first prize, but also to chart how these seventy-seven years have been a story of swings and roundabouts, with some successes, some failures, and the hope of recovery from a life-threatening condition.

When it was suggested that I might consider writing a memoir for public consumption, my first reaction was a definite 'no'. That is because, quite apart from the issue I have mentioned in the first paragraph, there are few more boring experiences than ploughing through the reminiscences of retired barristers and judges. These tend to be a recital of the cases they participated in, most of which are of no interest to anyone outside (or indeed usually inside) the profession. They are almost invariably designed to point out the brilliance of the author, who has been a member of a profession populated by prima donnas who are not lacking in an appreciation of their own talents.

Consequently this will not be a rehearsal of 'famous cases I won as a result of my own brilliance'. It is the story of a reasonably successful criminal hack; that is to say, someone whose working life was spent at the coal-face of the criminal justice system. It may be the story of a relatively big fish in a pretty small pond. But, most importantly, it is the story of a man who might be said to have been lucky enough to be able to make the most of the limited talent with which he was born and, in order to do so, had to deal with mental health conditions that could well have spelt total disaster. It is, I hope, a story that might give encouragement to others who have to grapple with similar setbacks.

I was tempted to use as a sub-title of this book 'It Changes', because the story of my life is reflected in that short phrase. It is a demonstration of how, if ever one thinks that things can't get much worse, they will almost certainly get better if one can ride the wave. Equally important, if one is ever tempted to think 'I am on the hog's back, and I will remain on it', then life will almost certainly soon kick you in the teeth.

Acknowledgements

I realised, as soon as I started writing, that I would need an enormous amount of help if I was going to produce something with which I could feel in any way satisfied. I would need help for a number of reasons, foremost among them my inadequate memory of events, some of which took place many decades ago. I was also very conscious of the tendency in all of us to mis-remember events and yet to be quite certain that they happened in the way we are convinced they did. All of us are tempted to overestimate our achievements and to underplay our failures: to justify our actions, and to excuse our mistakes.

For all those reasons I decided I would try to put together Team Boal, to make sure that I was kept, more or less, on track. I was amazed and gratified at the way that everyone I approached so readily agreed to play the part I asked of them. Nobody 'made an excuse and left', nor suggested that it might not be something worth doing. That was particularly so when I explained that this was not simply going to be a recital of cases I had appeared in, but that there were other reasons why I felt that this account might be worth recording. Those reasons will be found in the last chapter of the book.

Julian Bevan QC, Sir Allan Green QC and Timothy Langdale QC, all of whom practised with me at the criminal Bar, have held my hand as I committed to paper my recollection of cases, making sure as best they could that I did not fall into too many elephant traps. To those who wonder whether my recollection of the facts of those cases can possibly be as detailed as they may appear, and whether the quotations can be as accurate, I can give the assurance that I have not relied solely on my own memory: rather, I have relied on research by Alastair Young, Olivia Hill and Sarah J. Booth, to all of whom I am immensely grateful for the work they have done on my behalf. To Stephanie Mocatta, for trying to instil some basic computer skills in me, and to Christopher Penn for his contribution, I want to register my gratitude.

I also have most particularly to thank my 'board of censors and critics', who have given me the benefit of their views, and whose criticisms and vetoes I think I have, on almost all occasions, accepted: most important in that category are my wife Lizzie, our son Thomas, and our daughter-in-law Miranda, all of whom have been kind enough to say that the finished product does not embarrass them.

Last, but by no means least, I express my thanks to Heather Holden-Brown, to whom I now proudly refer as 'my literary agent', and to Andrew and Gilly Johnston, and all those at Quiller Publishing, who have shown sufficient faith to enable the book to appear. Quiller chose Kirsty Ennever to be the editor of this book. They could not have made a better choice. Kirsty and I have worked together like two instruments in a duet, and I could not be more grateful to her. Should I also thank Patrick Clarkson QC for suggesting to Heather that she contact me, as well as for his edits? Time will tell.

Chapter 1

THE BEGINNING

How did it come about that I went to the Bar, and practised at the criminal Bar for thirty years before becoming an Old Bailey Judge? There was no background of law in my family; indeed, although I know precious little about my antecedents, there was no hint that my future lay in that direction until a doctor in Eastbourne was charged with murder.

My father had retired from the Royal Navy in 1947 and, aged sixty-one, took the job of school doctor at Eastbourne College, where, for the next ten years, he ministered to the boys at the public school and its preparatory school. I was an only child and my parents and I lived in a small but comfortable house in the grounds of the prep school.

In the twenty-first century there is much talk of austerity, but nothing we have encountered as a result of recent economic crises and even the Covid-19 pandemic could compare with the state of the nation in 1947. It was only two years after a war that had not only killed and maimed a very significant number of people, including thousands of civilians, but this country was virtually bankrupt. Bomb sites were everywhere (I even remember one or two in Eastbourne, caused by German bombers offloading surplus armaments before flying back across the Channel), rationing was strict and punitive, and people were beginning to realise that peace did not spell prosperity.

My first recollection is of the winter of 1947–48, the harshest in living memory, and of going round our small frozen garden looking for sticks to be used as firewood. Life was much tougher for most people than it was for me. After nursery school I went to Ascham, the prep school, but living in the school grounds meant that, between the ages of eight and thirteen, with my father a member of staff, I was neither fish nor fowl. Our house overlooked the playing field between the two boarding houses, and I was a dayboy, regarded, as happened in private education in those days, as a second-class citizen. During school breaks, or after the other dayboys had gone home, the boarders played on the field, and my mother spent most of her time looking out of the kitchen window to make sure that her 'Petty' had not fallen over and grazed his knee. My father was too old, too ill or too weak to try to impose much influence on either mother or son. I was brought up by a mother whose protective instincts amounted to an obsession.

Perhaps this rather unusual upbringing, which today might even be described as bordering on dysfunctional, contributed to my problems later in life. While my mother doted on me and tried to wrap me in cotton wool, my father concentrated on his work in the college sanatorium. In the course of his work he necessarily issued prescriptions.

Dr John Bodkin Adams was a GP in Eastbourne. In 1956 he was highly respected and was idolised by many of the elderly widows who lived in that respectable seaside town, with one of the oldest, and best off, populations in the country. The unfortunate fact was that too many of those elderly matrons seemed to be dying whilst under the care of Dr Adams, who coincidentally seemed to be getting quite rich via bequests made under the wills of his late patients. In due course a police investigation uncovered extensive misuse of drugs which, if administered by the doctor, had hastened the death of some of those patients. Dr Adams was charged with two counts of murder and a number of offences under the dangerous drugs legislation current at the time. I should add immediately, that after a trial at the Old Bailey that enthralled the public and the media, the accused was acquitted of murder.

If convicted, Dr Adams would undoubtedly have been hanged. Capital punishment was widely supported, indeed hardly questioned, as the sentence for murder, and this was an age in which the criminal law was harsh. The principles upon which the criminal justice system was based were largely unaltered since Victorian times, and the popular press usually had as its main story a murder trial from the Old Bailey. In 1952 the public had been absorbed by the trial of R v Craig and Bentley, after which the nineteen-year-old Bentley was hanged in circumstances which would horrify us today. A year later, Reginald Christie, a serial killer of women at 10 Rillington Place was hanged for murder, and it became blindingly obvious that he had murdered Beryl Evans, whose husband Timothy had been wrongly hanged for killing her. It was that undoubted miscarriage of justice that led me to a lifelong opposition to capital punishment.

So how did the arrest of John Bodkin Adams lead me to the Bar? Dr Adams had covered his traces by forging the signatures of other doctors in the town, including my father's. This so intrigued the thirteen-year-old me that I determined to try to see Dr Adams in court. My memory tells me that I managed to insert myself into the public gallery at the first remand hearing at Eastbourne Magistrates' Court, but it may have been the first day of the committal proceedings in Lewes: wherever it was, my brief moment in the public gallery before being thrown out for being under age was enough. In my mind's eye I can imagine myself gazing down upon the bald head of Dr Adams and thinking 'you will hang'. Whether this vision is real or not, just being in the court was a life-changing experience, as

I was instantly captured by the drama in front of me. I went straight to a second-hand bookshop and bought the rather dog-eared copy of the biography of Sir Edward Marshall Hall KC by Marjoribanks that sits on my bookshelf to this day. I was spellbound. I couldn't put it down. From then on there was nothing else I wanted to do in life. I didn't want to be 'a lawyer'; I was determined to be a criminal barrister, and dreamt of the day that Graham Boal QC would address a jury in Court One of the Central Criminal Court, Old Bailey. I don't suppose that I imagined, in even the wildest of those dreams, that such a thing would ever come to pass.

My father died shortly after the Adams trial, aged seventy-three, and I was left to grow up with my widowed mother, herself now in her fifties. It was a rather isolated existence, and my mother became even more protective of me. Not unnaturally, she was anxious for me not to stray too far from home and, knowing of my interest in the law, she determined that I should become a solicitor in Eastbourne. There was no way that I intended to sit in a solicitor's office in a provincial town, conveying houses, drafting wills and attending meetings of Rotary. Even then, the thought of that way of life, however respectable, sent shivers down my spine.

At Eastbourne College I did not shine academically, nor indeed in any other way, unless it was on a tennis court as the result of sustained coaching. The absurd system by which boys were educated in public schools in those days meant that our education was unbalanced. I was reasonably, but not very, clever, and at the age of fifteen was required to specialise. I found myself studying modern languages, for which I had little aptitude, and spent not a single term being taught any science whatsoever. In my last year I was allowed to take up the subject which appealed to me most, namely modern history.

My housemaster, 'Teddy' Craig, like many other schoolmasters in the 1950s and 1960s, had been to university before the war, then served as an officer for its duration, and become a teacher afterwards largely because he wasn't cut out to do much else. Having accepted that it would be pointless to try to divert me from my ridiculous ambition to be a barrister (and thinking that it would be a good idea anyway for me to struggle free of my mother's apron strings), he realised that I would have only very limited resources with which to set off down the precarious path I had set for myself, and so took advice as to how this might be done. He thought that I had a reasonable chance of securing a place at Trinity Hall, the premier Cambridge college for aspiring lawyers, but advised me to take up an offer to read law at King's College London, where I would be studying within a stone's throw of The Temple, and would be in easy reach of an Inn of Court. That turned out to be one of the best pieces of advice I ever received.

I arrived in London at the beginning of the Swinging Sixties, but life for me, although new and exciting, did not exactly swing. That was mainly due to the fact that I had very little money. My father had left me £10,000, and I knew that was all I had to see me through university, studying for the Bar, pupillage and the first precarious years of practice. Although I was conscious of the life others were living in Carnaby Street and the King's Road, Chelsea, I did not have the wherewithal to participate. I lived first in a university hall of residence, then in a hostel in Lancaster Gate, and finally in a two-bedroomed flat beside a tube line, which I shared with three others, two medical students and a trainee stockbroker. In Lancaster Gate, my hostel was all of 400 yards from the tube station, but I remember many days when the London smog meant that I quite literally could not see my hand in front of my face as I walked from one to the other. This description is not intended to be a hard luck story: I thoroughly enjoyed my life.

At King's I immediately got an immensely lucky break. By chance I found my personal tutor to be a man called Jimmy Wellwood. Wellwood was one of those academic lawyers who, although called to the Bar, was never cut out to practise in court, and so taught at university. Once he too had failed to persuade me to desist from my ambition, he took me under his wing. He was not only the student adviser at Gray's Inn, which I immediately joined, but a great friend of one of the leading juniors at the criminal Bar, Roger Frisby. Without the coincidence of Jimmy Wellwood being assigned my personal tutor, I believe that none of what follows would have occurred. Roger Frisby was to play a very important role in my life, part positive and part negative, as we will see in due course.

I found the law degree punishingly turgid. I had no interest whatsoever in how citizens of the Roman Empire contracted to sell slaves under Roman law; I was bored to distraction by the Law of Property Acts, and how I got through the exam on equity will always amaze me. The only subjects that interested me were jurisprudence (marginally), criminal evidence (because I had to master it), and criminal law itself, parts of which fascinated me. I regarded getting a degree in law as being a necessary step, but I managed only a 2:2 (known nowadays as a Desmond', after Archbishop Desmond Tutu).

At university I lived a 'flat' life, rather than a student life. I never bought a college scarf, I only rarely went to The Chesham (the college club), and I dressed rather more conventionally than most students. My life involved going to lectures by Tube, coming back to the flat, and spending most of my time either in the pub with the boys or trying to 'pull birds'.

As to the latter activity I was singularly unsuccessful. I put that down to the fact that I was not particularly physically attractive, the fact that I had even less money to spend than most of my peers, and to my complexion. For as long as I can remember I have had vulnerable skin. As a teenager I had bad acne, which in the end was treated by a new drug called Roaccutane. This caused my lips to parch and had other mildly unpleasant side-effects. What was unknown at the time, however, and remained undetected for many years, was that one of the drug's side-effects could be to cause serious depression. By the time I was in my late teens I was suffering what I now realise were episodes of depression, leading to loss of self-esteem and anxiety. With the benefit of hindsight, I have no doubt that therein lay the seeds of the serious depression I suffered later in life and, as I will argue later in this memoir, depression and alcoholism go together like the proverbial horse and carriage.

After university, those entering the legal profession with the intention of practising divide into those intent upon qualifying as barristers and those who want to practise as solicitors. I of course had already decided upon my path, and so the next step was to pass my Bar Finals. To do so as quickly as possible, and with funds running out fast, I enrolled in a crammer in Chancery Lane called Gibson and Weldon. At the same time I was eating my dinners at Gray's Inn.

The Bar is an ancient profession, and some of its traditions seemed old-fashioned even in 1966; some have been significantly relaxed since then, but remain basically the same. In 1966, to qualify as a barrister one had to join one of the four Inns of Court (Lincoln's Inn, Gray's Inn, Middle Temple and Inner Temple), and eat thirty-six dinners in Hall, twelve a year over a period of three years. The idea was to allow the student to be baptised into the traditions of the profession, and to meet and mix with the barristers in practice as well as the Benchers, the senior barristers and judges, and in effect the 'prefects'. To the outsider it must all appear arcane and pompous, but it did serve a purpose. There was a collegiate atmosphere, and one learnt, almost by a process of osmosis, the rules of the game.

Much to my surprise, I passed the Bar Finals, and was called to the Bar by The Honourable Society of Gray's Inn in the summer of 1966. I was now a barrister. Jimmy Wellwood had persuaded Roger Frisby to meet me with a view to offering me a pupillage, and one day in the autumn of 1966 I made my terrified way to 3 King's Bench Walk, the chambers occupied by Roger and about eight other barristers. Somehow Roger was persuaded to accept me as his pupil for six months and, having paid him the customary fee of fifty guineas, I took my place at a desk in his room.

This country in the 1960s was one which, despite our retreat from Empire (emphasised by the recent humiliation of Suez), was still a major player in the world. The old order may have begun to lose control, with such events as the Profumo scandal undermining an establishment that was increasingly out of touch with the mood of the age, but London was still regarded as the capital of the world and it was an exciting place to live. The Swinging Sixties was a time of sexual freedom encouraged by the availability of the contraceptive pill, and John Lennon declared, to no one's great surprise, that The Beatles were 'more popular than Jesus'.

The year 1966 was a momentous one, quite apart from the fact that it was the year in which I was called to the Bar. Harold Wilson was Prime Minister and had hugely increased Labour's majority in the March election. In May, Ian Brady and Myra Hindley were convicted of the notorious Moors murders, in August the nation was shocked by the shooting dead of three unarmed policemen in Shepherd's Bush, and in October 144 people (including 116 children) died at Aberfan in South Wales when a coal spoil tip collapsed and engulfed a school. The coal grime we all saw on our television screens in many ways reflected the state of a nation slowly emerging from a dark age: though on 30th July the whole nation had been uplifted by England defeating Germany 4-2 in the final of the World Cup at Wembley. All over the country, in pubs and bars, the politically incorrect chant of 'two world wars and one world cup; we are the champions' could be heard. I probably sang it myself.

Chapter 2

PUPILLAGE

Pupillage means apprenticeship. In 1966 it did not quite mean sitting at a tall Dickensian-style desk with a quill pen and a pot of ink, but the young barrister of today would find what we did all those years ago almost incomprehensible.

There were no computers, and everything was done on hard copy: there was no internet, no mobile phones (let alone smart ones), no Google and no apps. If we needed to consult a law report, we took the book off the shelf; if we needed to take a law report into court, we either took the book itself or a photocopy, which was regarded as ultra-modern. The statements of witnesses were all on paper, as were the documentary exhibits. All serious criminal cases started with committal proceedings in the magistrates' court, before being 'committed' to the assizes or quarter sessions (it was some years before the Crown Court replaced them); and the 'deposition' of each prosecution witness had to be recorded, either in handwriting or on a typewriter, by the clerk of the court. Every witness had to attend in person, even the plan drawer and the photographer. That was the world I entered.

Roger Frisby was a tenant in the chambers of William Howard QC, at 3 King's Bench Walk (KBW) in the Inner Temple.

So what exactly is a tenant, and what is/are chambers? Barristers practising at the independent Bar are all self-employed. Each is an individual practitioner, dependent on the fees he himself can command, and in no form of partnership or fee-sharing arrangement with other barristers.

Here I must post three health warnings. The first is that I have referred to a barrister as 'he'. Throughout this memoir I may refer to barristers and judges by using that pronoun. I will do that simply to avoid writing he/she and him/her all the time; it is not intended as some form of chauvinism, and I hope it will be accepted in the way it is intended.

The second is that I will, from time to time, when referring to judges, even of great eminence, do so without according to them their full titles. Instead of, for instance, always writing Lord Chief Justice Lane, I may refer to him as just Geoffrey Lane. That is not out of disrespect or impertinence, but because, if asked in a robing room, 'who are you appearing in front of?', one would inevitably reply using the more familiar form of address.

The third warning I should utter, at this very early stage, is that, although I have checked my sources to the best of my ability, and with the help of those I have mentioned in the acknowledgements, I am largely reliant on my own fragile memory. With the passing of time, memory fades, and can become distorted, and one can come to the honestly held belief that something happened which in fact did not. I will be subject to all those fallibilities, but all I can do is assure the reader that if my attempts at accuracy do not succeed, it will not be because of any attempt to deceive. As one gets older, I think there is a tendency for the human mind to blot out things its owner wants to forget, to embellish others to his own advantage, and to make a good story even better by subconsciously 'adding a little parsley to the dish', as my father-in-law once described it.

With those three caveats in mind, I will return to my theme.

There is no fee-sharing among barristers, but there is expense-sharing: barristers form sets of chambers so that they can share premises, share administrative costs, and operate the return system, which is critical to any set, particularly a criminal one. I will explain returns in due course.

A typical set of criminal chambers, like ours, consisted in the 1960s of about ten barristers, ranging in seniority (or 'call') from one or two silks (QCs – Queen's Counsel) down to junior tenants who had qualified relatively recently. The best balanced sets would try to achieve quality on all rungs of the ladder. That is because the only way a barrister gets work is if he is instructed (briefed) to conduct a lay client's case by a solicitor, and a firm of solicitors tends to want to instruct only one or two sets, and to be able to rely on finding quality counsel to conduct their cases all the way up and down the scale of the seriousness of the alleged offences. Thus the solicitor prefers to go to the same set to instruct a particular QC to represent an alleged murderer, and to the most junior tenant to defend a client charged with shoplifting.

A QC is a senior barrister who has been awarded 'silk' by the Lord Chancellor. Every year the Lord Chancellor appoints new ones, and the list, in my day, was always published on Maundy Thursday. If a barrister felt, usually after twenty or more years in practice, that he wanted and deserved to take silk, he would apply to the Lord Chancellor and try to garner the support of senior judges in front of whom he had appeared. Why might someone decide not to apply for silk? The answer is that it represented a risk. In those days (although the rule has been watered down considerably since then), no silk could appear in court without a junior, which meant that the client then had to pay for both, or the legal aid authorities must be persuaded to issue 'a certificate for two counsel'. Thus, although the potential for higher earnings existed if one took silk, it was equally possible for a junior who did so to price himself out of the market. Why 'silk'? Simply because, whereas juniors wore 'stuff' (wool or cotton) gowns in court, QCs wore gowns that were not only different in design, but were made of real or artificial silk. On ceremonial occasions, a silk also wore a full-bottomed wig, which made him look like a basset hound, rather than the ordinary barrister's wig. (May I add, that I don't think I have ever seen a film or television programme in which they have got the robes right!)

In practical terms, how does a solicitor instruct counsel to conduct a case? This is where the engine-room of chambers is to be found. Each set employs clerks; a head clerk, and maybe two or three junior clerks. A barristers' clerk is a unique animal! He is not legally qualified; he is a mixture between a market trader and an NCO in the army but in some ways a CEO. He (and again, it could be he or she) is the go-between, the negotiator, the diary-keeper, the business manager, indeed the lifeline upon which the barristers depend. Traditionally (and while I was in practice it was the reality), a barrister has nothing whatsoever to do with the rather distasteful and vulgar matter of being paid for his services; it would have been serious professional misconduct for a barrister to be found on the telephone to a solicitor negotiating a fee for a privately funded case. Mostly, of course, the defence of alleged criminals was funded by legal aid (i.e. state funded), so the negotiation was either non-existent, because the fee was fixed, or was an *ex post facto* haggle with a civil servant, acting as a taxing officer. For prosecution work, rarely and only in important cases, the negotiation was in advance of the case and was with someone in the prosecuting authority; most of the time it was again a case of *ex post facto* bargaining with a civil servant.

The senior clerk was in a position of great authority; he could make or break a young barrister. The best way of describing the relationship between a senior clerk and a barrister in his early years is to draw the analogy of the junior army officer and his CSM or even RSM. Apparently the renowned RSM Brittain would shout at a young man fresh out of Sandhurst: 'I call you Sir, and you call me Sir; the only difference is that you mean it and I don't.' That says it all. The senior clerk would address the most junior tenant as 'Sir', and the young man called his senior clerk 'Fred'; but there was no doubt about who held the whip hand.

The senior clerk at 3 King's Bench Walk (3 KBW to us all) was Diana; clerks never had surnames in my time. Diana, who was then almost unique as a female senior clerk, was known throughout the Temple as 'the Duchess'. She was a lady of ample girth, and she presided over chambers from behind a director's desk, with rather too much of her elastic knee-length stockings visible through the knee-hole opening. The only possible description of Diana was 'formidable', and she looked after her charges like a benevolent, but firm, mother hen. The job of chief clerk to a successful set of chambers was jealously guarded, and tended to be passed from father to son in a way that would have made freemasonry look open and above-board. I never discovered how Diana managed to penetrate this secret, and almost exclusively male, society, except that she had been a junior clerk-cum-typist in the chambers two doors down from ours at 5 KBW.

If you were unwise enough to go into Diana's room when she was on the telephone to a solicitor, you might, before she shooed you from the room, have overheard a conversation that involved elements of horse-trading, bargaining for a carpet in a souk, and negotiating the transfer of a Premier League footballer. The returns system, as this process was known, meant that if solicitors and lay clients could not obtain the services of the counsel of their choice, provided that the solicitor concerned felt confident in chambers as a whole, he could be assured that he would get someone who would do the job to the best of his ability. That is how young tenants got their first briefs and, if they performed in that first case satisfactorily, then next time that solicitor might even specifically ask for Mr McSnooks. If even McSnooks was unavailable, and Diana had no one else to offer who might be acceptable, then it might well be that in The Feathers (a local hostelry, much frequented by barristers' and solicitors' clerks) that the I'll-scratch-your-back-today-if-you-scratch-mine-tomorrow returns system would operate between clerks from different chambers. We, the principals, were never let into the secrets of how work was distributed. If anyone dared to pry, he would probably be told to do his job and 'I'll do mine . . . Sir'. Being a pretty non-commercial animal, I was delighted that, throughout my career, I never had to negotiate my own fees, which I would have found excruciatingly embarrassing. It was bad enough occasionally hearing one's clerk telling a solicitor complete fibs about one's abilities, experience and successes!

That is the world into which I walked in the autumn of 1966 to start my pupillage with Roger Frisby. To my recollection there were then perhaps ten tenants and a couple of other pupils. They were, as was typical in those days, all male, white, and had been educated, I suspect, at public schools. But, although Bill Howard (William Howard QC) was head of chambers, as with the RSM in a good regiment, the entire edifice in many ways rested on the broad shoulders of Diana, assisted by one or two junior clerks.

I was lucky enough to be pupilled to one of the most able and respected advocates at the criminal Bar. He was also one of the nicest and kindest. I could not have had a better tutor. Within a week Roger had taught me many of the most important lessons that aspiring criminal barristers should learn, none of which are taught in the course of obtaining a law degree or studying for Bar Finals. One of the first things he said to me was this: 'I hope you haven't come here with any grandiose ideas about putting the world to rights, reforming the law, or upholding human rights. A barrister is a hired advocate, here to do a specific job and to represent a specific interest, whether he believes in it or not.' In other words, he was explaining the cab rank principle, of which much more anon. He went on to put the job of a criminal barrister in very simple terms. 'If you are prosecuting, you are not there to obtain a conviction at all costs; you are there to present the evidence and, if that evidence justifies it, to point out to the tribunal that it would be open to it, magistrates or jury, to find the case proved. If you are defending, however, and if your client maintains that he is innocent of the charge he faces, then it is your duty, while obeying the rules, and without misleading the court, to do your very best to obtain his acquittal.' He also quickly taught me some basic rules of advocacy, perhaps the most important of which was that if you could possibly avoid it, do not ask a question to which you do not know the answer. Another sage piece of advice, to which I have not always paid attention in my life, was 'if in doubt, don't'.

Roger's practice at that time, and until he took silk shortly after my pupillage, was predominantly prosecuting, and he was probably the first choice of the Solicitor to the Metropolitan Police (known to all of us as 'Sol Met Pol' or SMP). Roger was almost always first choice for cases prosecuted by SMP at the Central Criminal Court (the Old Bailey). He was such a good prosecutor because he was meticulous and scrupulously fair. Juries loved him. He was good-looking, had a mellifluous voice, and presented the case with such clarity that every juror understood what he was saying. In every case the proceedings start with the prosecution opening, at which the prosecutor outlines the case for the Crown (all prosecutions are brought in the name of the Crown: hence R v John Smith) and Roger's presentation was such that I often heard it said that 'when Frisby has sat down after opening the case, the defendant is dead before a word of evidence is uttered'. In due course, in silk, Roger became an equally formidable defender, until the demon alcohol got to him.

So what did I do as Roger's pupil? The pupil follows his master everywhere, and is not excluded from any aspect of his practice. He sits in his room preparing cases with him; he attends 'conferences' (meetings with professional and lay clients; when prosecuting, including the police officers in charge of the case); he goes into court with him, where he keeps a note of the evidence for him;

after court goes back to chambers with him to mull over that day's proceedings and prepare for the next. In Roger's case, and in the case of this pupil, it also involved going to El Vino's with him. It should be said at this juncture that El Vino's, situated in Fleet Street just outside the Temple, epitomised the hard-drinking culture of the Bar, and particularly the criminal Bar, at the time.

How could I help Roger prepare for a case? From day one, Roger would ask me to help draft his opening speech. That meant reading every word of the police report, every word of every witness statement, researching any law that applied to the case, and summarising the issues of law and fact with which the jury would be concerned. Obviously my early attempts were pathetically inadequate, but as time went by, and to my great satisfaction, I found increasingly that chunks of my draft were included in the finished product.

Crime, like ladies' clothing, goes in fashions. In the 1960s two of the most popular ways for the professional criminal to earn his living were by armed robbery (blagging) and disguising stolen cars for resale to an unsuspecting public (known as ringing or cut-and-shut). Because he was so meticulous, Roger was renowned as the most effective prosecutor of ringers.

For the uninitiated, ringing meant stealing a car, usually quite an expensive one, then buying a wrecked car of the same description and cutting them both in half. By attaching the undamaged half of the wreck to one half of the stolen car, the stolen one could then assume the identity of the legitimate wreck, and be sold on the open market to an unsuspecting purchaser. Well done, it was almost a work of art. At that time, a man known as 'Wingie' Cope (so called because he had lost an arm when a hoist fell on him whilst plying his trade) was the professor of ringing. To achieve the perfect job, not only did the criminal have to be a skilled welder, but he had to perfect the art of transferring the chassis and engine numbers of the straight car to the bent one.

To present the case convincingly to a jury entailed explaining all this, and showing in meticulous detail how it was done in the particular case. This involved drafting schedules (but without the benefit of Excel!), which gave registration, chassis and engine numbers, dates, details of re-sprayings, and all the other bits of the jigsaw, so that the jury could see exactly what had happened. I spent many hours and days of my pupillage drafting these schedules. Tedious it might have been, but rewarding when it passed muster with Roger and found its way in front of the jury to be explained by him. One of my finest hours was when Roger showed me a note that had been passed to him by an aficionado in the dock which read: 'Bloody marvellous schedule, Mr F. We're fucked.' Such was the respect between two professionals, each at the top of his game, that the crook could rely on Roger not to use that note against him. He subsequently had quite a few years during which to reflect upon the beauty of my schedule.

Blaggers were a different kettle of fish altogether. Armed robbers were, on the whole, ruthless professional criminals, who were quite prepared to use serious violence. Blagging, which was extremely prevalent in the sixties and seventies – and indeed until criminals discovered that dealing in drugs was a safer occupation – referred to holding up security vans carrying large amounts of cash. Very often there was an 'inside man', who might even be one of the security guards in the target van, but sometimes the guards were taken totally by surprise and subjected to the threat or actuality of serious violence by men carrying loaded, sawn-off shotguns. Two of the most dangerous armed robbers in the late 1960s were the notorious John McVicar (about whom a great deal has been written, including by himself) and a man called Tony Baldessare.

Roger's work while I was his pupil was not exclusively for the prosecution, and I was privileged to see him defend Baldessare when he, McVicar, and two others were tried for armed robbery at the Old Bailey. Trials for armed robbery followed a pattern. The prosecution evidence was almost exclusively that of police officers, usually from the Flying Squad (aka the Sweeney, from cockney rhyming slang, Sweeney Todd). Their evidence would include observation of the robbers, often over weeks, and then the actual scene at the robbery, where there would be an armed stand-off: all of this was possible because of 'information received' from an underworld 'grass'. The icing was sometimes put on the cake by 'verballing' the defendants, i.e. putting alleged admissions into their mouths. At trial the police would be accused of all kinds of chicanery. The defence would be alibi ('elsewhere' in Latin): this almost always involved calling the villain's 'moll', who would swear blind that she and the defendant were tucked up at the time of the robbery with a cup of Horlicks watching *Coronation Street* or similar, which had indeed been watched (no recording in those days!) and scrupulously noted by some associate. The trials were always no-holds-barred bloodbaths of suggestions and counter-suggestions of perjury.

This case was no different, and although Roger performed brilliantly, exposing a number of inconsistencies and porky-pies in the evidence of the police officers, all four defendants received substantial prison sentences. John McVicar, who subsequently turned over a new leaf and became a well-known author, journalist and social worker, was at the time of this trial one of the most dangerous criminals in England. He was immensely strong and spent his lunch hours in the bowels of the Old Bailey bending the bars on the window of his cell. He acquired further notoriety two years later in 1968 by pulling off an incredibly daring escape from HMP Durham.

At court, my primary job was to keep a note of the evidence. There were no laptops, and my shorthand (by which I mean secretaries' shorthand) was non-existent. But in every case, whether prosecuting or defending, my note had to be relied upon when Roger closed the case for the prosecution or defence at the end of all the evidence, and occasionally when there was a dispute as to what a witness had said. Towards the end of my pupillage Roger would ask my views on how to cross-examine a witness, and even how to compose his final speech. Of course he didn't always adopt those views, but it was a sign that he thought I was beginning to learn my trade.

I could not possibly have had a better pupillage, and the first indication that I was passing muster came when Roger offered to keep me on for a second six months as his pupil. I gladly paid him another fifty guineas. After that – the crunch! Was I going to be offered a tenancy at 3 KBW, or would I have to hawk myself around the Temple, looking for a tenancy elsewhere, or even abandon the project altogether?

Chapter 3

THE SECOND SIX MONTHS

During the second six months of my pupillage I was able to do work of my own. Although the majority of my working life was little different from what it had been in the previous half-year, occasionally a junior clerk would tell me there was a case for me to do. That would inevitably be to prosecute a case of shoplifting in a London magistrates' court, to defend in some minor matter in a magistrates' or youth court, or to attend a court of quarter sessions to make an unopposed application, for instance to change the date of a trial. When it was the latter I would proudly don the robes and virgin-white wig of a barrister, and try to look like one.

I vividly remember my very first case. Prosecutions for shoplifting were conducted by solicitors acting for the store in question, and I was sent to South-Western Magistrates' Court on Lavender Hill to prosecute a lady for stealing something fairly trivial from Selfridges in Oxford Street. I was instructed by Jeffrey Gordon, the senior partner of a small firm, whose offices were near the court. Prosecuting such a case involved calling to give evidence the shop detective who spotted the misdemeanour and the police officer who was called to the store to arrest the miscreant, and then finally cross-examining the defendant. The usual defence was 'I left the store having totally forgotten to pay'; if that was indeed the defence, then it could be that one question in cross-examination would suffice, namely 'if that were the case, Madam, could you explain to the magistrate(s) why the offending item was stuffed up your jumper?' (Incidentally, I refer to magistrate(s) because sometimes the bench consisted of three lay magistrates but more often, especially in central London, a stipendiary magistrate, who would be a qualified barrister or solicitor who spent his working life sitting in these courts. Not a job that ever appealed to me!)

That first outing to South-Western Magistrates' Court in early 1967 earned me the princely sum of £4 6s 6d (four pounds, six shillings and sixpence) or, in today's coinage, about £4.40; that amount might represent nearer £60 today. Of that, probably the shillings and sixpence went to my clerk. That fee represented part of my first year's income, the totality of which resulted in my having to pay Her Majesty's Inland Revenue something a little in excess of £6 as my contribution to the national debt. So proud of that first fee was I that, once I had paid it into my bank, I persuaded Jeffrey Gordon to retrieve the paid cheque from his bank and send it to me. It hangs in my loo to this day.

Since the main object of pupillage is to learn one's trade from one's elders and betters, part of that second six months was spent going to court with other members of chambers, for the obvious reason that if I had spent my time exclusively with Roger Frisby, I would never have seen, and thus learnt how to conduct, a case of burglary or assault occasioning actual bodily harm, which was the daily fare of the young criminal barrister. Thus there occurred one of the first of many embarrassing moments in my career.

Before the Courts Act 1971, cases too serious to be tried in the magistrates' courts (which tried well over ninety per cent of criminal cases) were tried either at quarter sessions, presided over by judges or senior barristers, or at assizes, which tried the most serious cases, and were presided over by High Court ('red') judges.

I was lucky enough to go to the Bar just as legal aid was beginning to pay for the defence in almost all criminal cases, and which provided reasonable fees for the work done, but it did not cover all cases. There remained two ways in which a defendant without legal aid could be represented. The first was 'court legal aid', whereby the judge could order that the barrister would be paid *ex post facto* by queuing up at the taxing office in the court building, to be paid whatever the taxing officer deemed appropriate; that was usually worth having. The second method, a hangover from time immemorial, was 'the dock brief'.

I had first come across the dock brief at school, when I acted the part of a barrister in the play with that title by the great John Mortimer QC. I had already decided that I wanted to be a criminal barrister, and I think that I was in charge of the Eastbourne College Dramatic Society, and thus able to choose the play and my part in it. Much later in life I was to be against John in a number of cases and we became firm friends. When our son Thomas was at school and due to play the part of John or his father in *Voyage Round My Father*, John was kind enough to dine with Thomas, Lizzie and me at The Garrick, and to give Thomas valuable tips on how to play the part. Now I was to find out what a dock brief was in real life.

The macabre way in which some defendants acquired representation at assizes was that they would be brought up into the dock at the beginning of the day's proceedings and allowed to choose any barrister then sitting in court to represent him on a 'dock brief'. Many barristers, whether they had briefs or not, would attend the assizes, and so, after the rush for the door of more senior counsel who had no desire to be chosen had abated, the defendant would be confronted by those who remained, of whom he could see only the backs of their wigs. It was well known that the wiliest of old hands would often deliberately choose the whitest wig, in the hope that judge and/or jury might feel pity for him being so inadequately represented. If singled out, the barrister was bound to take the case, and the prisoner would be required to hand over the £4 6s 6d, which was usually provided by some friend or relative in the public gallery.

One day it was suggested that I go with two or three members of chambers to Hertford Assizes, as there was a spare seat in someone's car. They all had briefs; I was there to observe. As soon as 'the dockers' were put up, my three friends disappeared, and I was left, with one or two others equally wet behind the ears, facing The Honourable Mr Justice Gerald Howard, one of the most feared judges ever to grace the High Court bench. The hairs on the back of my neck rose in terror as I heard the old lag immediately behind me say 'I'll have this one' and then, in even greater terror, as the judge in his red robes, prompted by the clerk in front of him, looked me straight in the eye and said 'Mr... er... Boil, take the money which will be handed to you, go below and take instructions'. Wishing that the earth would swallow me up or I might be allowed to crawl back to London and become an accountant, I pocketed the money collected from the public gallery, grasped in a sweaty paw the copies of the prosecution witness statements I was given, and retired to the robing room to read the case against the unfortunate man who was now my client.

The defendant was charged with 'the abominable offence' of buggery. He had a list of previous convictions as long as your arm for offences ranging from dishonesty to almost every sexual offence in the criminal calendar. When I met him in the cells he appeared as revolting as his record might suggest. The evidence against him in the instant case could only be described as overwhelming, including an alleged confession of guilt to the police. In a visiting room below the court he started to explain to me how he had been fitted up, 'verballed' by the police, and falsely accused by a young complainant whom he had never met, and whose determination to frame an innocent man he could not explain.

For the next two and a half hours, and in increasing desperation, I tried to explain to my client how hopeless his proposed plea of 'not guilty' would be, and how much he would incur the wrath of the merciless old judge who would sentence him after he'd inevitably been found guilty. I am quite sure that my endeavours were motivated more by the panic in my breast at the thought of putting this defence forward to a hostile court than by concern for my client's interests but, at about 12.45, my client asked: 'What do you think you could get off if I pleaded guilty . . . which I am not?' After obeying, as succinctly as possible, the rule that a barrister must say to his client 'you must only plead guilty if you are in fact guilty', I said that I thought that a plea of guilty might reduce the sentence by a third, particularly as I had been told that the judge wanted to get back to London that afternoon. Breathing the biggest sigh of relief of my life, I walked up the steps into the well of the court and told the clerk that he could inform the judge that my client would be pleading guilty at two o'clock.

One of the great traditions of the Bar was the Bar mess. It was where the barristers, of all seniorities and on both sides, had lunch together. Although it was an ancient tradition, it also served a purpose; one could ask questions, seek advice and experience the camaraderie of the profession. In Hertford the Bar mess was in The White Hart, a pub in the high street, which set aside a private room at lunchtime during the assizes. When I arrived in the mess that day, and gave the others the good news that I would not have to conduct a hopeless contested case, I was persuaded to sit at the table and order something to eat, even though I knew that, with the prospect of addressing Howard J in mitigation that afternoon, I would not be able to consume a morsel. I paid for the lunch I did not eat, and the glass of wine I did indeed drink to give me Dutch courage, with the better part of the dock brief fee.

When I got back into court, I found myself on the receiving end of one of the few acts of benevolence ever attributed to

Gerald Howard. As soon as he came into court he looked at me and, with the hint of what passed for a smile, he said 'Mr Ball, my clerk tells me that you spent the entire morning making this man see sense' (yes, those were the words a judge felt able to use in those days), 'and so I have decided to grant you court legal aid. Give back the dock brief money.' Horror – I only had half of it left! Luckily others in counsel's row appreciated my dilemma, and notes and coins were hastily passed along the bench.

The stress of this whole experience has wiped from my mind any recollection of my plea in mitigation or the ensuing sentence. Suffice it to say, that when I went down to see him afterwards, my client greeted me with a smile and a warm handshake, and said 'well done young man; you'll do; I'll have you again next time'. I am pleased to say that I never saw him again.

Having been blooded by this experience, I felt that nothing could ever be as bad again. I spent the rest of those six months either with Roger, or going to see how it was done by other tenants, or by earning the occasional crust on my own behalf, until one day towards the end of the period I was summoned to go and see Bill Howard, the head of chambers. I had hardly exchanged a word with him thus far, and I think that if we passed in chambers he may well have thought I was the junior clerk. After a few preliminaries, he began: 'Roger tells me you may have some potential, although I doubt it, and he has persuaded me to offer you a tenancy. Would you like to join 3 KBW?'

I need hardly describe my reaction. I was about to become a fully-fledged barrister, practising in one of the most respected sets of criminal barristers.

Chapter 4

THE EARLY YEARS

Any ideas that the aspiring barrister may have about the glamour of practice in the early years, or upholding human rights and righting injustices, are dispelled as he stands on a cold, wet platform of Liverpool Street station, waiting to catch an early morning train to attend Grays Magistrates' Court in Essex.

Very soon after the bubbles have evaporated from the bottle of champagne opened to celebrate the award of a tenancy, the young man or woman is confronted with the realities of scraping a living in one of the most challenging and competitive professions in this country.

One of the first things that happens after you are admitted as a tenant is that the senior clerk tells you the terms and conditions of your tenancy. You are now effectively a sub-tenant of the head of chambers, who has a tenancy agreement with the Inn of Court that owns the building. When I arrived we were crammed into the first floor of 3 King's Bench Walk, which consisted of three rooms, and what passed for a fourth room, which was more like a cupboard squeezed between the two larger rooms. The largest room, overlooking the Temple was, in comparison to the others, relatively spacious, and was the silks' room. Bill Howard QC had a large desk, Roger Frisby QC, as he became shortly after my pupillage, had another, slightly smaller, one, and a third desk was shared by 'door tenants' in silk. Door tenants were those whose main practice was in other parts of the country, but who needed a base when their practices brought them to London. Mark Carlisle QC MP, who practised in Manchester and was briefly Secretary of State for Education in Margaret Thatcher's government, was one. Charles Mantell, who ultimately became Mantell LJ, was another. As we expanded, others had to be squeezed in, including Robin Grey QC. Jeremy Connor, who became a highly regarded stipendiary magistrate, occupied the cupboard. The rest of us, including David Jeffreys, the 'senior junior' (in other words, the most senior barrister not in silk), were crammed into another room like sardines. The one opposite the front door was occupied by the clerks, from where Diana could observe all who came and went. She shared her room with her junior clerk, Graham (who left to become a milkman), and Peter, who I think came to us straight from school. The Health and Safety Executive, if it had existed, would not have tolerated the conditions in which we worked.

A special mention must be made of Julian Bevan. Julian was three years older and had been called to the Bar two years before me. Just as at school, that two-year seniority meant that at first I treated him like a prefect, but we soon became very close friends. He was my best man when I married in 1978, we climbed the greasy pole together with me just behind him, he became one of the most sought-after silks at the criminal Bar, and to this day in retirement we speak on the telephone at least once a week. At one time, I have been told, we were described as 'the two golden boys of the criminal Bar', but that was probably when we were in our thirties and had full heads of hair. Julian was far better looking than I was.

Although we were the best of friends, Julian and I, like all barristers, were, at least in theory, in competition with each other for work, and could at any time have found ourselves on opposite sides in court. More by luck than good judgement, this happened only once, much later in our careers, in a case he prosecuted and I defended. Needless to say, my client was convicted. I say more by luck, because it could easily have happened more often and neither of us could have refused. That is because of the 'cab rank principle', to my mind one of the most hallowed of all principles of the Bar, and one which I will explain in due course. Although we found ourselves co-defending (defending two co-accused in the same case) more than once, the only other time we found ourselves on opposite sides of the fence was decades later when Julian appeared in front of me at the Old Bailey.

Not long after I became a tenant, we acquired the tenancy of the ground floor of the building and so, not only could we spread our wings a little, but we took on a few more tenants to share the increased rent. On the ground floor I found myself sharing a small room with James Kynoch. I soon discovered, because he told me, that James was 'a recovering alcoholic'. That phrase meant little more to me at the time than that he drank sparkling water at chambers' dinners and parties and didn't come with us to El Vino's. I was to learn a lot more about it later in my life.

After telling me what my share of the rent would be, Diana then turned to what was for her the more pressing issue of clerks' fees. At that time it was pure and simple: ten per cent of every fee. At the end of each month I would get a bill which would record the fees that had come in that month, my chambers' bill for rent and other expenditure, and the percentage I owed Diana. I quickly worked out that the amount due to go into my pocket could amount to a minus figure.

Those of a mathematical bent will have already worked out that ten per cent of the gross fees of ten barristers might mean that the senior clerk should earn about the same as a middle-ranking tenant. The senior clerk had to pay the junior clerk(s) but, as chambers expanded to about fifteen tenants, some of whom were making a pretty good living, Diana never seemed to be on the breadline.

Like all barristers, I was self-employed, meaning that we had to pay, in addition to our chambers' rent and clerks' fees, for everything we needed; moreover nobody paid us if we were off sick, or for such luxuries as health insurance or pension provisions, and every day's holiday was a day upon which one was not earning.

The very early days of my tenancy weren't very different to the last months of my pupillage so far as my practice was concerned. I flogged round the magistrates' courts of London, and sometimes into the Home Counties, mainly to Hertfordshire and Essex. My first dock brief, as described above, was at Hertford Assizes because we at 3 KBW were all members of the South Eastern Circuit and Hertford was one of the assize towns on our circuit, as were Chelmsford and Lewes amongst others.

The circuit system dates back to when High Court judges, as His/Her Majesty's Judges of the King's/Queen's Bench Division went out on assize to administer justice. They went from one assize town to the next, dealing with the serious cases in one court before moving on to the next, and the Bar travelled with them; hence the Bar messes in assize towns like Hertford. All barristers had to be members of one or other of the six circuits in the country: the South Eastern (or 'home') Circuit, the Western, the Midland and Oxford, the Northern, the North-Eastern and the Wales and Chester. This mattered because the circuits, together with the Inns of Court, provided the regulatory and disciplinary machinery for the profession, and venturing onto another circuit cost you not only 'place money' in compensation for pilfering their work, but usually the displeasure of those into whose robing rooms one dared to tread.

As well as being a member of a circuit, a barrister would join county Bar messes, which also jealously guarded their boundaries and did their best to repel boarders. As I write this I am conscious of how anachronistic all this must appear to a twenty-first century reader, and how such procedures would today fall foul of the Monopolies' Commission and several other bodies designed to minimise any apparent restraint of trade or discrimination. But at the time we all accepted these archaic arrangements because, as well as upholding professional standards, they helped give everyone a fair crack of the whip. In my own case it helps to explain why, at least in my early years, if I went out of London, it would almost always be to courts in Hertfordshire and Essex, because I, together with others at 3 KBW, was a member of the Herts and Essex Bar Mess.

What was my daily fare in those difficult but stimulating initial years? The only prosecuting work available to me at first was those shoplifting cases, but any defence work I got could be anything from representing a motorist charged with driving without due care and attention to representing a murderer or armed robber at 'the first remand': that was usually the day after arrest, when the defendant was first put before the court and, as is reported frequently in the media, 'the accused said nothing other than to confirm his name and address'. His young brief had to stand up and say nothing more than 'on behalf of X I have no application to make at this stage'.

That is how I met Ronnie and Reggie Kray. The Kray twins, whom we all knew to be notorious and vicious criminals, were finally arrested by a hand-picked and dedicated team of police officers under the command of Superintendent Leonard 'Nipper' Read on 8th May 1968. Nipper had conducted a long and perilous investigation over many months, trying to persuade a terrified East End underworld that they would be better off without the reign of terror the twins had presided over for years. They had murdered, terrorised, blackmailed and stolen, and such was the power they exerted that for years the territory over which they ruled was populated by people who, like the monkeys, saw nothing, heard nothing, and spoke to no copper. Ronnie Kray had shot George Cornell in the public bar of the Blind Beggar pub in the Whitechapel Road, at point-blank range and in front of numerous witnesses, not one of whom saw or heard a thing. Read finally breached this wall of silence by donning a dog-collar, which allowed him access to pubs and cafés, thus gaining the confidence of ordinary witnesses and some of the Krays' lesser confederates.

The Kray twins were arrested with about fifteen other members of 'The Firm', including elder brother Charlie, and would have to be brought before a magistrates' court as soon as practicable after they were charged. The twins, and most of the others, were invariably represented by the East End firm of solicitors Sampson & Co, and whenever they were nicked they would always shout for a managing clerk called Manny Freyde. Manny, who was 'standing brief' to The Firm, was South African by birth, had qualified there, and then, under slightly mysterious circumstances, had come to London where his reputation, at least with the police and prosecuting authorities, was such that he was not regarded as a man of the highest integrity. He was not a qualified solicitor in this country, but he effectively ran Sampson's, with the solicitor of that name always acting, in criminal matters, almost as a front-man, since only a qualified solicitor could have his name on the brief. As soon as The Firm was banged up on 8th May, Freyde started ringing round the Temple to rustle up the appropriate number of young barristers, ability immaterial, to make sure that each of his clients was represented at the first remand hearing. In court each brief would rise in turn, intone that he had no application to make, and resume his seat, whereupon the accused would be remanded in custody.

Sampson's had instructed 3 KBW from time to time (Bill Howard had represented one of the Great Train Robbers for them) and so Diana was obviously one of the clerks Manny Freyde telephoned, probably as follows: 'Anyone will do; he won't have to do anything; I've told the boys there'll be no bail applications; three and two,

Diana, take it or leave it.' This meant that the fee would be a total of five guineas – three for the court appearance and two for the non-existent 'conference' beforehand.

The first remand hearing took place at Bow Street Magistrates' Court. My memory of that morning is a bit vague and blurred but I do remember certain things clearly. The first was the media scrum outside the court; I had never experienced anything remotely like it before. Security was tight, even if nothing like the circus that accompanies high profile cases today. As I said, there was a young barrister for each prisoner, and once we had all satisfied the authorities of our identity and purpose, we fought ourselves into the small foyer and then, after more checks, into the cell area. I can't remember for sure who my client was – I think it was one of the Lambrianou brothers – but somehow the prison officer must have thought I was representing one of the twins. The melee in the tiny cell holding area was about as thick as the media scrum outside, and in the confusion I found myself 'meeting' Ronnie and Reggie. The encounter lasted only a matter of seconds, and before you could say much more than 'Good morning – Mr Freyde says there'll be no bail applications today', we were all whisked into court and out again in a matter of minutes. I don't know whether I had expected 'Violet Kray's boys' to have horns or exude the scent of evil but, handcuffed to burly guards (probably police, as opposed to prison, officers) they appeared quite small and insignificant.

The next day I would most likely have come back down to earth and represented an unfortunate driver in a far off 'police court', as magistrates' courts were known. They were correctly so identified, because probably the most difficult feat of advocacy that any representative could ever be asked to attempt was to secure the acquittal, on a plea of 'not guilty', in front of a bench of lay magistrates when the client's defence involved an attack upon the credibility of police officers. It was more difficult than pushing the biblical camel through the eye of a needle.

I defer to no man in my admiration of the lay magistracy. Men and women, from increasingly varied walks of life, give, and have given for centuries, of their time and experience to deal with well over ninety per cent of all crime tried in this country. They do it, I am convinced, to the best of their ability, and as best they can observe the judicial oath to try cases 'without fear or favour, affection or ill will'. Nevertheless, by the very fact that they sit in a localised jurisdiction, and tend to regard the local police force as 'our policemen', the tendency to accept a prosecution case, even in the face of an objectively reasonable doubt, is sometimes something lay justices find difficult to overcome. I will give two examples from my own personal experience of the unique perils of defending in such courts, particularly if one's client has the impudence to plead 'not guilty'.

I went to Tottenham Magistrates' Court one day in the late sixties or early seventies to defend a young man, doubtless with little to recommend him, on a charge on which the evidence was paper-thin. The chairman of the bench was a local butcher, who had the reputation of being as tough as some of the meat he purveyed. At the end of the evidence I made an impassioned speech, reminding the bench, probably ad nauseam, that they could only convict if they were sure of guilt, and that if they felt there was a reasonable doubt, then that doubt had to be resolved in favour of the defendant.

The bench retired, and were out for longer than the time usually taken for the normal statutory coffee break. When they returned, the butcher's face was even redder than it had been when he left the bench; there had clearly been disagreement in the retiring room. He told the defendant to stand, and addressed him in these terms: 'Your solicitor' (one was addressed as such in most magistrates' courts) 'has urged us to find a doubt in this case; reluctantly we agree that there is a doubt, but we cannot give you the benefit of it. We find you guilty.' I got to my feet and, addressing the clerk of the court, told him, I hope politely, that he only had two choices: either to take the magistrates out again and explain to them the error of their ways or I would be off to the Divisional Court – the court that dealt with appeals from magistrates' courts on a point of law. The clerk duly invited the bench to retire again with him, and about ten minutes later the butcher and his colleagues returned, with the chairman even redder in the face. 'I'm told we've got to say not guilty; so we will.'

Another peril was that, in some magistrates' courts, the prosecution was not always represented by a qualified lawyer, but by 'the court officer', usually a police inspector. One day I went to Guildford Magistrates' Court to defend a man charged with dangerous driving. Whenever dangerous driving was alleged, there was always the alternative lesser verdict of 'not guilty of dangerous driving; guilty of careless driving'. Before the case started I tried as hard as I could to persuade my client that his best chance of avoiding disqualification would be to allow me to see if I could persuade the prosecution to accept a plea of guilty to the lesser offence. My client would have none of it. Nonetheless I thought I would put my toe in the water and explore the possibility with the police inspector who was conducting the prosecution. To cut to the chase of the story, the cross-examination of my client went like this:

> 'Are you saying that there was nothing wrong with your driving?'
> 'Yes.'
> 'You weren't driving either dangerously or without due care and attention?'
> 'Certainly not.'
> 'In that case, could you explain why your solicitor came up to me and asked if I would accept a plea to careless driving?'

My client looked daggers at me, the inspector couldn't understand why I was on my feet objecting and the chairman of the bench looked equally perplexed. Only the court clerk understood when I said: 'Either you order a retrial in front of a new bench, and explain to the inspector that "counsel-to-counsel" conversations cannot be used like that, or I am off to the Divisional Court . . .'

A few days later, there was a retrial in front of another bench, and my client was (rightly) convicted of dangerous driving and disqualified. The solicitor who had instructed me on his behalf, quite understandably, refused to pay me a second brief fee. The moral of this story? Know your court!

A young barrister, with the help of his clerk, should always try to establish a tiny corner which becomes his own niche area of practice. I was lucky enough to find mine when I became, for some unknown reason, counsel of choice for taxi drivers who were members of the London Taxi Drivers' Association and who themselves had a niche practice at Heathrow Airport. The LTDA was an old-fashioned trade union, which defended its members through thick and thin in every aspect of their working lives, including in court. A tight little group of cabbies ran a closed shop at Heathrow, enforcing an unwritten rule that only members of their closed-shop community could force their way to the front of the queue at the arrivals' cab rank, from where they drove foreign passengers who asked to be driven to central London halfway round the Home Counties before depositing them at their destination. They were known as 'the Heathrow cowboys', and there was constant warfare between them and the airport police, who would charge them over and over again with such heinous crimes as 'failing to conform to a lawful instruction' to move on.

Day after day, week after week, I would drive my old Triumph Herald to Uxbridge Magistrates' Court to defend these cabbies, usually repeat offenders. They invariably pleaded not guilty but they were always convicted. Two weeks later I would be defending the same client, who regarded the fines he received as a form of income tax, to be offset against the exorbitant fares with which they were fleecing unsuspecting foreigners. This little corner of work was for me what the cabbies would describe as 'a nice little earner'.

Uxbridge Magistrates' Court was presided over by a lady called Mrs Fisher, who seemed to me to bear a remarkable resemblance to Mrs Bucket (pronounced Bouquet) in the television comedy *Keeping Up Appearances*. She appeared in court wearing a suit and pearls and always wore a hat that seemed to be adorned with fruit salad. She and I struck up a kind of relationship, particularly after the nice clerk of the court told me that he had informed her that barristers did not necessarily always believe their clients, but were duty-bound to advance the case with which they were presented. Once that was understood, Mrs Fisher treated me with courtesy and respect, but invariably went on to utter the words 'we find the case proved'.

It was in front of Mrs Fisher that I first played the word game. This involved opposing barristers each nominating a word which his opponent had somehow to incorporate into his submissions to the bench, obviously the more outlandish and irrelevant the better; nothing, other than downright obscenity, was out of bounds. On this occasion I was prosecuting for a change, and the defendant, whose alleged motoring offence is irrelevant to the story, was represented by my great friend Roger Henderson, one of whose daughters is now my goddaughter. The bet was for five pounds. Roger gave me 'lawnmower' while I gave him 'sodomy', thinking I was on to a sure winner. My task was relatively easy; I suggested to the driver in cross-examination that he was being so unobservant that he would not have noticed if a gardener had been wheeling a lawnmower across the road. Job done. I sat back and waited to see how Roger could possibly bring my word into his final address to Mrs Fisher and her colleagues. In a speech of which Perry Mason would have been proud, Roger solemnly said this: 'Madam, I hope you will forgive me if I remind a bench even as experienced as this of the burden and standard of proof that applies to every case in these courts, from a case at the bottom end of the scale such as this, right up to a case as serious as murder or sodomy.' The five-pound note that Roger had placed on the bench between us went straight back into his pocket, and I felt obliged to push another one back along the bench towards him.

Everything seemed to happen in Uxbridge. On another occasion I was sent there to conduct a prosecution under the Dangerous Dogs Act. The offending animal had savaged a postman and the application, which the owner stoutly resisted, was to have the offender put down. The owner, and indeed the dog vicariously, was represented by Roy Amlot. As soon as we met, Roy told me that, despite the overwhelming evidence, the case would be defended: 'I'm afraid it's a fight, Boaly.' When I suggested that I would give him a lift back to London, after which we might have lunch together, Roy went off to make one final attempt to persuade his client to accept the inevitable. Ten minutes later he came back with a blood-stained handkerchief wrapped round his hand and exclaimed 'it's a plea, Boaly'! Roy went into court, pleaded guilty on his client's behalf and mitigated with one hand behind his back. We were in the car shortly thereafter. Happy days!

Within three or four years of becoming a tenant I was beginning to make occasional appearances, for both prosecution and defence, in the quarter sessions courts of Hertfordshire and Essex; that is to say at Chelmsford, Southend and St Albans; or even, very occasionally, a plea in mitigation of sentence after a plea of 'guilty' at Essex Assizes, Hertford Assizes, or the Old Bailey (the Central Criminal Court, but always referred to as 'the Old Bailey' because that was the name of the street upon which it was built).

In the days before the Courts Act 1971, prosecutions in the counties were undertaken, if not by the Director of Public Prosecutions, as in very serious cases, in one of two ways. Either there was a County Prosecuting Solicitor, as in Essex, or by private firms of solicitors instructed directly by the police, as in Hertfordshire. The latter method worked surprisingly well; solicitors in private practice were able to do what barristers applying 'the cab rank principle' did all the time, namely acting for the prosecution in a case one day, and acting for a defendant the next day in another. To my mind, the method worked particularly well, because it gave the solicitor the balanced approach that I believe it gives a barrister, enabling him to appreciate the problems faced by the other side. I found the Essex County Solicitor far more inflexible, and more difficult to deal with if trying to negotiate a plea: in other words, agreeing that a defendant would plead guilty to a lesser offence if the prosecution would drop the more serious one. That sort of perfectly respectable deal would also save the public the unnecessary expense of a contested trial.

My practice first took off at Southend Quarter Sessions, to which I would travel from Fenchurch Street station, in due course often with a fistful of small briefs; sometimes the entire list of 'pleas' (of guilty), appeals from the magistrates' courts, applications of one kind and another and so on, in the list for that day in one of the two courts. That 'nice little earner' was something I inherited from a more senior member of chambers when his practice took him up to a higher rung on the ladder, and I was found to pass muster with the then county prosecuting solicitor, Mr T. Hambrey Jones. In due course the odd Essex solicitor, having seen me in court, decided to brief me, and that in turn led to work in Chelmsford as well.

But it was at St Albans that I really found my niche and started to establish a reputation of sorts. I spent much of the next few years driving my (now increasingly ancient) Triumph Herald up to St Albans, to appear before the chairman and deputy-chairmen of Hertfordshire Quarter Sessions, and it was here that I cut my teeth in front of juries. Strangely, I have no clear recollection of my first jury trial, but I would be prepared to bet that it was at

St Albans that I first addressed that body of twelve citizens that I had set my heart on addressing all those years ago in Eastbourne. I prosecuted or defended, taking on any case that came my way; mostly burglary, minor assault and minor fraud. For some reason there was at the time a spate of dishonest milkmen in Hertfordshire, who overcharged the housewives of the county.

By 1970 I was earning the sort of income that allowed me to upgrade my Triumph, and to pay the instalments on a hundred per cent mortgage of £18,000 on a small terraced house in Peel Street, in then non-trendy Notting Hill Gate. In those days it wasn't known for celebrities, expensive restaurants and fashionable clothes shops. Only twelve years earlier, the terrible Notting Hill race riots of 1958 had occurred just up the road: and when I moved in, cars very like my own were parked in Peel Street, rather than the Range Rovers, Mercedes and Porsches that you might find there today. To give some context, in 1970 the voting age was reduced from twenty-one to eighteen, the half-crown ceased to be legal tender, Prince Charles joined the Royal Navy, Edward Heath succeeded Harold Wilson as Prime Minister, and feminists disrupted the Miss World contest hosted by Bob Hope.

On New Year's Day 1972, however, the criminal justice system in England and Wales underwent a huge transformation.

Chapter 5

THE MIDDLE YEARS

British currency may have gone decimal in 1971 but, for the criminal barrister, the most important thing that happened that year was the passing of the Courts Act 1971. Originally the brainchild of a Lord Chancellor's Office under the then incumbent, Lord Gardiner, Harold Wilson's Lord Chancellor, the act was actually passed during Edward Heath's tenure, with Lord Hailsham (Quintin Hogg) as Lord Chancellor. It came into effect on 1st January 1972. Notably, four days later (and nothing to do with the passing of the act), Rose Heilbron became the first female judge to sit at the Old Bailey. That is worth remembering when one hears suggestions in the twenty-first century that there are not enough female judges. Judges are usually appointed perhaps thirty to thirty-five years after they are called to the Bar, and when Rose Heilbron was called there were very few female barristers.

The Courts Act, designed to modernise the criminal justice system, abolished assizes and quarter sessions and replaced them by a single Crown Court, which would deal with all 'trials on indictment' (i.e. all cases too serious to be disposed of in the magistrates' courts). These Crown Courts, which would sit in court centres all over England and Wales, would be presided over by circuit judges (an entirely new name), or by a new breed of judicial animal altogether, namely Recorders – senior barristers who would sit as judges, not full-time, but for stints of about a month at a time. In practical terms, the passing of the Courts Act didn't make much difference to the day-to-day workings of the court, except that the circuit judges were now to be referred to as 'Your Honour', and would wear what most of us regarded as very unattractive robes. These included a kind of belt of a singularly insipid mauve colour, set off, when the judge was trying crime, by a sash of bright red, which clashed violently with the belt.

A word of explanation might be required at this stage. The uninitiated might suspect that circuit judges would go out on circuit. Wrong. They didn't go anywhere; they sat at their court centres. Meanwhile, High Court judges did not remain at the High Court at the Royal Courts of Justice in the Strand; as well as sitting there, they went out, as before, to try the most serious cases on circuit. Confused?

Did that mean that all cases of murder and other very serious offences would now be tried in Crown Courts on circuit? Not quite! The Old Bailey retained its jurisdiction to try cases that would otherwise have to be tried by 'red' judges (so called because, when trying crime, they wore scarlet robes). These were cases in which the crime had usually, but not necessarily, been committed within the Greater London area. Before the reader's confusion becomes any greater, we will move on to something more digestible, and return to the jurisdiction of the Central Criminal Court (the Old Bailey) later.

The year 1972 was a particularly violent one of the Irish Troubles. So far as my future practice was concerned, perhaps the most significant events were what became known as Bloody Sunday on 30th January, and the IRA bombing of Aldershot Barracks on 22nd February, which left six dead. On 30th March the Parliament of Northern Ireland was suspended, and in April a report (subsequently described as a whitewash) by the then Lord

Chief Justice, Lord Widgery, exonerated all the British soldiers who had been present at the events that had taken place in Londonderry (Derry to republicans) on that fateful January Sunday. Little did I know at the time how much influence those events arising from Irish nationalism might later have on my professional life.

Around that time I passed an important milestone: I got onto 'the Yard list'. This meant that I became eligible to prosecute for the Solicitor to the Metropolitan Police (SMP), whose main office was still then at New Scotland Yard. Getting onto the Yard list was an essential hurdle for any criminal barrister practising in London to jump, unless he was content not to prosecute within the metropolis. It was a critical moment when my clerk came to me with 'a blueback'. All briefs in which the prosecution was conducted by SMP were wrapped in a pale blue back-sheet and tied with white ribbon; all other briefs had white or cream back-sheets and were tied with red (or pink) ribbon.

The arrival of the blueback meant that I was to undergo the Yard test: I was to go to some outlying court, in my case Wallington in south-west London, to conduct an insignificant case for the prosecution. I knew that sitting at the back of the court in a corner of the public gallery, supposedly unobtrusively, would be a Yard clerk (an experienced managing clerk who had seen it all before), who would observe my performance and report back to head office. I have no recollection of the case I was entrusted with (I was probably too frightened to remember), but I do remember my own clerk coming into my room perhaps a week later with another brief with a blue back-sheet and white tape. I had passed the Yard test. This meant that I could add another, very important, dish to the menu of what I was now qualified to do. At first, of course, it would mean doing the rounds of London magistrates' courts, but in due course I found myself briefed to prosecute in the higher courts.

In the new decade, my practice began to include more and more jury trials. These were now probably almost equally divided between prosecution and defence and involved my appearing in Crown Courts all over London and in St Albans, Chelmsford and Southend, with the occasional foray to the Old Bailey. The latter usually involved me being led. In those days, silks (QCs) could only appear in court accompanied by a junior – a barrister, of whatever call, not in silk. These junior briefs were, in many ways, the jam on the bread and butter; usually one had little to do, other than taking a note for one's leader and making the occasional suggestion on the conduct of the case, which was usually rejected. It was still the almost invariable custom that the junior was paid two-thirds of the silk's fee, though there was always the exception. One of these was a case where I was led by Bill Howard in a plea of guilty. When Diana had completed the usual hard-fought battle with the aforementioned Manny Freyde for Bill's fee, she dared to ask about mine, to which Freyde replied: 'Sod the junior!' Diana persuaded him that it would be improper for me to go into court without any fee marked on my brief but Freyde's response was that she could write anything she liked on my brief, provided that that amount was deducted from Bill's fee. I didn't get much. A 'sod-the-junior brief' became a term of art in our chambers.

Obviously, appearing in my own right, I had days I cared to remember, and days when things didn't go quite to plan. A case that I still regard as constituting one of my few genuine forensic triumphs was heard in these comparatively early days at either Middlesex Quarter Sessions or Middlesex Crown Court (I can't remember exactly which side of the implementation of the Courts Act it took place). In any event, the case was tried in the building the other side of Parliament Square from the Houses of Parliament, now occupied by the Supreme Court. I was briefed to appear for a doctor, who was charged with driving whilst under the influence of alcohol. These were pre-breathalyser days, and the evidence to support the charge came, as always, from police officers and the police doctor, a medical practitioner who was on a rota of doctors who could be called to the police station, day or night, to examine motorists arrested for the offence.

My client had been stopped by the police after apparently committing some road traffic offence on his way home late at night, having attended the annual dinner of the London Irish Medical Golfing Association. That was not a good start; indeed, if I had been prosecuting, I might have been tempted to use the American expression, never uttered in our courts, of 'I rest my case'. Things got worse. The evidence of the police officers was that as soon as my client opened the driver's door, he vomited over their boots. Then on the way into the police station he repeatedly fell up the steps. When my hero was examined by the police doctor, he fell over twice while trying to walk the statutory white line, and the nystagmus in his eyes (a sure sign of disability) was the worst the doctor had seen in years.

By the end of the prosecution case it looked hopeless: hopeless, that is, until I called in evidence three doctors who had attended the abstemious dinner with my client. The first doctor gave evidence that the vomiting must have been due to the fact that, when my client felt a little unwell towards the end of the dinner, he, the witness, had prescribed a little warm milk which, with the benefit of hindsight, he thought might have been a mistake. The second witness told the jury of the accused's appalling in-growing toenail, which would have caused him to fall almost any time he tried to walk. With the jury, if not the judge or prosecutor, beginning to enjoy this greatly, the third learned medico described in great detail how the nystagmus was the result of an unusual condition of the inner ear, only recently diagnosed. At the end of the trial the jury retired, barely able to conceal the smiles on their faces, and returned ten minutes later with a resounding verdict of 'not guilty'.

One of the days at the other end of the spectrum was when a client of mine, at the end of a searching cross-examination by my opponent, suddenly exclaimed 'Oh, fuck it; have it your own way', and strode out of the witness box and down into the cells.

The courts then were full of personalities. Two of them frequently crossed swords at the Middlesex Quarter Sessions. The judge was Ewen Montagu who, as a naval intelligence officer in the war, had come up with the idea of 'the man who never was' for Operation Mincemeat. The barrister was Sir Harold Cassel Bt, who had suffered terribly in a Japanese prisoner-of-war camp, and who always said that, as a result of that experience, he now feared no man. These two men loathed each other, probably for reasons obscured by the mists of time, but every time Harold appeared in front of Ewen the sparks would fly. On one occasion I was privileged to witness, when Harold was defending, his final speech to the jury included the words: 'His Lordship is, as you will see from the shields that adorn the walls of this court, the latest in the line of chairmen of these quarter sessions, going all the way back to Judge Jeffreys, who presided over the notorious Bloody Assizes. It will be up to you to decide, members of the jury, whether you think much has changed in the intervening three centuries.'

Harold Cassel teased Ewen Montagu mercilessly. One of Harold's more irritating eccentricities was that, when prosecuting and addressing the jury in his final speech, commenting disparagingly on the evidence of the defendant, instead of looking at the jury to whom he was talking he would put one foot up on the bench, exposing an expanse of brightly-coloured sock, whilst staring at the man in the dock. It was an effective technique, but one that Ewen Montagu rightly thought was bordering on the unfair. On one occasion, when Ewen could restrain himself no longer, he snarled at Harold:

'Mister Cassel,' he deliberately omitted the sir, *'when you are addressing the jury, please do them the courtesy of looking at them.'*

'If Your Lordship pleases,' replied Harold. *'Would Your Lordship be kind enough to give me further and better directions?'*
'What on earth do you mean?'
'Would Your Lordship please give me a direction as to which particular juror Your Lordship would like me to look at?'
'Don't be so insolent!' was all the learned judge could spit in response.

Game, set and match!

Although there were moments of great mirth in court, the majority of the time one was dealing with accounts of humans behaving badly, sometimes very badly, and it was important to try to keep a sense of perspective; a kind of gallows humour often relieved moments of stress and tension.

My appointment to 'the Yard list' radically changed my life. Increasingly I found myself doing more prosecuting than defending, and appearing more often in Crown Courts in London, particularly at the Inner London Crown Court at Newington Causeway. 'London Sessions', as we continued to call it, dealt with the bulk of London crime, and I always felt it was a singularly unhappy place. I seldom enjoyed going there: it felt like just a production line and the advocacy was never of the highest order. The whole place smelt of stale cabbage.

The judges were a mixed bunch. The senior judge was one Reggie Seaton, who was a tough nut. He sat in Court One, and dealt with all manner of court work. A sad array of failed barristers sat in there, day after day, hoping to live off the crumbs that fell from Reggie's table as he distributed 'court legal aid' to minor villains. These unfortunates were brought into the dock in droves, having failed so far to obtain legal aid, mainly because they didn't know how to go about it.

By contrast, Henry Elam sat in Court Two. He was a charming man, whose inclinations were always to extend the quality of mercy if he possibly could. It was often the case that he would hear pleas in mitigation in the morning, and at the end of each one say to defending counsel: 'I will pass sentence at two o'clock; nobody need attend.' This meant, we thought, that he wanted to address the defendant alone, without having to meet the eyes of his counsel. I will always remember the occasion when Henry interrupted his summing-up to the jury to tell them that Englishwoman Ann Jones had just won a match at Wimbledon, adding, addressing his shorthand writer, 'don't write that down, otherwise they' (meaning the Court of Appeal) 'will think I've gone potty'! Another story about Henry, probably apocryphal, is that once when consulting Archbold (the criminal 'bible'), in order to perfect his direction to the jury on what needed to be proved in a case of burglary, he said to them: 'A man commits burglary if he inserts his penis into another man's . . . oh dear, I seem to have turned over too many pages . . .' In front of him was the page in Archbold upon which appeared the definition of buggery.

If one was lucky enough to see one's case listed in Court Three, one would find oneself in front of David West-Russell. David was one of the nicest and best judges ever to grace the bench. However, if one was unlucky enough to find oneself listed over the corridor in Court Four, one would find oneself in front of a judge called Ossie McCleay.

As so often, the wise barrister made sure he 'knew his court'. In my experience, Ossie was one of the laziest and most short-tempered of the judicial breed. He lived somewhere in the south-eastern suburbs (I think in Ted Heath's constituency), and he liked to take the earliest possible train home in the afternoon. The worst possible form of mitigation in Ossie's court was one that took place in the afternoon and went on a moment longer than absolutely necessary. He sat in a chair with a kind of canopy over it, which meant that his desk was so badly lit that an overhead light was required. When he got bored, he would ostentatiously flick the switch to turn off the light, and sit back, picking his nose.

One day I was sent to Ossie's court to mitigate for an old lag; both he and the judge were old hands, and had met on a number of occasions before. To my horror I saw that our case was last in a list of pleas of guilty, and was unlikely to be called on much before 3pm. When I went to see my client in the cells, we discussed the points I could raise in mitigation, which were extremely few and unmeritorious to boot. We both knew the form; and my client agreed to trust me to do the best I could with what little I had. 'Okay, guv, you know best,' he said. Not every client had the same faith in my ability. When he asked how long I thought he would get, I replied 'anything under four would be a result', an estimate with which he agreed.

I think I may have asked my client one pertinent question during our short conference: 'Did you ever serve in the Royal Navy?' Unfortunately the answer was 'no'. This was a pity, because it was well known that Ossie had served in the Navy in World War II, and that any defendant who could claim similar service to King/Queen and country could expect a healthy discount. I went back into court to await my turn, and watched as Ossie got more and more irritable as each plea in mitigation was presented to him. At about three o'clock my case was called on, and after a brief prosecution opening of the facts, I rose tentatively to my feet. 'My Lord, through me Mr X has only one thing to say, and that is "please not too long".' In a flash, the learned judge passed sentence thus: "X, you should be very grateful to your counsel. Thirty months.' The light flicked off and His Honour Judge McLeay disappeared, doubtless to enjoy a cup of tea with Mrs McLeay. My client was indeed very grateful.

Throughout the early 1970s, the quality of my prosecution practice steadily improved, until the momentous day when I got my first brief to prosecute at the Old Bailey. And that is when I met Mr McRory and learnt how to draft indictments. As part of my pupillage I had made my first tentative attempts at doing so, but now it was for real, and in a case in which I might have to defend my own handiwork.

The indictment is the formal document that 'indicts' the defendant, and upon which he is 'put in charge' of the jury that is to try him. It is the basis of the whole case, and getting it wrong can bring the whole edifice, however strong the evidence, crashing to the ground. Typically it can look like this:

R v John Henry Smith

Statement of Offence
Murder

Particulars of Offence
On the 1st January 1970, you murdered Jane Smith

That is perfectly simple, and a pupil in his first week could draft such an indictment. They can get very complicated though, if, for instance, there is more than one defendant (it is 'multi-handed'); a number of offences are alleged, some of which involve all defendants, others only one or some; and when the Crown wishes to indict for 'alternative offences'. An example of that would be when the prosecutions want to guard against the possibility of a jury finding the most serious offence unproved but give it the opportunity to find the defendant guilty of an alternative (lesser) offence.

Mr McRory ('Mac' to us all) was a highly experienced managing clerk, who was in practical terms in charge of all prosecutions conducted by SMP at the Old Bailey. He sat in his own office on the fourth floor, was responsible for instructing counsel, and was the one man on earth whom any barrister who hoped to have a future prosecuting needed to impress. Mac was not only experienced, he was extremely clever, wise and self-effacing. He addressed all counsel as 'sir' but, rather like the relationship between the young barrister and his clerk in chambers, we all knew, when we walked into Mac's room, who was the boss. Many a time he asked to see me to 'discuss' an indictment I had drafted, and as soon as he said '. . . with the greatest of respect, sir, although it is your decision, may I suggest for your consideration that . . . ' I knew I had made a terrible howler. I would leave his room with the draft indictment suitably amended.

Prosecuting 'up the Bailey' was stimulating but challenging. It was a wonderful place to appear, not only because the work was, almost by definition, more interesting, but everyone there, from usher to judge (with one or two exceptions), and including one's opponents, tended to be of a high calibre. There was also a solemnity and aura that was not always to be found elsewhere. By the mid-seventies, the bulk of my work was prosecuting for Sol Met Pol at the Central Criminal Court, with an occasional bit of defending, there and in other places, thrown in.

On 14th May 1974, I had the most important encounter of my life. That evening I met my future wife, Elizabeth Mary East. Six days after I met Lizzie, who was to have the most profound and beneficial effect on my life, Ian Ball attempted to kidnap HRH Princess Anne as she was being driven down The Mall. At his trial I was led for his defence by John Hazan QC and instructed by Kingsley Napley and Co. I say 'his trial': it was over in less than an hour, because everyone agreed that Ball was clearly suffering from mental illness and was in urgent need of psychiatric treatment, so he was quickly dispatched to Broadmoor. My part was to stand in the dock beside him to make sure that he uttered the word 'guilty' as the various counts on the indictment were put to him. The words 'instructed by Kingsley Napley' have a particular significance in my story.

One day, I can't remember exactly when it was, I had been sent off to Old Street Magistrates' Court to defend in a case. About a fortnight later, my clerk came to me with a brief from a firm of solicitors of whom I had heard, because they were acknowledged to be the foremost firm doing criminal work in London, if not in the whole country. Diana was as surprised as I was, because Kingsley Napley had seldom, if ever, briefed 3 KBW before. Neither of us could understand what had happened. I discovered afterwards that at Old Street that morning, waiting for his case to come on, which was listed behind mine, was David Napley, the senior partner of that firm. Apparently he had returned to his office and remarked to a junior partner: 'I've just seen a young man who I think may have some potential; send him a brief, so that we can see what he's really like.' That turned out to be about the luckiest break that anyone plying my trade could possibly get.

In due course a brief arrived, I suspect from Christopher Murray, one of Napley's junior partners. He and I thus began a professional relationship for which I am extremely grateful, and which lasted up to the day I went onto the bench in 1996. I must have done that case to his satisfaction because over the next few years I was the fortunate recipient of many more briefs from 'KN', increasing over the course of time in size and seriousness, and therefore in financial reward.

The 1970s were the absolute nadir for the reputation of the Metropolitan Police. Stories of corruption and many other kinds of malpractice began to gain common currency, encouraged by increasingly critical stories written by investigative journalists. Police officers were routinely accused of racism, corruption, planting evidence and concocting interviews, and at the coal-face it became increasingly difficult to persuade juries to convict defendants on the basis of police evidence alone, however strong and in other respects convincing it was.

In many ways the Met had only themselves to blame, and were their own worst enemies. They refused to wake up and smell the coffee. For instance, they persisted in ridiculous fictions about how they compiled their notes of an incident or interview. I believe that they were taught at Hendon Police College that they should maintain through thick and thin that their notes were made independently of each other, at different times and in different rooms, despite the fact that the notes were often word-for-word identical. Juries understandably did not believe a word of it, and the officers giving evidence were made to look, not only silly, but unworthy of belief. I remember sitting in court on many occasions as juries were visibly disbelieving of the assertion that two men, sitting in different locations, could make a record of incidents and conversations lasting half-an-hour or more, in identical terms, using exactly the same words, without any form of collaboration. I have no doubt that many a serious criminal went free because juries could not swallow such obvious lies.

On one occasion, some years later, I was invited to give a lecture at Hendon Police College on the subject 'How to give evidence'. I vividly remember the audience sitting there with metaphorically open mouths when I said that giving evidence should be perfectly straightforward: just tell the truth. I was not invited again.

The other bone of contention was the 'statement under caution'. This document would come into existence in police stations after a suspect had 'coughed', and was admitting guilt. It was headed in this way: 'I, John Smith, wish to make a statement. I have been told that I need not say anything unless I wish to do so and that anything I say will be taken down and recorded in evidence. I make this statement of my own free will.' After the body of the statement, recorded in the hand of a police officer, but supposedly at the dictation of the accused, there appeared this caption: 'I have been told that I can correct, alter or add anything I wish. This statement is true. I have made it of my own free will.' The police officers would then solemnly swear that the words in the body of the statement had been dictated, word for word, by the defendant, as he now was, and that they had in no way assisted or contributed. I will now exaggerate to make the point, but if the jury, who would usually have copies of the statement in front of them, then read the words 'I now proceeded down the western footpath in a southerly direction until I reached the automatic traffic signal at the intersection that was showing green', and it was suggested that these were the words of the police officer, rather than those of John Smith, a suggestion stoutly denied by the officers, they, the jury, often had little difficulty in disbelieving that part of the policemen's evidence. The real mischief was that those 'porkies' tainted the whole of the rest of the evidence, so that when unlikely allegations of 'plant' were made against those same officers in the same case, all defending counsel often had to do was to say to the jury 'if you believe what that officer said about the taking of that statement, then you'll believe anything', for that defendant to go free.

And that was without 'the verbals'. Verbals was slang for the allegation, true or false, that police officers untruthfully put into the mouths of criminals they were arresting, i.e. admissions of guilt that had not been made. Sometimes they were subtle, sometimes less so. I well remember a case of robbery I was prosecuting, in which officers from the Flying Squad (the Sweeney) attributed to a hardened criminal the words 'Okay guv, you've got me bang to rights this time'. This might have been a case of double-bluff, but when the accused went into the witness box, voluntarily revealed his many previous convictions, asserted 'fit-up' and told the jury, 'I would not have admitted even my name to the Old Bill', I am afraid I knew whom I believed. Sadly, since I had no doubt as to the man's guilt of a very serious violent crime, the jury did not believe the police evidence either and acquitted him.

I don't believe that the majority of the policemen who stepped off the straight and narrow were inherently bad, or even dishonest, people. I think their misdemeanours were due to a culture, laziness, a misguided belief that they were somehow entitled to be believed, that the ends justified the means, and, most of all, a lack of good leadership. Nor do I want to give the impression that these transgressions were being committed by every detective in the Met; far from it. This malfunction was mostly confined to the large, close-knit and homogeneous specialised squads like the Flying Squad, the Obscene Publications Squad, the Dangerous Drugs Squad and for that matter, the various Regional Crime Squads around the country.

What exactly do I mean by a lack of good leadership? Here I might tread on a politically incorrect minefield. I have maintained for as long as I can remember that there is a fundamental flaw in the structure of the police, and that is that there is no officer cadre. I am certainly not suggesting that I would like to see an elite of men and women exclusively drawn from the middle classes, or educated at private schools. The armed forces (and the police force is increasingly becoming an armed force too) have a structure based upon the fact that certain people, hopefully the brightest and best, are specifically trained to lead others. They learn that art at Sandhurst, Cranwell or Dartmouth. Leading means setting an example. The trouble with the police in those days was that, with very limited exceptions, they all started in the ranks, and learnt the culture of the force in the police canteen, where rule one was 'support your colleague, whatever he says or does, through thick and thin, regardless of whether what he is doing is right or wrong'. This meant that if six policeman in a patrol van arrested a man in the street, and one of them decided to give him a good thumping before depositing him in the back of the van, the other five, regardless of whether they approved or not of what their mate had done, would swear black and blue (if that is a permissible pun) that no such thing had happened. To break ranks and 'grass' would require a courage few would possess, because, if one of them did, then his future in the canteen would have been an unhappy one, and would probably have ended in resignation. In a similar military situation, one would hope that the officer would stop such a thing happening or, if it did, then call it out.

I wouldn't want to give the impression that my professional experience overall led me to the view that the police were institutionally dishonest, or that any more than a small minority were up to no good. Quite the contrary; I thought most of the police officers I worked with when prosecuting, or 'against' when defending, did an admirable job, often under very difficult circumstances. But human nature being what it is, some officers, observing at close quarters the sometimes huge rewards that professional criminals achieved by their ill-gotten gains, were tempted to supplement their incomes by 'having a bit of it'. Others adopted the cynical approach that the ends justified the means, so they were entitled to take shortcuts and obtain convictions, not by hard graft, but by gilding the lily. Thus the criminal was granted his just deserts, even if at the expense of the oath the officers took in court to tell the truth, the whole truth, and nothing but the truth.

Many of those officers might have sought to defend taking shortcuts by the argument I heard so often, that the scales of justice were so heavily loaded in favour of the defence, that a little bit of 'rebalancing' was called for to achieve what they would have described as justice. Central to that assertion, for which I had some sympathy but to which I would never subscribe, was one of the central tenets of the criminal justice system: that 'it is far better that ten guilty men go free than that one innocent man be convicted'. That is the basis of the rule that juries have to be sure of guilt before they are entitled to convict, and it is for the prosecution to prove that guilt. Some police officers regarded this as being far too favourable to criminals, and decided to add a little grist to the prosecution mill. I once heard a senior officer, in charge of a case that I had prosecuted, and which resulted in what both of us regarded as a slightly dubious verdict of 'not guilty' by the jury, say 'don't worry, sir, he'll come again'. He did not add 'and we'll make sure he does', but it wouldn't have surprised me if that had happened.

The kind of bending of the rules that I have been describing was later dubbed 'noble cause corruption', another phrase to which I would never subscribe. Such behaviour was never 'noble', and the real mischief it created was that, for years after the corruption cases of the 1970s, juries would acquit criminals who on any objective view were plainly guilty, because they simply would not accept the evidence of Metropolitan Police officers.

Talking of painting or gilding the lily, it is slightly ironical that I was instructed to defend Detective Constable Nigel Lilley in one of the first trials in the 1970s that exposed terrible corruption in parts of the Metropolitan Police. Lilley was a member of the Drugs Squad, and he and five others, including his DI, Inspector Kelaher, his DS, Norman Pilcher, and a WDC (woman detective constable) were tried for perjury and conspiracy to pervert the course of justice. The story, put quite shortly, was that this squad had been put in charge of investigations into a family called Salah, who were suspected of, and were quite plainly guilty of, international drug-smuggling on an industrial scale. The investigation involved months of observation on the activities of the extended family, all of whom were at it. Just as the net was about to close, while the squad waited for a Land Rover to return from the Continent laden with drugs, the Bulgarian police rather unsportingly arrested the major players, and our Drug Squad was left to pursue, and ultimately prosecute, only some of the relative minnows within the family.

The trial of the remaining Salahs involved these officers giving evidence of the activities of the family after they heard of the arrests in Bulgaria. Those activities were, if the evidence of the officers was to be believed, more than capable of proving involvement and guilt. All went swimmingly from the prosecution's point of view until the officers – accused of fabricating their observations by defending counsel, on the instructions of their clients – were cross-examined. Police officers are almost always allowed to refresh their recollections by referring to their notes in regulation police notebooks, provided certain conditions are met. In giving evidence, these officers maintained that the observations in their notebooks had been made at or near the suspects' homes. One of the defence counsel, having asked to look at one of the notebooks, then asked to see the same officer's official diary. A police diary is again a regulation record, in which the officer is required to record his movements every day. Presented in court the next day, this diary revealed that the officer was recorded as being in an entirely different place, miles away. As one notebook after another was compared with the corresponding diary, a very disturbing pattern emerged: time and again the officer concerned was recorded as being in two completely different places at the same time. The case began to unravel.

The result of the case against the Salahs was that they were convicted, because the evidence, taken as a whole, was overwhelming; but as more and more doubts were raised about the officers' integrity, further investigations eventually led to them being prosecuted, and to the Salahs' convictions being quashed by the Court of Appeal.

In the trial of R v Kelaher, Pilcher, Lilley, Prichard, Acworth and McGibbon, which started at the Old Bailey in September 1973, I was led by Michael Parker QC for Lilley. The defence of the officers was that the evidence they had given at the trial of the Salahs was indeed true, that their notebook entries were accurate and recorded what they had seen. That required an explanation as to why their diaries recorded them as being, on a number of occasions, elsewhere. The explanations were tortuous and complicated, but basically amounted to this: 'we disguised our true movements in our diaries because there were a lot of very naughty and corrupt officers at New Scotland Yard who might have looked at them, and that might have resulted in a lot of our work, particularly our relationships with informers, being compromised'. The more the detail was explored, however, the less those explanations held water. Whereas Kelaher,

Acworth and McGibbon were acquitted, for good reasons it would be unnecessary to go into here, Pilcher, Lilley and Prichard were convicted. The judge, Melford Stevenson J, who was not regarded at the Bar as being exactly a pushover, in sentencing rightly said that he regarded Lilley and Prichard as 'victims of dishonest superiors'; he sentenced them to eighteen months each for perjury, by any account a lenient sentence. Pilcher, the detective sergeant and puppet-master who, according to the judge, had 'poisoned the wells of criminal justice', was given a sentence of four years.

Two features of that trial stand out in my recollection. The first was watching the painful contortions Pilcher went through when he was pinned into a corner and forced to admit that he had taken his official police diary apart, torn pages out, substituted pages with different entries, and then sewn the diary together again, in order to produce it in court as though it contained only the original pages and entries. It felt as though we were watching the man himself being torn apart – but without any prospect of being sewn back together.

The other vivid recollection I have is of advising Lilley that, although it was a matter entirely for him to decide what clothes to wear in court, he might think it sensible not to continue to wear a different, beautifully cut, Savile Row suit every day. Although the case did not contain any allegation that these men had profited from their offences, there hung over the entire proceedings an unstated suggestion, which was beginning to find its way into the press, that officers in the Drugs Squad were making a lot of money out of 'recycling' the drugs they were seizing. Nigel Lilley, immaculate and slightly arrogant, although personally quite likeable, didn't actually take my advice, and started his sentence in a very smart suit.

If the Drug Squad trial was one of the first cases of corruption in the Met to hit the headlines, it proved to represent only the tip of a very large iceberg, and later in the decade I was to defend in a far more serious case.

The mid-1970s represented a watershed in my professional life. I was beginning to find myself instructed in ever more significant cases, and was working far harder than I ever had before. Hard work for me brought stress, which I coped with through what I then believed to be my friend – alcohol. Looking back now, perhaps the first warning sign should have been that I was having to get up increasingly early in the morning to do the work that others would have done before going to bed the previous night. If asked, I would probably have said 'I work hard and I play hard'. My social life was by now considerably enhanced by the fact that I was increasingly escorting Lizzie, who both I and others thought bore a striking resemblance to Grace Kelly. Dinner parties in those days rarely concluded before midnight, and I consumed more than my fair share of wine. I have no doubt now that my drinking started to become a problem at that time; indeed, I remember having a bad hangover on the day Ian Ball was sentenced for kidnapping Princess Anne.

Chapter 6

WORKING WITH 'GOD'

In late 1975 or early 1976 I experienced my first professional encounter with God. Not the God with whom I had had at least a partial relationship for as long as I could remember, but 'God' meaning John Mathew, who was almost universally referred to at the criminal Bar by that nickname. At that time, John was First Senior Prosecuting Counsel to the Crown at the Central Criminal Court. That is a bit of a mouthful and requires explanation.

The most serious cases throughout the country have, ever since the nineteenth century, been prosecuted by the Director of Public Prosecutions (DPP). Until very recently the DPP has always been drawn from the upper echelons of the Bar. John Mathew's father, Theobald, known as Theo, was among the most distinguished, but it was in no way the result of nepotism that John became the most respected advocate at the criminal Bar. The DPP presided over a staff of lawyers, clerks and administrators, almost all of whom were of the highest calibre.

In London there was a list of counsel, known as 'Treasury Counsel', only for the anachronistic reason that, in the nineteenth century, they were instructed by the Treasury Solicitor and their fees were met by the Treasury. These barristers, known to everyone as TCs, were usually twelve in number, and held a permanent 'nomination' to prosecute the Director's work at the Old Bailey. To be made a TC was a highly coveted appointment, and was regarded as a very important achievement which marked recognition as a trusted performer. These TCs even occupied an especially designated room at the Old Bailey. Although they remained members of their several chambers, they were effectively clerked by the DPP's representatives at that court. The rationale behind this elite cadre was that, unlike on circuit, where QCs might be forced to return cases at the last minute with no obviously suitable replacement available, TC briefs could be returned within the group, while the Director could be confident of the ability of the returnee. Indeed, TCs were all trained to prepare their work in the same way, so that it was said that a TC, who had only received the brief the night before, could go into court and open the case to the jury from his predecessor's opening note without having read the entire brief. That would be an exaggeration, but the point was well made.

By the mid-1970s, with serious crime increasing at an alarming pace, there came into existence what was known as 'the supplementary list', i.e. barristers thought to be suitable for consideration as future Treasury Counsel. These barristers would be led in cases by a TC, and if their performance merited it, they would gradually rise like cream to the top of the milk. As established Treasury Counsel retired – either to take silk and return to 'the cab rank' or onto the bench – that was the moment when the lucky candidate who had risen to the top would be promoted to be the most junior TC. TCs were themselves divided into Senior TCs (usually about six of them) and Junior TCs (usually also about six in number). In most cases an STC would lead a JTC, or a JTC would lead someone on the supplementary list. Occasionally, in very big cases, an STC would lead a JTC leading someone on the supplementary list. It was in those latter circumstances that I first spoke to 'God', or rather he first spoke to me.

Since I have now introduced the DPP, Treasury Counsel and the phrase 'the cab rank' into this account, this may be the moment to pause and consider the ethos of the criminal Bar, at least as I saw it all those years ago.

To me, the cab rank was possibly the most important principle upon which the Bar operated. The relationship between solicitors and barristers, in a criminal context at least, is perhaps best explained by the, albeit partially inaccurate, analogy of the medical profession. You go to your GP for anything from a headache to a sprained ankle. If the GP diagnoses something serious, or something that he thinks needs specialist attention, he will refer you to a consultant, and if you require surgery, then you will be operated upon by a surgeon, and not by your GP. In a similar way, your solicitor will draft your will, convey your house, and represent you in a magistrates' court (where he has a right of audience) if you are caught speeding in your car. But if you are charged with a serious criminal offence, and must stand trial in the Crown Court, at least until comparatively recently, you would be represented there by 'counsel', i.e. a barrister. Until 1990, except in limited circumstances, solicitors had no right of audience in the Crown Court.

I considered that the cab rank principle was both necessary and right. It meant that, in effect, all barristers were plying their trade like black-cab taxi drivers and, provided they had their yellow light showing because they were not otherwise engaged, they could be flagged down by any solicitor to represent any client. It meant that, provided the barrister held himself out as practising in that field, provided he was not otherwise engaged for another client, and provided the fee, either privately or on legal aid, was commensurate with the seriousness of the case and the barrister's experience, then the solicitor could flag down counsel of his (and his client's) choice. It meant that no barrister could say 'I don't prosecute' or 'I don't defend', or 'I don't like what he's accused of', or 'now I've met him, I don't like him'. If one pauses to think about it, the obvious corollary of not having the rule is that the Yorkshire Ripper, the Moors murderers, or the Soham child murderer might never have found anyone to act for them, and might have been forced to face those grave charges without representation. That must never happen.

I am afraid to say that, much to my regret, that rule has been increasingly watered down, so that some so-called 'human rights barristers' now announce with some pride that they will not prosecute or represent a man charged with rape. I will return to this subject in due course, because I confess it to be something of a bee in my bonnet, but let me state, here and now, that I regard that approach as nothing less than an abrogation of professional duty.

The Treasury Counsel system is regarded by some as an exception to the cab rank rule, in that it is permissible for TCs to say that they have opted out of it for the duration of their tenure of that office; indeed some TCs do only prosecute during that time. I am not sure whether I have ever approved of such an opt-out and indeed, as we shall see in due course, I never attempted to avail myself of it.

I climbed another rung of the professional ladder when I was appointed to the supplementary Treasury Counsel list, and started to be led by Treasury Counsel. I was well aware that I was on probation and that if I performed to the satisfaction of my leaders, then I stood a chance of entering the room on the third floor of the Old Bailey which I came to regard as the holy of holies. In 1976 my chance came, when I was briefed as second junior, to be led by John Mathew and David Jeffreys in what became known as the Balcombe Street trial.

This trial took place in the middle of a turbulent decade, memorable for the so-called winter of discontent, the miners' strike and the three-day week, when rubbish piled up in our city streets and rats ran amok ; and at the end of it, in 1979, Margaret Thatcher was elected. The summer of 1976 was the hottest on record, resulting in serious water shortages and a hosepipe ban that turned our gardens into parched earth and brown lawns. The next summer we celebrated the Queen's Silver Jubilee, and we all tried to keep our spirits up, the men in platform shoes and flared trousers, the girls in hotpants.

It was also the decade in which the IRA, and later the Provisional IRA, embarked upon a sustained campaign of bombings and other outrages on the mainland, including the Birmingham pub bombings of November 1974, which at times made many people feel as though the country was at war.

The Balcombe Street Four, as they became known, were part of an IRA Active Service Unit (ASU) that wrought havoc upon London and the Home Counties between October 1974 and December 1975. They were later described as 'the most violent, ruthless and highly-trained unit ever sent to Britain by the Provisional IRA (PIRA)'. They carried out approximately forty bomb and gun attacks, almost certainly murdered upwards of thirty people, and maimed countless others.

The IRA had extended its bombing campaign to mainland Britain in the spring of 1973. On 8th March, an ASU bombed the Old Bailey (I happened to be in chambers at the time). Photographs in the press the next morning showed the dishevelled, twenty-one-stone figure of my great friend, James Crespi, who announced that he had 'saved the fabric of the Central Criminal Court by inserting my body between the bomb and the building'. As he later regaled his friends and acquaintances in El Vino's and the Garrick Club with the story, he always added that he would carry 'bits of Michael Mansfield's bicycle' in his torso for the rest of his life. Michael Mansfield was not James's favourite member of the Bar. The members of that ASU were caught trying to leave England by plane.

Having learnt from their mistakes, the IRA then sent over four-man 'sleeper cells', who carried out an increasing number of attacks; the campaign intensified throughout 1974 and included the Birmingham pub bombings, which were to play such an important part in my life nearly twenty years later. In August, the ASU which became known as the Balcombe Street Gang moved into their first 'safe house', in Waldemar Avenue, Fulham.

The Balcombe Street Four comprised four of the six members of this ASU. They were Hugh Doherty, Joseph O'Connell, Eddie Butler and Harry Duggan. Two others, Liam Quinn and Brendan Dowd, were also active within the unit, but were not in the terrorists' car on the last night of the incident which resulted in the four being holed up in Balcombe Street and subsequently arrested.

The campaign conducted by these four terrorists and the other two members of their ASU was one of ever-increasing violence, and day after day the people of London were subjected to the terror which was intended to bring the government to a point when it would 'negotiate' with the IRA. It is to the credit of the government and the population as a whole that, despite news, day after day and week after week, of further outrages, no form of surrender to terror was ever seriously contemplated.

The highlights of this campaign of over forty attacks (if 'highlights' is a word that can properly be used in this context) included the murder of PC Stephen Tibble in February 1975; the killing of a brave explosives officer called Roger Goad a few months later; the bomb placed at the London Hilton that killed two and injured sixty-three; a bomb placed under the car of Conservative MP Hugh Fraser, that instead killed the cancer researcher Gordon Hamilton Fairley, an innocent passer-by; and the shooting dead of Ross McWhirter, twin brother of Norris, and together the founders of *The Guinness Book of Records*. Finally, shots were fired into Scott's restaurant in Mayfair, which proved to be the group's swansong, on 2nd December. About a week before, they had thrown a bomb into the same restaurant, killing one diner and injuring fifteen more, and by now the gang were under surveillance by the Anti-Terrorist

Department at New Scotland Yard, the Bomb Squad. As soon as the shots had been fired into Scott's from the terrorists' stolen car, two extremely brave police officers pursued them by commandeering a passing taxi. There then followed a high-speed chase as other police units joined in, north over the Marylebone Road and into Balcombe Street, very close to Marylebone Station. There the four decamped from their car, ran into a block of flats, and burst into flat 22B on the second floor, occupied by an elderly couple named Mr and Mrs Matthews. The men demanded a plane to fly them and their hostages to Ireland, and a six-day stand-off ensued.

The Balcombe Street siege was front page news throughout the world as we all watched events unfold on television. The police operation to secure the arrest of the four terrorists without further loss of life was nothing short of masterful, combining restraint and patience with a firmness of resolve which made it plain to the kidnappers inside the flat that there were only two ways in which they would leave that building: either under arrest or in body bags. The police were under the command of Detective Chief Superintendent Jim Nevill, and the negotiator who kept a conversation going for six whole days was Detective Superintendent Peter Imbert, the most talented police officer I ever encountered. He went on to become Chief Constable of Thames Valley, Commissioner of the Metropolitan Police, Lord Lieutenant of Greater London, and then Lord Imbert. He also, as we will see later, was a police officer who, before many others, saw the folly in persisting with the fiction concerning 'contemporaneous notes', and thus restored a deal of credibility to the evidence given by police officers.

I later had the privilege of listening to the full recordings of the conversations between the terrorists inside the flat and the police officers outside the building, after the four men allowed wireless communication to be set up. Peter Imbert, assisted by an expert psychologist, spoke from a telephone outside, whilst Joe O'Connell (calling himself 'Tom') had one inside the flat. The negotiations were painstaking and immaculate. Little by little, Imbert persuaded 'Tom' that there was no way out alive other than by the terms dictated by the police, and those terms were unconditional surrender. I listened to the tapes with increasing admiration, and in due course was responsible for helping to redact the transcripts to make sure that nothing injurious to national security was revealed in court. The police, aware that the terrorists were watching television and listening to the radio in the flat, also used what would now be called misinformation: they persuaded the media to drop subtle hints, such as that the SAS were about to be ordered into the flat in an operation reminiscent of the raid on the Iranian Embassy, though in fact no such thing was contemplated, because it would have gravely imperilled the hostages. Eventually the terrorists were winkled out and arrested.

Unsurprisingly, the Balcombe Street Four did not thereafter co-operate with the police in any way other than, to my recollection, making limited admissions in interview. Indeed they did their best to introduce red herrings into the investigation, and in due course literally turned their backs on the court, which they suggested, through their counsel, had no jurisdiction to try them on the spurious ground that they were 'prisoners of war'.

By section ten of the Criminal Justice Act 1967, it was possible for defendants in criminal trials to make, through their counsel, formal admissions as to fact. This was a particularly welcome reform, which meant, for instance, that the plan-drawers and photographers need no longer attend to give evidence. Defending counsel could be invited to make formal admissions on a whole range of evidential and procedural matters. By section nine of the same Act, written statements made by witnesses to the police, provided certain requirements were fulfilled and only if the defence agreed, might be read to the jury and constitute evidence, just as though the witness was standing in the witness box. These two provisions did more to shorten trials and mitigate inconvenience to witnesses than any other in my professional lifetime. Both those procedural shortcuts, however, required the co-operation of the defence. We knew well in advance of the Balcombe Street trial that the defence would not co-operate in any way, and that we would be 'put to proof' all the way down the line. This had two important repercussions on the preparation for trial.

The first was that decisions had to be made concerning the size and scope of the case to be presented to a jury. To have added counts (charges) to the indictment covering every offence we believed we could prove would have made a trial cumbersome, unwieldy and almost unmanageable. So a process of selection was inevitable. The police had produced a huge wall-chart, in the form of a schedule, which set out the incidents and the evidence available to prove complicity by each of the four defendants, bearing in mind that two of the ASU would not be on trial. John Mathew, David Jeffreys and I had a number of consultations with Mr Nevill and Mr Imbert and representatives of the DPP to hammer out the shape of the indictment. From recollection, we set as a limit a maximum of twenty incidents upon which we would seek verdicts from the jury on substantive crimes (which would mean eighty verdicts), together with some general counts, alleging such offences as conspiracy to commit offences under the explosives and firearms legislation. I think that, in all, the defendants were to be 'put in charge of the jury' on counts which required something like a hundred verdicts. So question one was: 'Which offences would be on the indictment and which would be omitted?' The answers to that question were to be found in the answers to two more, namely 'Which are the most serious offences?', and 'On which counts would our evidence be watertight and easily established?' Obviously counts of murder would, almost inevitably, take precedence over others which had resulted in less serious harm.

The next series of decisions involved determining how, in the absence of any form of co-operation from the defence, and bearing in mind that we would have to prove every fact every step of the way, we could present a digestible case to a jury. It was an absolute pleasure working with John, David and a team of such dedicated police officers, and in the end we worked out solutions to both problems. It was decided, for instance, that I would have sub-contracted to me the presentation of all the fingerprint evidence. That would mean my making sure that every necessary piece of evidence required to prove this part of the case was in place, and that, come the trial, I would 'call' that evidence.

Most people understand the rudiments of fingerprinting, and it can be among the most compelling kinds of scientific evidence. At this juncture I hope I will be forgiven if I allow another bee to escape from my bonnet. I say 'scientific evidence' deliberately, because the misuse of the phrase 'forensic evidence' for some reason irritates me intensely. 'Forensic' means 'used in a court of law', so all evidence in court is 'forensic'. Fingerprint evidence, together with evidence concerning DNA, blood analysis and firearms residue, amongst many other things, is part of the 'scientific evidence' adduced in court.

After many months of preparation, the case of R v Doherty, O'Connell, Butler and Duggan began at the Old Bailey in front of Mr Justice Cantley, or Cantley J, as High Court judges were always described, on 24th January 1977. Joe Cantley was aged sixty-seven, had been a High Court judge for over ten years, and had married for the first and only time the year after his appointment. He had a slight lisp and was not regarded as the most user-friendly of judges. His portrait in the National Portrait Gallery captures his usual expression quite well.

John Mathew opened the case to the jury in a way that instantly reminded me of the way Roger Frisby had opened cases. It was crisp, economical, totally comprehensible, and fair, while being, at the same time, devastatingly compelling. When I first came to the Bar, Roger and John were acknowledged as the two masters of their craft, and it was therefore the more tragic when alcoholism finally destroyed Roger's career. By the time 'Matty' had finished opening the case, judge and jury already had a canvas onto which the colours were now to be applied. The opening was indeed a work of art, to which David and I, rather like the pupils of Michelangelo, had added the occasional brushstroke.

We then set about the laborious business of calling the evidence. We had to dot every 'i' and cross every 't'. Defending counsel had instructions from their clients to do two things. The first was to 'put us to proof' so that if, by the end of the Crown's case, there was any lacuna which might allow counsel to submit that there was 'no case to answer' on any count on the indictment, then full advantage was to be taken of that. The second and, as we soon discovered, primary objective, was to try to help the IRA cause as a whole, not by trying to prove that these defendants did not commit the offences with which they were charged, but ironically to prove that they had committed further offences, of which other IRA suspects had either been convicted, or of which they were suspected. To that extent the whole trial was bizarre.

I will not attempt to outline all the evidence called by John and David, but I myself had to spend many days calling the evidence to prove that fingerprints found at the scene of the crimes, or upon devices used to perpetrate them, were the fingerprints of these defendants. Fingerprint officer after fingerprint officer, and the experts who examined their work, came in and out of the witness box, as I tried to deal, count by count, defendant by defendant, with the evidence in a logical, comprehensible and chronological way. The experts painstakingly took the jury through their methods, using photographs of the prints found at the scene and comparing them with photographs of the defendants' prints. Without going into great detail, their conclusions were based on 'ridge characteristics', visible as 'hills' and 'valleys' on the photographs, which, if they showed that sixteen or more in number were in agreement, proved guilt to a universally accepted standard. I could see that Mr Justice Cantley was getting increasingly restive as this unexciting and repetitive evidence went on and on, hour after hour, and I remember that there came a time when, after one rather acerbic judicial intervention, 'God' had, in the absence of the jury, to call His Lordship to order in a way which, to the *cognoscenti*, made it abundantly plain who was in charge of these proceedings. The judge then allowed me to do my job without further interruption.

On the 9th February 1977, the Balcombe Street Four were convicted of, I think, seventy-four offences, including multiple counts of murder, and were sentenced to life imprisonment, with a recommendation that they serve a minimum of thirty years. On the 14th April 1999, they were released as a result of the Good Friday Agreement, and I vividly remember feeling physically sick when I heard that news.

For me, the trial proved a watershed in my professional career, because not very long after it I discovered that John Mathew had recommended that I be appointed Treasury Counsel. That recommendation went, through the DPP, to Sam Silkin, the then Attorney General, and since what God ordained almost automatically came to pass, I was appointed Junior Treasury Counsel on 21st July 1977. David Jeffreys, who had been appointed two years earlier, was the first ever to be appointed from 3 KBW, while Julian Bevan was appointed on the same day as myself.

On 8th December 1976 I had gone to a dinner party given by Lizzie in her flat in Pimlico. Since we had by then been going out for some time, I stupidly and presumptuously assumed that I would not be driving home that night: but Lizzie had other ideas. The result was that at about two o'clock the following morning, I slid gently into the back of a police car in Kensington High Street. I was breathalysed and taken to Kensington Police Station. In due course I was summoned to appear at West London Magistrates' Court on a date to be fixed, for 'driving a motor vehicle with a blood-alcohol concentration (considerably) above the prescribed limit'. I remember sheepishly telephoning John Mathew to tell him that he now needed to withdraw his Treasury Counsel recommendation. His response was to reprimand me for being so stupid and irresponsible, but to say that it would not cause him to withdraw his support. On 12th February 1977 I pleaded guilty, was fined £30 plus £9.70 for the costs of the police doctor, and disqualified from driving for twelve months, a penalty that was par for the course. I was represented at court by John Mathew.

As I recite those facts I am reminded that this was another milestone on my alcoholic journey, and that my career might justifiably have come to as shuddering a halt as my car had done when it slid into the back of the police car. In the event, however, I was blessed with two pieces of amazing luck. The first was that this unfortunate occurrence did not prevent my being appointed Treasury Counsel. The second was that, rather than drive her Mini back and forth between Pimlico and Notting Hill, Lizzie decided to move in with me. Those were two of the most defining events of my life.

Chapter 7

THE DIRTY SQUAD

I have deliberately altered the chronological order of events slightly in order to sandwich an example of policing at its best (the resolution of the Balcombe Street siege) between two examples of quite unacceptable policing at its worst. If the Drugs Squad trial did indeed, as I have suggested, represent the exposure of the tip of the iceberg of police corruption in the Metropolitan Police, I also appeared for the defence in a trial that exposed much more of that extremely unsightly iceberg.

In the late sixties and early seventies, rumours of institutional malpractice in the Met were rife in my profession, and many of us were witnessing things in court that caused serious concern. This wasn't simply about police officers cutting corners to convict men they knew were serious criminals, against whom they thought it legitimate to 'adjust' the evidence so as to rebalance the scales of justice, which they believed were too heavily weighted in favour of the criminal. It wasn't just about 'verballing' or planting evidence to ensure that guilty men got their just deserts, however unsavoury those practices were. It was beginning to be obvious to many of us at the coal-face that there was a cancer of corruption at the heart of New Scotland Yard; not the entire force, of which the vast majority were decent, honest men fighting crime on behalf of society, but a hard core of detectives in specialist squads, rubbing shoulders with hard core criminals, and becoming as dishonest and corrupt as those they were supposed to be bringing to book. And, talking of hard core and books, one of the places where it was suspected that the cancer was at an advanced stage was the Obscene Publications Squad, otherwise known as 'the Porn Squad' or 'the Dirty Squad'.

This country had just got used to the permissive society of the Swinging Sixties, which had revolutionised attitudes to sex. Of course it is not true that sexual intercourse was invented in the sixties, but what occurred in those heady days was a relaxation of the sexual mores that those born before World War II had taken for granted. One of the consequences was a positive explosion onto the market of literature that would have made our forebears turn in their graves. It had been a swift and far-reaching revolution. In 1970 it was only ten years since Mervyn Griffith-Jones had prosecuted Penguin Books for publishing *Lady Chatterley's Lover*. Mervyn had served with distinction in the Coldstream Guards in World War II and won the Military Cross; he had been junior prosecuting counsel at the Nuremberg War Trials, and also junior counsel for the Crown in the prosecution of Ruth Ellis, the last woman to be hanged in Great Britain. Mervyn couldn't understand why some sniggered behind their hands when he asked the Lady Chatterley jury (at least half of whom were from what Mervyn would have described as 'other ranks'): 'Would you even wish your wife or servant to read such a disgusting book?' When the Porn Squad officers ultimately stood trial at the Old Bailey, Mervyn Griffith-Jones was sitting in another court as Common Serjeant, the second senior permanent judge at the Central Criminal Court.

I have spoken in another context of how crime, rather like the clothes industry, has fashions. By the beginning of the seventies, some professional criminals had discovered that pornography was a ripe, low-hanging fruit just waiting to be plucked, and they moved into Soho to take advantage of such rich pickings. Among those criminals was James 'Jimmy' Humphreys, aka The Emperor of Porn.

The law on obscenity, and in particular obscene publications, had been a minefield of uncertainty for many years, the test eventually being whether the offending article 'had a tendency to deprave and corrupt', but in many ways depravity was in the eye of the beholder. Theo Mathew, when he was DPP, had been asked by a number of senior officers to bring prosecutions against pornographers, and his response was 'if you think I am going to sit here like King Canute and bid the tide of pornography recede, then you've got another think coming'. By the beginning of the 1970s though, not only was the porn becoming harder and harder, often imported from the Netherlands and Scandinavia, but the incoming tide had become a positive tsunami. Humphreys and his fellow pornographers were opening shop after shop in Soho, peddling books, magazines and videos that passed the obscenity test by anyone's standards; meanwhile the purveyors were making huge amounts of money.

The Obscene Publications Squad was supposed to enforce the law, but a group of officers saw this trade as a golden opportunity to 'have some of it', and started what was, in effect, a protection racket. Either the shop owners paid up, or they were raided.

As 1971 drew to a close, Home Secretary Reginald Maudling announced the appointment of Robert Mark as the new Commissioner of the Metropolitan Police. He took office in April 1972. Mark's brief was simple and specific: clean up the Met. Known as 'the Manchester Martinet' and 'the Lone Ranger from Leicester', Mark made it plain from the beginning that he would institute a root-and-branch spring-clean and that no officer against whom he found evidence of corruption, be he commander or constable, would be safe. At the end of a three-year investigation, headed by Deputy Assistant Commissioner Gilbert Kelland, fifteen officers, including two retired commanders, were eventually tried at the Old Bailey on corruption charges; thirteen went to prison for a total of ninety-six years. Obviously those thirteen officers were not tried in one trial.

The trial in which I appeared started on the 8th November 1976. Six officers were in the dock: DCI George Fenwick, DI Clive Miles, DS (but recently promoted Inspector) Charles O'Hanlon, DS David Jones, DS Peter Fisher and DC Michael Chamberlain. They were charged with conspiracy to accept money and other considerations from people trading in pornography, and various specimen counts of bribery. I represented Charlie O'Hanlon, led by my Head of Chambers, Bill Howard QC. The case was tried by Mr Justice Mars-Jones whilst John Mathew led for the Crown. In all, seventeen pornographers were called by the prosecution, their evidence being supported by that of four former officers who had served in the Obscene Publications Squad.

The Crown's case was formidable. Pornographer after pornographer told the same story: a crude but effective, and extremely lucrative, protection racket – 'pay up or we'll close you down'. Usually on a weekly basis, an officer from the squad would visit to collect the money. The amounts varied, depending on the size of the shop, its turnover, and the criminal record of the pornographer, whose willingness to pay was often commensurate to the size of his CRO (Criminal Record Office) file. Each defendant's case was also much the same: basically that no such thing had happened and the witnesses were all lying.

The case for the defence might have had some chance of success if the Crown's evidence had been confined to that of seedy pornographers with very dubious pasts; a jury might have been disinclined to convict 'upright defenders of the thin blue line' on the word of proven London criminals. Unfortunately, as far as the defendants were concerned, the prosecution case was not so confined. Kelland and his team had persuaded three former colleagues of the accused to spill the beans. Detective Inspector Kilkerr and two Detective Sergeants, Munro and Tomlin, went into the witness box to tell the jury, from the inside, about how the ill-gotten gains were collected and then distributed. Every Friday evening the squad would meet for a drink in The Tank, a bar in the basement of New Scotland Yard, and Fenwick would distribute the week's takings: each officer would leave with a wedge of notes in his back pocket.

Only a few moments during my career in court remain vividly in the memory, but the evidence of the clean-cut, upright, rather good-looking Kilkerr's account of one Friday night is one of them. He told the jury how he had gone to St James's Park tube station, walked down to the platform, taken the notes out of his pocket, torn them up, and vomited onto the track. As he gave that evidence, it felt as though the temperature in the courtroom fell by several degrees. I remember thinking well, that's it then. According to our instructions (what our clients insisted was the truth), Kilkerr and the other two police officers were cross-examined by counsel for the accused on the basis that they too were telling a pack of lies.

It will not surprise you to learn that five of the defendants, with the exception of Miles, who was acquitted for good reasons I needn't go into, were convicted, I think on all counts of the indictment. In passing sentence, Mars-Jones J, with a curl of the lip I came to recognise, passed swingeing sentences. Fenwick (whom the judge described as the 'arch villain') received ten years' imprisonment; O'Hanlon, seven; Chamberlain, eight; Jones, seven; Fisher, four· a total of thirty-six years.

All the convicted officers appealed against their sentences. On 15th March 1978, all appeals were dismissed in a damning judgement of Lord Justice Geoffrey Lane. (Two years later, he was appointed Lord Chief Justice and went on to become, in the opinion of many including myself, the best holder of that office in modern times.) The applications were heard together with those of other officers, including Bill Moody, formerly Detective Chief Superintendent and head of the OPS, who appealed against a sentence of twelve years imposed by Mars-Jones at the end of his trial. Lane LJ acknowledged that none of the officers in the trial in which I took part was responsible for initiating the corruption, and indeed each had found himself posted to a squad in which corruption was the order of the day; but he went on to say that heavy sentences were undoubtedly called for because 'one of the unpleasant tasks which faces this court is to ensure that the level of sentence in this type of case is sufficient in the future to provide the stimulus to the faint-hearted so that they will not permit themselves to become embroiled should they find themselves facing temptation'.

Robert Mark, when he took over as Commissioner, is said to have described the CID in the Met as 'the most routinely corrupt organisation in London'. With many exceptions it was rotten from the head downwards, and in due course Commander Ken Drury, head of the Flying Squad, was tried, convicted and sentenced to eight years. Commander Wally Virgo was also tried for corruption, convicted and sentenced to twelve years; his conviction was quashed on appeal, and he died quite shortly afterwards.

Perhaps the last word should belong to Gilbert Kelland, who had led the investigation into the Porn Squad, who remarked that 'the crow of corruption had been nailed to the barn door'. Nothing but praise should go to him and his team of straight officers, who had perhaps the worst job any policeman can be asked to perform, namely reaching deep into the barrel to extract the rotten apples. An example of what straight and honourable officers had to face in those bad old days could be found in a notice that appeared in a police magazine after the death of Bert Wickstead, the tough and uncompromising head of the Serious Crime Squad in the 1970s: it read 'A memorial service for the late Mr Wickstead will be held in the telephone box opposite the Blind Beggar public house.'

The conviction and sentencing of the officers I have mentioned did, as Geoffrey Lane had predicted, seem to bring to an end a period of institutional corruption in the Met. Of course, individual cases of malpractice continued to occur, and no doubt still occur, but gradually the Met began to recover its self-respect, and indeed regain the confidence and respect of the population it serves.

Three months after the appeal of Charlie O'Hanlon had been dismissed, Lizzie and I were married, at 5pm on 28th June 1978 in Gray's Inn Chapel. It was a Wednesday, and the reception was held in Gray's Inn Hall at 6pm, to allow all the barristers to do a day's work in court before attending. Julian Bevan was my best man. I allowed myself, and more importantly Diana allowed me, and my bride a five-day honeymoon in Italy before I returned to the grindstone. After all, I had a 'fixture' at the Old Bailey the following Wednesday.

When we had got engaged, a great friend of Lizzie's had asked her how she could marry 'a paid liar'. I would be a rich man if I had a pound for every time over the years when I have been asked, as every criminal practitioner has been: 'How can you defend someone you know is guilty?' I will now try to deal with such common misconceptions.

The answer Lizzie might have given to her friend would be 'he's not'; whilst the short answer to the second question, the one every barrister dreads, is: 'I don't, but if you would like a more informative response, then I will try to explain before you fall into your soup through boredom.' Here is that longer explanation.

Barristers do not invent defences for defendants. Neither, I hope, do solicitors. Barristers do not tell defendants what to say in evidence. Neither, I hope, do solicitors. To do any such thing would not only be the grossest professional misconduct, it would amount to the criminal offence of conspiracy to pervert the course of justice. What barristers do is 'abide by their instructions', which is a rather pompous way of saying that we are, in effect, the defendant's mouthpiece. Our job, if we are briefed for the defence, is to represent our client; in other words to say to magistrate, judge or jury what he, the client, would want to say, ideally in a more articulate way.

In practical terms, what does all that mean? If the client maintains his innocence, even if the weight of the evidence looks insurmountable, then his counsel 'puts his case' as fearlessly and skilfully as possible, and with as much credibility as possible. All his counsel can do to avoid his client making his position even worse than it is already, is to point out to him that the evidence is so strong that, if the accused is in fact guilty, then he would be well advised to come clean, plead guilty, and allow his counsel, by a plea in mitigation, to reduce the sentence that would otherwise be imposed if he fought the case to the bitter end. Bearing in mind that it is always counsel's duty to do his utmost to obtain the best possible result for his client, then to give that advice is his duty.

If acquittal seems impossible, then the next best result is a reduced sentence. I spent more hours than I care to remember telling clients that if, but only if, they were in fact guilty, then a timely plea of guilty would inevitably reduce the severity of the sentence. Judges were always advised by the powers-that-be to observe, as a guideline, the rule that timely pleas of guilty should attract at least a one-third reduction. Remember my 'docker' at Hertford Assizes, and my old lag appearing in front of Ossie McLeay? Indeed, a plea of guilty could, in the right case, allow a non-custodial sentence to be passed instead of a sentence of imprisonment. The reduction in sentence was not because the courts operated a 'last day of the sale' or 'bargain basement' policy; it is because the timely plea saved public time and expense and, more importantly in my view, meant that the defendant did not compound his crime by going into the witness box, commit perjury, and try to pull the wool over the eyes of a jury.

On the subject of pleas in mitigation of sentence, I was led for Charlie O'Hanlon by one of the best mitigators in the business; my head of chambers, Bill Howard. Bill did not have the reputation of being a great master of detail, but I saw him soften many a judicial heart, even ones as impervious as Geoffrey Lane's. In giving judgement in the Court of Appeal in that case, the future Lord Chief Justice referred to Bill's submission as 'a moving plea', and I remember thinking, as I sat behind him, that I was listening to a master of that art. I sensed that Geoffrey Lane was indeed moved by Bill's submission and that, had he felt that his duty would allow him to do so, he might have knocked a year or so off our client's sentence. Although I wasn't half as good at it as Bill, on the occasions when a plea in mitigation that I had presented seemed to achieve some real and tangible result for a client, I regarded that as the most rewarding form of advocacy.

No chapter containing the names of Mervyn Griffith-Jones and Bill Howard, and touching on the art of mitigation, would be complete without reference to the case of an Old Etonian former Guards officer, who had inexplicably turned attempted bank robber. The defendant had, in an incredibly ham-fisted way, tried to rob two banks on Guildford High Street, armed with a sawn-off shotgun. Bill led me for the defence, and after a consultation, Bill asked me to summon Diana to his room. He asked her to make sure that the case was listed as a plea of guilty before the Common Serjeant at the Old Bailey. This was an unusual request because, although meetings were held daily in the list office, for clerks and list officers to arrange the business of the court, it was part of the folklore of the Temple that the Duchess (Diana) always sent one of her junior clerks.

In due course the case was indeed listed in front of the Common Serjeant, Old Etonian and former Coldstream Guards officer Mervyn Griffith-Jones. After the case was opened for the prosecution, Bill then embarked upon probably the best, and certainly the most effective, plea in mitigation that I had ever heard. It was spellbinding; without being ostensibly over-emotional, his words tugged at the (not always visible) heart-strings of the judge.

He emphasised the previous impeccable character of the accused, and suggested that this episode must have represented some form of brainstorm, caused by a temporary attack of depression. By the time Bill sat down, one wondered whether there could be a dry eye in the house. The result? A completely unexpected suspended sentence for an armed robber.

Since I have included this episode in a chapter about corruption, should I question the authenticity of that result? Knowing Mervyn Griffith-Jones as well as I came to, I have absolutely no doubt whatsoever that the whole thing was totally above board; Mervyn was as straight as his Guards-trained backbone.

A postscript, however, perhaps demonstrates how different attitudes were in those days. In an exchange between judge and leading counsel during the course of Bill's address, the judge asked to examine the offending weapon. After it had been handed to him, Mervyn examined it with great care, and then, looking solemnly over his half-glasses, exclaimed:

'Mr Howard, this man applied a saw to a Purdey!'
'Yes, my Lord; I regret to say that that is indeed the case.'

Both men shook their heads sadly. (This *was* nearly fifty years ago!)

Chapter 8

THE TRIAL OF THE CENTURY

Julian Bevan and I were appointed Junior Treasury Counsel on 21st July 1977. Shortly before that I had been summoned to attend the chambers of the Attorney General, Sam Silkin, in the Royal Courts of Justice in the Strand. As I walked from 3 KBW in the Temple across to the Law Courts, having a pretty shrewd idea of the purpose of the summons, I wondered whether I would have to decline the expected appointment. To say that I was determined to impose two conditions before accepting the job might appear pretentious, pompous and precocious, but I had decided that I had to raise both issues as they were very important to me.

The first was my total opposition to capital punishment. The last hangings in this country had taken place in 1964, and capital punishment had been suspended in 1965, but the clamour for its restoration during the IRA bombing campaign had reached a crescendo after the events at Balcombe Street. The public were voting heavily in favour in opinion polls and most of us were predicting that within two years Mrs Thatcher, a known supporter of restoration, would be in 10 Downing Street.

My opposition to capital punishment went all the way back to 10 Rillington Place. As I have mentioned earlier, in March 1950

Timothy Evans had been hanged for the murder of his wife. In July 1953 John Reginald Christie was hanged for murdering at least eight women in the house they had both occupied. It became indisputable that the hanging of Evans was a terrible miscarriage of justice, which Ludovic Kennedy proved in his book *10 Rillington Place* beyond a peradventure. From the moment I read that book I became, even in my teenage years, a passionate abolitionist, and cases such as Craig and Bentley, Ruth Ellis and others, cemented my views. It wasn't just the possibility of mistake that convinced me; I found the whole concept of the state killing in cold blood, albeit in retribution for another killing, morally repugnant. I also rejected the argument that capital punishment deterred potential killers. I did so because most murders are committed in the heat of the moment, and the killer has no time to reflect upon the consequences of his actions; but also because research in the USA suggested that the murder rate in states that had abolished the death penalty was no higher than that in states that had retained it; indeed the research suggested the opposite. For all those reasons, I determined that I would have to say to the AG that I would not prosecute in a capital case.

The second issue I felt very strongly about was the so-called cab rank principle, which I hope I have already adequately explained. To my mind, the whole justification for the existence of the independent Bar is that a barrister is an advocate who is available for hire, regardless of his own personal views, and regardless of the popularity of the cause, or indeed the client. If barristers could pick and choose which cases appealed to their own prejudices it would, in my view, undermine the entire *raison d'être* of the profession.

So I entered the Attorney's room in some trepidation. Sam Silkin had been appointed to serve in James Callaghan's government in 1974; he was regarded as 'a soft socialist', and a man with sound principles. Personally he was a very nice man, and he listened sympathetically to what I had to say. Rather to my surprise, he said that he had no problem with either of my 'conditions', and indeed wrote on my file, there and then, that I would not be required to prosecute in capital cases if the death penalty were to be restored, and also that I had his explicit permission to appear in at least one substantial case a year for the defence, if I were offered such a brief. Ironically it was only a matter of months before I took advantage of that latter indulgence.

Only a couple of days after our appointment, Julian and I stepped into the holy of holies – known to everyone simply as 'the room' – on the third floor of the Old Bailey, and took two of the desks placed back-to-back in that long room. With our arrival, it housed seventeen Treasury Counsel. Although I undertook a number of prosecution cases in the interim, it seems to my recollection, all these years after the event, that I had scarcely got my feet under one of the desks before Diana, back in 3 KBW, gave me the news that without any doubt changed my life.

Between July 1977 and October 1978 my practice had, as was right and proper, concentrated upon my duties as a Treasury Counsel (TC). As Junior Treasury Counsel (JTC), I was, more often than not, led in a succession of murder cases by a Senior Treasury Counsel (STC), but from time to time I conducted less serious cases in my own right. None of the murder cases in which I appeared in those fifteen months or so stands out in my memory. It may seem odd that I remember none of them, but the brutal fact is that most were run-of-the-mill for those of us whose duty it was to prosecute them. The majority were domestic murders, in the sense that they were committed within a domestic environment, and the issue was rarely one of who committed the fatal act, but rather whether that person was guilty of murder, or of the lesser offence of manslaughter, on the grounds of diminished responsibility, provocation, or lack of intent. Each case represented a dreadful loss of life, and a tragedy for at least one other person, but very few had any particular feature that would stick in the memory of the advocates some thirty years later. That reality, which might appear shocking to the outsider, might best be explained by the fact that it would be impossible to do one's job if one allowed oneself to become too involved in individual cases.

I think it was during the years when I started to do Treasury Counsel work that I first became aware of the feeling 'when are they going to find me out?', known I believe as imposter syndrome. As a profession, barristers are not prone to wearing their hearts on their sleeves; indeed many might even be described as being emotionally constipated. But most (and, dare I suggest, often the better ones) suffer, as most actors do, from stage fright, which can be almost crippling. In my case, the higher I climbed the greasy pole of the Bar, the worse this got. Outwardly, I am told, I exuded self-confidence and belief in my own ability, but inwardly the lack of self-confidence and insecurity led inexorably towards a depressive condition. Consequently I began to self-medicate, although never before or during the working day, with what I then believed to be my friend: alcohol.

The lack of confidence was far less debilitating when I was being led but, as I climbed, rung by rung, the Treasury ladder, more often than not I was either appearing on my own or, increasingly, leading a more junior barrister. As will be seen in due course, the depression, although it occasionally reared its ugly head, dissipated when I went onto the bench; but there was a very good reason for that, called recovery.

But let us return to the narrative. On 4th August 1978, The Rt Hon Jeremy Thorpe MP had been arrested on charges of conspiracy to murder and incitement to murder a man who allegedly had been his gay lover. Diana came into my room shortly thereafter to tell me that Sir David Napley, as he now was, the President of The Law Society (the governing body of the solicitors' profession), and Thorpe's solicitor, had telephoned to instruct me as Thorpe's junior counsel. It wasn't, however, quite as simple as that, Diana said.

What Sir David had in mind was that I should attend the committal proceedings at Minehead Magistrates' Court as his junior. The idea that counsel should act in proceedings as his instructing solicitor's junior was, to say the least, novel, and Diana had come to say that, on the advice, or indeed instructions, of the head of chambers, she was to countenance no such thing. I like to think that I too would have rejected the idea out of hand, and I am confident that I would have done, even if it meant that I would no longer be instructed in such a notorious and fascinating case.

I have earlier explained that committal proceedings (which by now could amount to little more than a paper transaction if the defence agreed), provided an opportunity, if the circumstances warranted it, to require prosecution witnesses to be called to give evidence and record 'depositions'. Such circumstances included causing the evidence to be called with a view to submitting that there was no case to answer, and that therefore the case should not be committed for trial at the Crown Court.

It was an unwritten rule at the Bar, and one that had been drummed into me by Roger Frisby during my pupillage, that it was only in rare and exceptional circumstances that the defending advocate would cross-examine a witness in committal proceedings. Ask a few questions to clarify a point maybe; try to emphasize a lacuna in a few questions in order to strengthen a submission in an already weak case perhaps; but never cross-examine in a way that might prepare a witness for a sustained cross-examination at trial, so that he could be forewarned and maybe forearmed. In other words, the golden rule was, as we young barristers were always taught, 'keep your powder dry'.

In the event, Sir David decided to adopt a rather different approach, and to cross-examine witnesses thoroughly at the committal proceedings. In particular, he cross-examined perhaps the two key prosecution witnesses, Peter Bessell and Norman Scott, at great length, and in detail. It is not, I am bound to say, what I would have done had I had the conduct of that hearing. Thousands of words have been written about David's conduct of those proceedings, and I do not intend to enter the fray, mainly because I was not there. David devotes a whole chapter of his memoir *Not Without Prejudice* (1982) to the Thorpe case, the majority of which is a justification of what happened at Minehead. I have no intention of examining his contentions here, but anyone who is interested should read the book.

Over the course of many years, I got to know David quite well, and to respect him, but I have to confess that he and I did not always agree. Regrettably, David is dead, and therefore has no right of reply. I also acknowledge that I owe him a huge debt of gratitude for the way he advanced my career. In his autobiography he was kind enough to be complimentary about me, and indeed wrote on the flyleaf of my copy of the book 'fulfilling all my expectations', but I would be less than frank if I did not say that some of our disagreements, always the subject of courteous discussion, were quite fundamental.

David was, without any doubt, one of the foremost solicitor-advocates of his generation. He always fought his corner valiantly, and one of the things he passionately believed was that some members of the Bar underestimated the value of solicitor-advocates. The phrase that I think riled him most was if barristers referred to solicitors as being members of 'the junior branch of the profession'. Some barristers seemed to go out of their way to be condescending, which only confirmed David's belief that not enough respect was accorded to him and his profession by some members of mine.

In the case of the Minehead committal proceedings, it is only fair to note that David did not take exception to my refusal, through my clerk, to appear as his junior. Immediately after Thorpe was duly committed for trial, David telephoned chambers again and instructed me as junior for the trial at the Old Bailey. My first question was to ask who was going to lead me. I thought a sure bet would have been John Mathew, who was by now, of course, in silk, and already viewed as the most effective gamekeeper-turned-poacher in the business and the criminal solicitor's first choice. Indeed, David says in his book that he had tried to secure John's services, but had been pipped at the post by Thorpe's co-defendant, David Holmes. If not Mathew, then I had a number of names in mind; I wondered if David would, as often happened, consult the junior about the choice of leader. He didn't, instead telling me that he had already instructed one George Carman. My immediate reaction was 'George who?'. I had never heard of George Carman.

It transpired that David had first seen George in action in a case at the Old Bailey known as 'the Big Dipper case', in which he had represented a co-defendant. David had not known of him before, but was so impressed with what he saw and heard that he started to brief him. When John Mathew proved unattainable, David had discussed various possible leaders with Jeremy; between them they decided to instruct George, who was practising on the Northern Circuit, mainly in Manchester, and mainly in civil cases.

I pause to add that I have now referred to my future lay client as 'Jeremy'. I can remember only one other client (Dr Leonard Arthur, of whom more anon) whom I ever addressed by his first or Christian name. By the time I came into the case, Jeremy, David, and George were all addressing each other like that, and obviously I fell into line, even though it took a little time for me to feel comfortable doing so, and with being called 'Graham' myself. Before anyone jumps to the conclusion that this was me being pompous and self-important, let me explain why I instinctively found this difficult.

I believe that one of the great strengths of having a split profession of barristers and solicitors is that it allows the lay client the luxury of two different approaches. The relationship patient-GP-surgeon is, as I have suggested earlier, not dissimilar to that of lay client-solicitor-counsel. Just as some of us get to know our GP quite well over the course of time, so some clients forge a quite personal relationship with their solicitor. I am not suggesting that Thorpe and Napley had ever met before Lord Goodman introduced them, but thereafter the two men, with David's junior partner Christopher Murray, spent countless hours together preparing the defence. Necessarily a fairly close relationship must have developed between them. Usually, counsel comes to a case 'cold', by which I mean he has not met his lay client until he has received his brief, mastered it, and formed views upon the conduct of the case. That allows, in my view, for a degree of objectivity and clear analysis that is sometimes not afforded to the solicitor. To take my medical analogy forward, it is sometimes the case that a GP fears the worst, which is why he refers his patient to a consultant, but it falls to that consultant to break the really bad news. Just as the consultant will lead in the operating theatre, so counsel will lead in court, because jury advocacy, in which no solicitor, however eminent, had in those days any experience, is the barrister's trade; his sole operating theatre was the courtroom.

The Thorpe case was unusual in many ways. I was not brought in until after the committal proceedings, but as soon as I started attending consultations (conferences with silks) I discovered that a lot had happened pre-committal to which I was not a party. This had led to the close relationship between Jeremy, David, and George, which was quite outside my previous experience. Jeremy was a qualified barrister, who had practised for a short time years ago, and I remember that at that first consultation he brought into the room an out-of-date edition of Archbold, the criminal practitioner's bible, from which he started quoting and expounding propositions in law. David was a criminal solicitor who passionately believed that solicitors should have greater rights of audience; I don't think I would be far wide of the mark if I suggested that, had he been allowed to, he would have liked to have represented Jeremy at the Old Bailey as his leading advocate. Jeremy had known George at Oxford, and sometimes I wondered who was in charge of the conduct of the case. George seemed sometimes to defer to David in a way that I found unusual. The term 'instructing solicitor' does not mean that the solicitor instructs counsel on how to conduct the case. Once the brief for trial is delivered, then counsel, and certainly leading counsel, should be in charge. Of course the whole process of consultation means there is discussion, during which ideas are canvassed back and forth, but there should be no doubt as to who holds the whip hand.

George's relationship with his juniors, or certainly with this one, was also unusual. One minute I was his confidant and even adviser, the next I found that he had made decisions behind my back. A huge amount has been written about George, including a book by his own son, Dominic, in which he mounts a scathing attack upon his father. It cannot be denied that George was unlike any other barrister I ever worked with, but it is not my intention to further blacken the name of a deceased man. In my view he was a brilliant but flawed man and there is plenty of opinion in the public domain that provides support for that proposition; some might go so far as to describe him as a genius in his own field, but a genius with feet of clay.

I must also acknowledge that I owe George a huge debt of gratitude because, for some years after the Thorpe trial, he asked instructing solicitors to brief me as his junior. I acted as such in three memorable cases that I will describe later. At this stage I will give my version of a number of incidents which may throw some light upon George's strengths and weaknesses. The most instructive of these may be to relate what happened on the night before George was due to cross-examine Peter Bessell, the most important prosecution witness because, if believed, he gave direct evidence of Thorpe suborning him to arrange for the murder of Norman Scott.

The trial of Holmes, Deakin, Le Mesurier and Thorpe (that is the order in which they appeared on the indictment) was, without doubt, rightly described as 'The Trial of the Century'. It probably attracted more worldwide media attention than those of the Yorkshire Ripper, Dr Crippen and the Moors Murderers all rolled into one. Never before had the leader of one of the UK's three major political parties been accused of a comparable offence. The Rt Hon Jeremy Thorpe MP was not only the leader of a resurgent Liberal Party: it was strongly rumoured at the time (and Jeremy showed me evidence in support of this) that Ted Heath, had it not been for this scandal, would have offered him the job of Foreign Secretary in the coalition government which most pundits saw as the only way Heath could form an administration.

I am not going to attempt to rehearse the alleged facts of the case in any great detail. If anyone needs reminding, there is a huge amount on Google and countless books have been written about it. The first two episodes of the 2018 BBC television series *A Very English Scandal* (based on the book of the same name by John Preston) provided a very accurate account of the prosecution's case. I must emphasise that it reflects their case, because our defence, on Jeremy's instructions, amounted to a denial of substantial parts of it. I must also add that the trial scene in the third episode is a travesty of what took place. A far better account of the trial is to be found in Thomas Grant's extremely good book *Court No. 1 The Old Bailey*.

For public consumption, the case had everything – gay sex, political intrigue, guns and corrupt financial transactions, in fact everything but a bishop; and I remember we even had one of them up our metaphorical sleeve in case Jeremy was convicted and it was decided to call witnesses in mitigation of sentence. Outside the court building, every day, photographers on ladders jostled to get the best pictures of the actors arriving at and leaving court. Inside the theatre of Court One (and it can only properly be described as such) the courts administrator, my friend Michael McKenzie (whom we shall meet again in twelve years' time) had to issue tickets to those he admitted to 'the City Lands benches' behind counsel.

When the four men took their places in the dock, all eyes were on one man: Jeremy Thorpe. No longer was he Jeremy Thorpe MP, because only days earlier he had lost his seat in North Devon when Margaret Thatcher swept to power.

I must set the scene with a short reminder (or, for younger readers, introduction) to what the prosecution was alleging. The case was that Jeremy Thorpe had had a homosexual affair with a much younger man, who was, when they met, a groom working for a friend of Jeremy's. The allegation that most appealed to the salacious 'red tops' was that Thorpe had first committed buggery on his 'victim' in Thorpe's mother's house while he, the unwilling victim, bit the pillow to dull the pain. The prosecution alleged that this young man, who went by the names Norman Josiffe and then Norman Scott, became emotionally dependent on the MP, who gave him some limited financial and other support. It was further alleged that Norman became an increasingly obsessive and embarrassing parasite, repeatedly making public utterances to the effect that Jeremy was his lover. Eventually, Jeremy supposedly consulted Peter Bessell, who was the Liberal MP in the neighbouring constituency, and in the end specifically asked Bessell to find someone who would rid him of the problem permanently. Bessell asserted that Thorpe made it crystal clear that he wanted Scott murdered. The Crown's case was that Bessell had contacted David Holmes, a prominent Liberal supporter who had been Jeremy's best man at his first wedding; that Holmes then contacted a businessman called John Le Mesurier, who in turn got in touch with a Welshman called Deakin, who had shady contacts. Deakin found a hitman called Andrew Newton to take on the contract. Newton then drove Scott, together with Scott's Great Dane Rinka, on to the moor near Minehead in Somerset, where the dog, rather than Scott, was shot and killed.

That is a very imperfect précis of a case that had all sorts of ramifications, including the suggestion that the money to pay for the contract came from a businessman in The Bahamas known as 'Union Jack' Hayward, whose contribution to Liberal Party funds had, unbeknownst to him, been diverted for that nefarious purpose.

The trial was presided over by Cantley J (who had tried the Balcombe Street Four); David Holmes was represented by John Mathew QC; John Le Mesurier by Dennis Cowley QC from the Midland Circuit; and Deakin by the mercurial Gareth Williams QC from the Wales and Chester Circuit. All four defendants were charged with conspiring to murder Norman Scott, and in addition Thorpe was charged with inciting Holmes to commit murder.

In many ways, the case against Thorpe rested on whether the jury accepted that Peter Bessell was a witness of truth, upon whose testimony they could safely rely. It was essential, from Thorpe's point of view, that Bessell's evidence, together with his general credibility, be undermined to the extent that the jury could be persuaded to, at the very least, be unwilling to accept the essential parts of his story. George, although he had a flat to stay at in London, often came round to our house in Holland Park to spend the evening, be fed by Lizzie (although he ate very little), be supplied with copious amounts of whisky by me, and to discuss, in a very discursive and disorganised way, the day's proceedings and the case in general. It must be said that George was socially very inept, had no small-talk whatsoever, and could talk about nothing other than the case.

The night before George had to cross-examine Bessell, he arrived as usual at about eight o'clock, having emerged from some Fleet Street hostelry, with some of the case papers in a plastic bag. For the next six or seven hours or so, with the papers strewn all over our kitchen table, we discussed how George might approach his task in the morning. I felt that his thinking was so scattergun and unstructured that I feared for the morrow. At about 2am I almost literally poured George into a taxi, and I went to bed in a state that amounted almost to terror. I could not believe that my leader would be in a fit state by 10.30 that day even to get himself into court, let alone conduct the most important cross-examination of his life. I lay awake, trying to prepare myself for the moment Cantley J might say, 'Mr Boal, I am not prepared to wait any longer for your leader to appear; you must cross-examine this witness'. I had drunk too much the night before as well, although nothing to compare with George's intake, but as I caught the tube to the Old Bailey that fateful morning the sickening feeling in the pit of my stomach was due, not so much to a hangover, as to fear almost amounting to panic.

By 10.25 that morning everyone was crammed into Court One, in anticipation of a day many expected to determine the fate of Jeremy Thorpe: everyone except George Carman. Were my worst fears about to be realised? At 10.27 the diminutive QC swept into court, his clerk ushering people aside, and proceeded to arrange his papers on his lectern; I leant forward to restore to him those that he had left in our house the night before. As I sat behind him, I noticed the tell-tale smell of peppermint, the beads of sweat on the back of his neck, and the slightest tremble of his hand as he rearranged his papers. At precisely 10.30, the instruction 'Be upstanding in court!' rang round the large room, and Cantley J took his place.

'Yes, Mr Carman,' said the judge, and George rose to his feet to confront the witness across the court. For the next two-and-a-half days I sat spell-bound, completely mesmerised by what is best described as an Oscar-winning performance. George began by playing Bessell, much as an expert angler plays a fish. Then he moved into a more combative gear, reminding one perhaps of Muhammad Ali 'floating like a butterfly and stinging like a bee' – the odd jab here, the odd feint there, and then the body contact. John Mathew had already cross-examined the witness in his own majestic way, but Bessell's evidence did not affect his client in the same direct way that it did ours, so it was for George to deliver, if he could, the knock-out blow.

John had already made the most of the best point we had: that Bessell had signed a contract with *The Daily Telegraph* to tell his story after the trial. The great bonus for us lay in the clause which stated that he would be paid £50,000 if Jeremy was convicted, but only £25,000 if he was acquitted. George took up the cudgels, when many others might have thought, point made, don't give the witness a second chance to slip out of it. He cross-examined Bessell for nearly three days. This is not the place to record the detail of the ordeal to which George, quite justifiably, subjected the man. To me it seemed to resemble medieval torture, as George administered the forensic equivalent of hanging, drawing and quartering. He teased Bessell about 'double-your-money evidence', enquiring sympathetically whether the witness could help the jury on the meaning of the word 'loyalty'; he jousted with him on the subject of the immunity from prosecution under which he had agreed to return from the USA to give evidence; he chided him on his relationship with journalists; but the *coup de théâtre* was delivered one afternoon. At about 3.30pm, George embarked upon a series of questions exposing inconsistencies in the accounts Bessell had given on various occasions, and suggesting one or other account was a lie. I saw George glance up at the clock, and at 4.15pm, which was usually the time when the judge rose for the day, he said to Bessell, 'before His Lordship rises, I want to ask you about one other matter'. Whatever this was, it certainly wasn't a very significant one, but once Bessell had given his answer, George rounded on him and raised his voice slightly:

'And so what you said previously, Mr Bessell, was a lie, wasn't it?'

'Yes, Mr Carman.'

'A whopper?'

'Yes, Mr Carman.'

Then, turning to the judge, George enquired:

'Would that be a convenient moment, My Lord?'

'Not quite,' replied the judge. 'I think there's time for one more whopper.'

There are dramatic moments in some trials when one feels the whole atmosphere has changed, and the balance of power with it. In my forty years in court, none was more dramatic than that. Up until that moment there had been no hint that the judge was favourably inclined towards the defence. From then on, however, judicial interventions appeared to us to be increasingly favourable to the defence.

If I have used over-dramatic language in the last paragraph, perhaps over-egged the pudding, or even misremembered something in my enthusiasm, I hope I will be forgiven. Put it down to the fact that I had witnessed, in those few hours, one of the most effective, indeed devastating, pieces of advocacy which that historic court had ever seen. In any event, by the time George sat down, we felt that the tide had turned, possibly conclusively, in our favour.

The next witness was Norman Scott. Whereas Bessell had been a sophisticated, intelligent and wily performer, Scott cut a rather pathetic figure in the witness box. Bessell had arrived in court suave and sun-tanned, straight from his adopted home in California. Scott, by way of total contrast, appeared pasty-faced and to be a troubled individual. George and I had decided that Scott had to be handled with extreme delicacy. The one thing that we wanted to avoid was a repetition of an incident that had occurred during the committal proceedings. Provoked by much tougher questioning from Napley, Scott had rounded on him and shouted out something to the effect that he could prove he had slept with Thorpe, because otherwise how would he know that Jeremy had nodules under an armpit. Those, George and I agreed, were potentially murky waters into which we did not want to be enticed. George therefore treated the witness, if not with kid gloves, then with velvet ones, inside which, Scott was led to believe, there lurked iron fists.

George addressed Norman Scott as a benevolent psychiatrist,

taking a history from his patient, might have done. Although he put our case, as he had to, he did so as succinctly as possible, keeping the witness on a tight rein. In one sense, whether or not the two men had had a homosexual relationship (the word 'gay' was not in currency in those days) was not directly relevant. The act of buggery, which is what Scott alleged and Thorpe vigorously denied, was a serious criminal offence at the time Scott alleged it to have first occurred at Thorpe's mother's house in 1960 or 1961. By 1979, by reason of the Sexual Offences Act 1967, the act would not have been a criminal offence if performed by two consenting adults in private. It was not, in any event, alleged on the indictment; but since the credibility of the actors in this drama was at stake, and since the prosecution suggested that the relationship provided the motive for the alleged conspiracy, then it was important that George made sure that the witness did not leave the witness box with his credibility intact. Having challenged as expeditiously as he could the central element of Scott's case, George went on to suggest, with considerable justification, that he was a fantasist, who had had to resort to psychiatric treatment on a number of occasions. Scott left the witness box without having exploded some unexpected bomb under us. As the interventions of the judge suggested, and his summing-up subsequently demonstrated, there was at least one person in court who doubted whether Norman Scott was a witness upon whom a jury could safely rely.

How were we going to deal with the whole issue of homosexuality? Jeremy was a twice-married man with a son, Rupert, from his first marriage to the lovely Caroline Alpass, whom I had, coincidentally, once met. Caroline had died in 1970 in a car accident when she was driving from Devon to London. What we knew Scott wanted to allege in court (but he was given no opportunity to do so) was that he had telephoned Caroline that morning to impart news of his affair with her husband, with the implied inference that she had, as a result, committed suicide. Every day of the trial, my first duty was to see that Rupert got safely to school without being hounded by a pack of photographers.

Subsequently, in 1973, Jeremy had married Marion, formerly the Countess of Harewood, who stuck by Jeremy throughout like glue. We suspected, rightly as it transpired, that if an unequivocal denial of any homosexual tendency in Jeremy was made, the prosecution had virtually conclusive evidence, primarily in the form of a letter to a gay acquaintance in the States, which would torpedo any such assertion. George and I toiled away for hours in the privacy of my kitchen as to how to get over this difficulty. The denial of homosexual activity with Norman Scott had been made, as it had to be on our instructions, but somehow we had to forestall that denial being undermined. At long last we came up with a formal admission that might suffice. I may have got it slightly wrong but I remember it as the following: 'It is admitted (formally) under section 10 (to which I have referred elsewhere) that Mr Scott had good reason to believe that Mr Thorpe had homosexual tendencies.'

I had no confidence that this would pass muster with the prosecution. Indeed, if I had been prosecuting, it would not have passed muster with me. But George, in one of those one-to-one, 'just between you and me, old boy' meetings that I discovered over the years was part of his stock-in-trade, got Peter Taylor to agree that it would suffice. Peter Taylor, later Taylor LCJ, brought down especially from the North-Eastern Circuit to lead for the Crown, was a man of huge integrity, and a robust but fair prosecutor. Any suggestion, later made, that he pulled his punches for pro-establishment reasons is, to my mind, totally unfounded, but how he let George dodge the whole issue of homosexuality in one banal, and highly equivocal, sentence still surprises me. One morning then, when nothing much else of note was happening, George rose to his full five feet six inches, and made the admission.

Andrew Newton was the next witness. He appeared to come

straight from central casting. He had already served a two-year sentence for firearms offences concerning the shooting of Rinka the dog on Exmoor. In the past he had been a commercial airline pilot, but in recent years had led a pretty rickety life. He had, he said, been recruited in a nightclub after being involved in a fight, and now said, contrary to what he had said at his own trial, that his brief was to shoot Scott rather than the dog. We, on Thorpe's behalf, did not need to concern ourselves with Newton, since he was so far down the line, and never claimed to have had any direct dealings with Jeremy. He was the concern of other defendants and their counsel. He was the last of a trio of crucial witnesses, each of whom in his own way could be described, at the very least, as out of the ordinary.

The rest of the prosecution case presented us with fewer problems, but was by no means plain-sailing. Whereas Newton was primarily John Mathew's problem, as well as Cowley's to a lesser extent and Williams's to a greater extent, 'Union Jack' Hayward and his accountant Dinshaw provided evidence which was uncomfortable for us. The prosecution wanted the inference to be drawn from it that the money that had come from Hayward had been used by Jack's friend Jeremy, not to assist the Liberal Party, but to pay a gunman to commit murder. George skated round Hayward's evidence with a skill that was not totally in accord with strict adherence to our specific instructions on the matter, and Jack left the witness box under the impression that he and Jeremy were not, nor had ever been, at odds. Jeremy, quite rightly, had answered 'no comment' to every question he was asked in the formal police interview, but since the police officer who was recording his answers got fed up with writing this every time, he resorted to putting ditto marks instead. Jeremy was immediately dubbed The Ditto Man by *Private Eye* magazine.

Submissions of 'no case to answer' were made on behalf of each defendant, and it came as no surprise to anyone that these were rejected. So now it was time for the four of them, each one in turn, to present his defence.

The afternoon the prosecution case was closed was followed by an evening I will never forget. Defence counsel, and defence counsel alone, gathered in a room that had been assigned to them. The meeting was called by John Mathew and George, and the objective was to see if we could hammer out a joint approach to the rest of the case. No lay client and no solicitor was present.

David Napley was not, and could not, be present at court on every day of the trial, as he had a practice to run and other cases to oversee. Indeed I do not recall his being at court very often during the trial. The day-to-day conduct of the case was left in the capable hands of his junior partner, Christopher Murray. Christopher had been involved in the case from the moment Kingsley Napley were instructed, and I found him, as I had in the previous cases in which he had instructed me, the almost perfect instructing solicitor. The suggestions he made were always helpful, he had an extremely good way of navigating the sometimes difficult interaction between lay client and counsel; he protected counsel against irrelevant distractions, and he was always willing to do anything asked of him. We got on extremely well, and each of us seemed to understand how the other worked. In passing I should add that the trial was made much less stressful than it might otherwise have been by the fact that I also knew the DPP's representative at court, Christopher Newell, very well, having also been instructed by him. The two Christophers had a relationship that allowed them to maintain professional distance but trusting interaction at the same time. The friendship between the three of us endures to this day.

I don't remember whether David Napley was at the Old Bailey that afternoon, but I rather think, bearing in mind his contention in his memoir that, had he been, he might have tried to insist on being present at the subsequent meeting that I am about to describe, that he was not. The reason why I have no recollection of any such potential dispute could be that, whatever has been said to the contrary elsewhere, George and I went into the meeting knowing exactly what our position would be, and David knew that only too well. Speculation has abounded ever since as to when, and in what circumstances, the decision was made that Jeremy Thorpe would not go into the witness box. George and I had discussed the issue from time to time ever since we had first met, and I have no doubt that we had arrived at a settled decision before that meeting that we would call no evidence. I am equally sure that we were all very careful to ensure that the decision did not leak to anyone beyond 'our team'.

I have already mentioned the, to me slightly unusual, relationship between George and David Napley. George was understandably keen not to offend this influential, and for him potentially lucrative, instructing solicitor. Indeed David had, as was his duty, tried to keep his client's brief fees to a minimum by telling both George's clerk and mine that this case could be the precursor to a future on the sunlit uplands. My recollection was that George had an 'all-in' fee of £15,000 on his brief, and that I had £10,000 on mine. Even in those days, those fees did not represent a king's ransom. I was not at all surprised that George did not voice a word of criticism of his instructing solicitor in his presence, but when we were alone together the QC was by no means as complimentary or supportive of David's tactics at Minehead. He believed, as I did, that a number of hostages to fortune lay in David's cross-examination. I have already pointed out that one of the reasons why the golden rule of keeping your powder dry at committal is usually observed, is that otherwise witnesses can arrive at trial forewarned and forearmed. Peter Bessell, for example, arrived at the Old Bailey aware of at least some of the issues that would be used in order to attack him. In fairness to David's approach, the other side of the coin was that George was aware of some of the heffalump traps that had been exposed at Minehead. That, for instance, was why he made sure that Norman Scott had no opportunity to start describing Jeremy's anatomy.

I entered the crucial meeting in no doubt that we were not going to call Jeremy to give evidence: but what transpired in that room can only be described as a game of cat-and-mouse between George and John Mathew. John (whom I last saw only months before his death, aged ninety-two, in February 2020), and I discussed the Thorpe trial many times during the last thirty years, and although our recollections did not always coincide precisely, as one might expect with the passage of time, we were able to compare notes about that meeting.

John, for whose ability and integrity I would be the stoutest champion, had not encountered George before this trial, but he told me that, although he felt that he could rely on a 'counsel-to-counsel assurance' by George, he would not have had the same confidence in our lay client. Indeed, only in 2020 John showed me a piece of paper, the significance of which was immediately apparent to me, but which I had never seen before. I will come to its significance in a moment or two. 'Counsel-to-counsel conversations', often criticised by those who have not been involved in them, sometimes allow cards to be laid on the table that would otherwise be held close to the chest, to the disadvantage of both. In this case, it was hoped that such an informal meeting might lead to an accord that would prove to be to the benefit of all four parties.

One of the weapons at the disposal of the Crown in a 'multi-handed' criminal trial is to put defendants in the order on the indictment which they, the prosecution, choose. Here they had chosen to put David Holmes first, with Thorpe last. That presented John Mathew with a problem. He had more or less come to the conclusion that he was not going to call Holmes to give evidence, but he was frightened that, once he had announced that in court, he had no control over what other defendants, further down the indictment, chose to do.

Why might John have decided not to call his client to give evidence? I do not know for sure, and John, loyal to the principle of client confidentiality, would never have told me, but it was not difficult to surmise. It is one of those mantras at the criminal Bar that 'the defence case is always at its highest at the end of the prosecution case' and that, in the experience of all of us, many a defence case that might have resulted in an acquittal had the jury retired to consider their verdict immediately the Crown closed its case, then at once went downhill, sometimes fatally, when the defendant gave evidence and was cross-examined.

With the Crown's case here primarily dependent on the reliability of the three main witnesses, whose credibility had, at even the lowest estimate, been severely dented, was it a possibility that the case for the defence might start to go downhill if defendants stepped into the witness box? In the meeting John was up-front. He required an undertaking from George and me that, if Holmes did not give evidence, then neither would Jeremy. John was acutely aware that the politician might have great faith in his own ability to fend off cross-examination, and he needed a cast-iron assurance that if we now said that Jeremy would not be giving evidence, that was an assurance upon which he could rely. What John feared was that even if Jeremy gave instructions to us now to the effect that we could give Holmes and his counsel the undertaking they sought, then, when it came to his turn, and after Holmes had committed himself to not giving evidence, there was nothing to stop Thorpe changing his mind and deciding to give evidence after all. It had become obvious to those with very keen perception that in fact the defences of Holmes and Thorpe were not by any means wholly in accord. From listening very carefully to the precise words that both Carman and Mathew had used when putting their respective cases to prosecution witnesses, it was clear that their clients' instructions were at variance. If Thorpe gave evidence, he would say that he neither participated in, nor knew anything of, any conspiracy to do anything to Scott; whereas Holmes would say that what he did to recruit others down the line amounted to a conspiracy to frighten Scott, so that he would desist from further embarrassing Jeremy, but was not in pursuance of a conspiracy to murder him.

From the start of the meeting, John and George played an elaborate game of bluff and counter-bluff until both were satisfied that they could announce to the other two teams that neither of their clients would be giving evidence. Right up until almost the end of the meeting, George was extremely careful to give the impression that a final decision had yet to be made about this. Until 2020, when John showed me the original document that I mentioned above, I had no idea, or at least no recollection, of its existence: but it was an undertaking that John had insisted that Jeremy should sign in his own hand. In effect, that document, signed and dated by Jeremy, said that if David Holmes did not give evidence, then neither would he, and if Jeremy later reneged on this undertaking and gave evidence, then he agreed that John Mathew could cross-examine him on the contents of the document. That meant that Jeremy could not risk ratting on his former friend.

That negotiation between counsel for Thorpe and Holmes had taken well over an hour, with counsel for the other two defendants taking little or no part in the discussion. Now John turned to counsel for John Le Mesurier, against whom there was not much evidence. Le Mesurier's leading counsel, Dennis Cowley, a portly gentleman with a walrus mustache, was observed quietly snoozing in a comfortable leather armchair. Once roused and told of John's and George's decisions, he was asked what he and his client intended to do. Dennis exclaimed: 'You two buggers have made my decision for me; of course I won't call evidence after that!' With that he sat back and closed his eyes once more. Then Gareth was asked the same question. The Welsh wizard replied that his client (Deakin) was going to give evidence, and 'it's no good you two trying to dissuade me'. They tried hard to change his mind, pointing out that a 'one out all out' display of disdain for the prosecution case would be ruined by a tacit admission from one of them that there was a case for him to answer. They also suggested that Deakin might bring everyone down if he failed to impress in the witness box; but all to no avail.

In court the next morning, John announced that he was calling no evidence, as did Cowley for Le Mesurier in due course. Deakin did go into the witness box, and all I need say was that he left it relatively unscathed; he certainly hadn't holed the ship in which all four defendants were sailing. By now the press, the broadcast media, and therefore the public had realised that the show they had all waited months to hear, namely Jeremy's evidence and his cross-examination by Peter Taylor, was either going to take place now or be denied them. When George rose and announced with great solemnity, 'My Lord, on behalf of Mr Thorpe, we call no evidence', there was an almost audible sigh of disappointment in court, and certainly outside, where the press and television crews were waiting for their pound of flesh. It was as though the spectators in the Colosseum had suddenly been told that no Christian would be thrown to the lions that day.

For the next part of the narrative, I am grateful to Thomas Grant, who has allowed me to crib from his book on Court One trials (full details on page 108): a very good read! He has provided me with the direct quotations from the speeches and summing-up.

Peter Taylor's closing speech for the Crown was a model of its kind. It was both fair and telling; persuasive and moderated in tone. It was a classic example of prosecuting counsel not trying to persuade a jury to convict against its better judgement, but laying out the evidence upon which he invites the members of that jury to the conclusion that they can be sure of guilt. I think the only touch of rhetoric in that speech was to suggest that the story of Jeremy Thorpe was 'a tragedy of truly Greek or Shakespearean proportions – the slow but inevitable destruction of a man by the stamp of one defect'. As I recall the future Lord Chief Justice's last closing speech at the Bar, I am reminded of the words of Johnny Nutting, my successor as First Senior Treasury Counsel, who said on a television programme that 'the Crown gains no victories nor suffers any defeats'. One of the greatest characteristics of our criminal justice system is that the prosecution is not there 'to get him down' at all costs.

It has been suggested, for some reason that nobody has been prepared to spell out in terms, that prosecuting counsel in some way pulled his punches, particularly in relation to Jeremy Thorpe. The underlying implication must be that Peter chose to go easy on our client because he, Jeremy, was a member of the establishment. That same criticism was also made, this time in spades redoubled, about the judge. I believe the slur in both cases to be totally unjustified, but particularly in the case of Peter Taylor. I have even heard it suggested that Peter, whom we all knew was probably conducting his last case as an advocate after a most distinguished career at the Bar (before going on to an equally distinguished career on the bench), had been 'instructed' to go easy on a defendant who, up until quite recently, had been a prominent member of the legislature. I reject any such suggestion or innuendo as defamatory rubbish, and I have seen nothing to convince me of a contrary view.

It was something of an irony that Peter was followed by the most effective gamekeeper, now turned formidable poacher. John Mathew was not there now to be fair, or even-handed; he was there to do all he could, within the bounds of propriety, to secure the acquittal of his client. He launched into a full-blooded attack on the credibility of the two witnesses whose evidence might, indeed would if believed, have convicted David Holmes. In words that seemed utterly appropriate as late as 1979, but would only be received with ridicule today, John said:

'I wonder whether the scales of justice held by that figure on the dome of this court are still trembling having heard the startling admissions from the witness Mister Peter Bessell.'

He then dealt with his client not giving evidence. He met the point head on.

'Through me, what Mister Holmes is saying to you is this: "I am not guilty of this offence. You (the Crown) have not proved through the evidence that I am, because the evidence you have brought defies belief. Therefore there is no need, because there is no evidence, for me to deny the charge."'

Suffice it to say that such a submission would not be as easy to make since the passing of the legislation that now allows both the prosecution and the judge to comment on the failure of a defendant to give evidence.

George and I had sweated (and drunk) over his final speech for hours on end. Unfortunately, 'working with George' almost always did mean 'drinking with George', and our kitchen table was again the scene of the action, with George's papers strewn all over the place once more. He didn't seem to want to make notes, just to try out ideas and rehearse the rhetoric. Now that I knew the man much better, I did not worry so much that he wouldn't perform; my worry was that he would say something out of place. In the event, he trod as close to the line as possible without going over it, except on one occasion. It was a *tour de force*.

George began with his own pen-portrait of his client:

'Privately, he is a man with a life that has had more than its fair share of grief and agony. Nature so fashioned him that at the

time he had the misfortune to meet Norman Scott he was a man with homosexual tendencies . . . Mister Jeremy Thorpe does not wish any advantage or disadvantage. He is now in your sole charge and he is content with that position. But inevitably because of the prominence he has achieved in the public life of this country, the case has centred to an extent on the life and times of Jeremy Thorpe – his frailties, his weaknesses have been exposed remorselessly to the public gaze . . . He is a man with a sense of humour, capable of real wit, and certainly a man to whom comedy was never absent for very long in his life. But tragedy has replaced it in large measure . . . At his age, if your conscience and oath permit you to say not guilty, there may still be a place somewhere in the public life and public service of this country for a man of his talents.'

George had not vouchsafed this passage to me in our discussions, and I remember thinking as I listened to it that I hoped the judge would not retort, 'Mister Carman, are you commenting on the evidence, or are you trying to give evidence, because I recall no evidence being given in this case upon which you can make those observations'. No such rebuke was administered, either at the time or in the summing-up:

Of Scott, George said '. . . *he is sad, mad or bad, or a combination of all three, I care not'. Of Bessell, '. . . he may go down at the end of this case as the Judas Iscariot of British politics of the twentieth century, because they have three things in common; one, he seeks to betray a friend; two, he seeks to betray him for money; and three, he seeks to betray a man who, I submit, is innocent of the charges laid against him. If, by your verdict you say not guilty, that may be the final epitaph of Mister Bessell.'*

Now that I have re-read that passage, I remember us drafting, re-drafting and perfecting it. In court, George said:

> 'We are not here to entertain the public or provide journalists with further copy. We are here for a much more serious purpose; to determine whether these charges are made out.'

Then to the peroration, which the two of us had similarly composed, refined and then perfected, well into the small hours. George spoke as follows:

> 'You have the right as citizens to vote in elections. But you have a much more important right and a much greater responsibility to vote guilty or not guilty. Mister Thorpe has spent twenty years in British politics and obtained thousands and thousands of votes in his favour. Now the most important twelve votes of all come from you . . .', George pointed at the juror in the back row on the extreme left of the jury box, 'and you . . .' to the next one, 'and you . . .', pointing in turn to each one of the twelve jurors. 'I say to you, on behalf of Jeremy Thorpe, this prosecution has not been made out. Let this prosecution fold their tents and silently steal away.' (This was a deliberate mis-quotation from Longfellow, omitting the reference to Arabs.)

After a dramatic pause, during which one could have heard a pin drop, George slowly resumed his seat. It felt as though he had dared the jury to convict at their peril. I left court that day quietly confident that even a summing-up designed to 'pot' us would not convince the jury to defy the diminutive genius who had challenged them to reject his masterful piece of advocacy.

The exception I mentioned earlier? This was the passage in his speech which, in my opinion and that of many others, crossed the line which separates what an advocate is entitled to say from what he should not say: George suggested that one possible interpretation of the evidence was that David Holmes had conspired with others behind Jeremy's back and without his knowledge. In view of the agreements we had reached with John Mathew, I felt extremely uncomfortable when I heard that, and John was understandably very cross. Many years later, John asked me if I had known that George was going to say that. I had not. Perhaps John Le Mesurier had a point when he was later quoted as commenting that, presuming Jeremy Thorpe was aware that his leading counsel was going to include this passage in his speech, then 'greater love hath no man than this, that he lay down his friends for his life'.

The summing-up of Mr Justice Cantley has been criticised, ridiculed and satirised. It has even been suggested that it was the product of a man who had been corrupted, and somehow persuaded, by the powers that be, and instructed to do his best to ensure the acquittal of Jeremy Thorpe. Whether that was the result of an agreement between the judge and leading counsel for the Crown has been hinted at but the implication never spelt out. In any event, I reject any such suggestions out of hand, and believe that they are largely the fantasies of those who felt cheated and disappointed at a result that deprived them of gloating over the corpse of a ruined man, conspiracy theorists who tend to find reasons to reject a result other than the one for which they were hoping.

The preceding paragraph should not be read as an assertion that Cantley J's summing-up was balanced or a model of its kind; it most certainly was not. Nor should my comments be seen as a rebuttal of the right of satirists and comedians like Auberon Waugh and Peter Cook to ply their trade. I found most of what Waugh wrote at the time quite amusing, and Cook's take-off of Cantley in *The Secret Policeman's Ball* hilarious. Waugh had waged a campaign against Thorpe for years, standing against him in the 1979 election as candidate for 'the Dogs' Party' (in memory of Rinka, Scott's deceased Great Dane), and coining as an election slogan 'vote Liberal and enlarge the circle of your friends'. Peter Cook's parody was the product of one of the most brilliant comedic minds of the time, as those of us who applauded *Beyond the Fringe* in the sixties knew – though he, too, was a flawed genius.

I suspect that most of the criticism of Cantley J stemmed from a fundamental misunderstanding of the functions of the judge when he sums up a case to a jury. More detail of this will appear later, accompanying my own experiences on the bench, but now might be the right moment to explain those functions with particular reference to this much publicised and much reviewed case. A judge is not simply a referee, sitting on the bench with a metaphorical whistle (not a gavel, as film-makers and television producers often wrongly portray). He is there, of course, to make sure that the rules are obeyed: that is his primary function up to the moment of his summing-up. But the summing-up itself must incorporate two distinct functions; first he must direct the jury on the law as it affects the case, and direct them on the elements of the offence(s) they must find established before they can convict; and secondly he must review the evidence, in order to remind them of the salient parts of it, and to help the jury arrive at their decisions. I repeat, help – not dictate. His review of the evidence, though, does not have to be a sterile and anodyne repetition of the words used by witnesses, i.e. simply reading from his notebook. The judge is perfectly entitled to express his own views on the cogency or otherwise of certain parts of the evidence, provided always that he makes it abundantly plain that it is the jury's view of that evidence that matters and not his own.

It is absolutely true to say that Cantley went about as far as it would be reasonable for a judge to go in some of the comments he made; many suggest he went too far. But another consideration must be brought to bear. If a judge feels with justification that it would be dangerous for a jury to rely upon any piece of evidence, or indeed on the evidence of a particular witness, then it is not only his right, but I would say his duty, to express that reservation, provided again that he makes it clear that, if the jury disagrees with him, it is not only its right but its duty to reject the judicial view and substitute its own. The judge has the same right to express a view, if he has formed it, that a piece of evidence, if accepted, points towards guilt, provided he accompanies that expression of opinion with the same caveat.

Judges have always had to be extremely careful when emphasising points that favour the prosecution. First, if they go too far, any conviction is liable to be quashed by the Court of Appeal. Secondly, and more immediately, if a jury thinks the judge is 'putting the boot in' it may, with its innate corporate sense of fairness, go in completely the opposite direction. I will deal with the best example I know of that in a later chapter.

Cantley did indeed indulge in strong expressions of his view as he reviewed the evidence of the three critical witnesses in this trial. During his review of Peter Bessell's evidence, he described him as a 'humbug' and his conduct as 'deplorable'. He described Andrew Newton as 'a conceited bungler' and remarked, 'what a chump the man is; to frighten or to murder, that is no way to go about it'. But he reserved his most caustic and disparaging remarks for Norman Scott. At the beginning of his review of Scott's evidence the judge said, 'You will remember him well . . . a hysterical, warped personality, accomplished sponger and very skilful at exciting and exploiting sympathy . . . he is a crook; he is a fraud; he is a sponger; he is a whiner; he is a parasite. But, of course, he could still be telling the truth. It is a question of belief.' Later he went on to describe Scott as 'a spineless neurotic character, addicted to hysteria and self-advertisement'.

There can be absolutely no doubt that the judge was warning the jury in the most cogent terms that they should be very wary indeed before relying on the evidence of any one of those three witnesses, but at every turn he peppered his observations with the phrases judges always use when commenting on the evidence; phrases like 'but it is entirely a matter for you' and 'it is your view of the evidence that counts, not mine'. Perhaps the phrase that pointed the jury in a certain direction more than any other was when he described the evidence against Jeremy Thorpe as 'almost entirely circumstantial'; that was extremely favourable to the defence, as there was one piece of evidence that was not circumstantial, but direct, namely Bessell's evidence that Jeremy, in the wording of Count Two which Thorpe alone faced, had 'incited' him to murder Scott.

Those who have most vociferously criticised the summing-up were almost certainly, with the exception of Auberon Waugh, not in court throughout the trial. It was only those who had been there consistently who would have been able to sense, as I think all counsel did, how the atmosphere changed as the trial proceeded, and how the tide had gone out on the prosecution case to a very large extent. I would hazard a guess that by the time the judge started his summing-up, very few who had been in court from start to finish would have put much money on convictions. I might even suggest that someone with an open mind, sitting in the public gallery throughout, might have wondered whether the judge should stop the case.

If that open-minded observer, unprejudiced by the media coverage over the past months, or the book written by Penrose and Courtier, had simply decided the issues according to the evidence and nothing else (as the jurors were obliged by their oath to do) and then been asked before the judge even started his summing-up, 'do you think the Crown has satisfied you, on the evidence you have heard, so that you can be sure of guilt?', then I think the odds are that that observer would have said no. If Cantley J's view was that it would be dangerous for the jury to be sure of guilt, he had every right to make that view known to them, albeit in a way that many regarded as ham-fisted, unsubtle and unsophisticated. To impute bad faith is, to me, a bridge too far.

I have a theory, and it is only speculation, that a clue to Joe Cantley's attitude to Norman Scott in particular may be found if one were to look back at another case he had tried in 1970, four years after he had married for the first and only time at the age of fifty-six. When trying a case involving a young man who had been severely injured in an accident with a bulldozer, and informed that the young man's injuries were affecting his sex life, Cantley had asked if the man was married; when told that he wasn't, the judge remarked, 'well, I can't see how it affects his sex life'. Could it be that nine years later, a slightly unworldly judge found Norman Scott's way of life so unpalatable that he could hardly believe that anyone who admitted to such 'deviance', as he might have described it, could give reliable testimony? I must repeat that this is pure conjecture on my part.

Before I move on from the summing-up, I want to acknowledge that I of course at the time observed it through rose-tinted spectacles, because it was indeed manna from heaven for our cause. Notwithstanding my own bias, I would suggest that Cantley's approach might have found favour with one of the most distinguished judges and jurists of the twentieth century, Lord Devlin.

In a strange irony, I revert to the case of Dr John Bodkin Adams, the doctor whose arrest for murder led me to the Bar. Devlin J, as he then was, was the trial judge when Adams was tried, and acquitted, at the Old Bailey in 1957. He, like Cantley J twenty-two years later, was trying the most high-profile case of the time, and he too formed a view of the quality of the prosecution evidence. Dr Adams, like Thorpe, did not give evidence, and the media, some of the commentators, and the public felt cheated by being deprived of the opportunity of reading about the defendant being cross-examined, and possibly humiliated.

This is a passage from Mr Justice Devlin's summing-up:

'I dare say, members of the jury, it is the first time you have sat in the jury box. It is not the first time I have sat in this chair and addressed juries. And not infrequently I have heard a case presented by the prosecution that seemed to me to be manifestly a strong one. And sometimes I have felt it my duty to tell the jury so, reminding them that the case for the prosecution must be strong if it is to be proved beyond reasonable doubt; and that it rests always with them to say whether it is strong enough. I do not think, therefore, that I ought to hesitate to tell you in this case that here the case for the defence seems to me to be manifestly a strong one and that you must not find for the Crown until after you have weighed and rejected all the arguments that have been put before you on behalf of the defence.'

That, I would suggest, was an even stronger indication than that given by Cantley J. It may therefore be an example of how times have changed, to compare what Devlin said only ten years before I was called to the Bar with what Cantley said little more than ten years after I started practising, and then to compare that with what I might have felt able to say when on the bench twenty years later. Judges were perhaps more robust in 1957 and 1979 than my generation thought it sensible to be. Whether that is viewed as a good thing or a bad thing may depend upon the age of the reader.

On Wednesday 19th June 1979, the judge finished his summing-up and asked the jury to retire to consider their verdicts with these words: 'You may go now. Take as long as you like; there is no hurry; we shall wait for you.' The defendants' bail was revoked (as was customary in those days), which meant that Thorpe and the others spent, as it turned out, two nights in HMP Brixton. A number of stories circulated about what happened over those two nights, most I suspect apocryphal. The nastiest of them was that a sadistic 'screw' had put Jeremy into a cell with a known homosexual; I have no idea whether that was true. What I do know is that at some stage we went to see Jeremy to take his instructions as to whether, in the event of conviction, George should address the court in mitigation of sentence, and/or call character witnesses, a number of whom were willing to come to court at short notice. Jeremy, having spent two nights in Brixton, albeit in the hospital wing, greeted George, who had probably spent the evening before having a good dinner, with 'hello George; you look as though you've had a rough night'. We set out what we referred to as the pros and cons of our various options, at the end of which Jeremy remarked, 'I will leave it to you to decide; after all, you are the pros and I hope we will not be the cons'. Whatever one's feelings about the man, one must give him credit for being able to crack a joke like that at such a time.

On Friday 22nd June, after a retirement of over fifty-two hours, the jury came back into court and delivered unanimous verdicts of 'not guilty' in respect of all four defendants on Count One (conspiracy to murder) and in respect of Count Two (the charge against Thorpe alone of inciting Holmes to commit murder). Something close to pandemonium erupted, despite shouts of 'silence in court!' from the ushers. Jeremy threw the three red cushions he had used during the trial out of the dock, leant over the rail to embrace the faithful Marion, and mouthed the words 'well rowed Balliol' across the court at George.

No application was made for our costs to be paid out of public funds; we had agreed beforehand that that might prove a bridge too far. George and I, having partially disrobed, accompanied Jeremy as he left the door of the Central Criminal Court and, with arms aloft, was guided by police officers through the scrum of photographers, journalists and other onlookers, as though he had just won another election victory. Later that evening he stood on the balcony of his house in Orme Square, again waving to those outside, as though he were still the MP for North Devon thanking his supporters after victory at the polls. I was inside the house drinking a glass of warm white sparkling wine, procured in a hurry by his friend, supporter and fellow Liberal MP, Clement Freud. I left as soon as I decently could.

Some time later, one of the jurors, contrary to the undertaking she had given not to reveal anything that occurred in the jury retiring room, allowed herself to be interviewed. She revealed that they had been eleven-one for an acquittal at the end of the first day of their deliberations, but that it had taken a further day and a half, at a time before majority verdicts were introduced, to persuade the twelfth juror to concur. She also said, according to the interviewer, that the jury had seen nothing wrong in the approach taken by the trial judge in his summing-up.

Three months later I received a letter, dated 19th September, from Jeremy Thorpe, the result, as I subsequently discovered, of David Napley urging him to write to both George Carman and me. I had asked Jeremy to sign a photograph I had obtained of him leaving court, in which I also appeared. His letter, comprising one side of a sheet of paper, read: 'Delighted to hear from you and equally pleased to sign the photograph recalling our joint venture.' The words 'thank you' did not appear; instead he told me about an intended trip to Africa 'to pull off a major business venture in Zambia and Zimbabwe', and the letter ended with 'When I am back let's meet'. No invitation ever arrived.

There is one strange postscript to the story. I play golf once a year at Aldeburgh, and every year stay with friends just up the road in Thorpeness. Theirs is the house Marion Thorpe sold to meet Jeremy's legal expenses, and I believe I sleep in the room once occupied by Jeremy.

Chapter 9

MORE CASES WITH CARMAN

The early 1980s represented a significant milestone, both in my professional and private life. They might be described as the years of onwards and upwards: for 1980 was the year in which I took a gamble on the housing market and the one in which Thomas Henry Boal was born.

In October 1979 I had celebrated my thirty-sixth birthday, and Margaret Thatcher had been Prime Minister for nearly six months. I sensed that the dreadful economic stagnation of the seventies was going to give way to a more buoyant outlook. Since we had married (and indeed for a year before that) Lizzie and I had lived in a small house, and now she was pregnant. I had been a treasury counsel for a couple of years, and the Thorpe trial had, in the words of my head clerk, 'got my face known'. I decided it was time to back my hunch and buy a family house. I was encouraged in this by my friend and accountant, Tony Campbell, to whom I still owe an enormous debt of gratitude; indeed, were it not for him, the turbulence in my life that was still to come might have reduced me to a pretty parlous state.

Tony had insisted, almost from the moment I was given a tenancy at 3 KBW, that I pay seven-and-a-half per cent of my gross earnings (the maximum allowed to avoid the incidence of taxation) into pension funds selected by him. He had acquired a substantial corner in the financial affairs of the criminal Bar. Barristers, as Tony would be the first to agree, were notoriously negligent about safeguarding their future; they tended to live from hand-to-mouth, running up huge overdrafts thanks to the late payment of fees, and always relying on their boat coming in some day soon. Although I was no more reliable than the majority of Tony's portfolio of criminal barristers, I was perhaps a little less foolhardy than some. I, like most others, spent most of my career at the Bar with a large overdraft, but I was a client of Barclays Bank in Fleet Street, just outside the Temple, and successive managers learnt to be extremely tolerant of us, provided we took the type of sensible precautions that Tony forced on me.

Tony persuaded me that now was the moment to take advantage of what we both recognised as a rising property market, and when we found a four-storey house in appalling condition (what the estate agent described as 'in need of modernisation'), I decided to take the plunge. It was a considerable risk but, as I subsequently learnt, risk-taking is a hallmark of the alcoholic. We bought this house, right on the border between respectable Holland Park and the bad-lands of North Kensington, for what was then the eye-watering amount of £80,000. At the time it consisted of four run-down flats, and we spent another £40,000 on converting it back into a single house. By the time we had finished, the project had cost £150,000, which, although it may seem like chicken-feed in the third decade of the twenty-first century, was stretching my resources beyond any sensible limit. I took out a huge mortgage, which I could scarcely afford, but encouraged by Tony's advice – 'it will hurt like hell now, but will get easier every year' – I ploughed on. How right he proved to be, and in the forty years since then, it feels as though I have hardly signed a cheque without Tony's approval.

The decision may have been risky, but perhaps it wasn't totally reckless as I had already been briefed in a case that promised to keep me lucratively employed for several months. George Carman and I had both received brief fees in the defence of Jeremy Thorpe that might have been regarded as modest, or even miserly, were it not for David Napley's assurance to both our senior clerks that the case could 'make us'. And so it proved. In the next few years we were both briefed in three potentially highly financially rewarding cases: the defence of Kagan Textiles Ltd; the defence of Dr Leonard Arthur; and the inquests into the death of Roberto Calvi ('God's banker').

I never quite got to the bottom of why George insisted to the solicitors involved in those three cases that he wanted me as his junior; indeed I only had his word that he did so insist. There was, however, a certain logic to it. We had worked together successfully in the Thorpe case, and few people knew that beneath the show of total unity, there was a tension that at times had threatened the effectiveness of 'the team'. Although George sometimes adopted tactics that I considered dubious, we had certainly found a *modus operandi*, and we had pulled off what many in the outside world regarded as a great victory. As I will explain later, when I deal with the Arthur case, there was, however, another reason why George wanted me by his side. His practice before Thorpe had been almost exclusively civil, and I doubt that he had ever prosecuted, other than small cases at the very beginning of his career. He used me, as treasury counsel, to explain some of the thinking and decision-making that lay behind prosecuting in serious cases; and indeed I would often hear him refer to me as treasury counsel, particularly if he thought that might give him some advantage over an opponent. I also think that George rather relished having as his junior an enthusiastic drinking companion.

Joseph Kagan was born Juozapas Kaganas in Lithuania in 1915. In common with many of his compatriots, he suffered terrible hardships under both the Russians and the Nazis before making it to Huddersfield in 1946. His family had been in the textile business back home for generations, and Kagan set up Kagan Textiles Ltd (KTL) in Elland, near Leeds. In 1951 Joe (as everyone knew him) invented Gannex, a rainproof material from which KTL manufactured raincoats. They were efficient (I was given one by KTL in due course, and wore it very occasionally) and became fashionable, thanks largely to the fact that Harold Wilson, then opposition spokesman for trade and industry, wore one ostentatiously when on an extensive international tour in 1956. In due course, Lyndon Johnson, Mao Zedong, Krushchev, and even our own Queen Elizabeth and the Duke of Edinburgh were all photographed wearing one of the garments.

The precise nature of the relationship between Kagan and Harold Wilson became a source of increasing speculation; suffice it to state that Kagan was knighted in Wilson's first resignation honours list in 1970, and ennobled as Baron Kagan of Elland in Wilson's second resignation honours list in 1976. Harold Wilson lived in Huddersfield, and it was said that all he was doing, in promoting Kagan's wares, was helping local industry, but Kagan's continuing links with Soviet Russia, together with Wilson's flirtations with the Communist regime in his earlier political life, gave rise to speculation which never totally subsided.

In 1980 Kagan had been arrested in Paris as a fugitive from justice, extradited to this country and in due course tried and convicted. The story behind that is where I became involved. Although the extradition treaty which allowed Kagan to be brought back to the UK did not include offences of conspiracy, the real case against him was that he had been involved in a massive tax and VAT fraud. The Crown alleged that he had conspired with others, including his sons, to effect the fraud, and chose to charge the corporate body KTL as one of the participants in that conspiracy. George Carman and I were instructed on behalf of KTL. Because of the extradition problem, Kagan himself was charged with theft of indigo dye and false accounting.

The directors of KTL were decent, and I believe honest, businessmen, and their reaction to the charge that they were guilty of a conspiracy with Kagan was (with Yorkshire expletives omitted), 'You must be joking! He was stealing indigo dye from us; he was defrauding us'. When Joe, at that time a fugitive in Spain, discovered that this would be his company's defence, he sprang into action. He sacked the entire board, put in a puppet board under the chairmanship of his wife, and told the new board to instruct us to plead guilty, thus avoiding our embarrassing defence ever seeing the light of day.

I remember sitting in my room in chambers, scratching my head and wondering what do we do now? This was not only in a professional capacity, but in the domestic context as well. We had sold our house, Thomas was only months old and we were about to put builders into our new house, which would be uninhabitable for at least six months. Previously, everything had seemed to fit in so neatly. In anticipation of a six-month trial at Leeds Crown Court, we had rented The Old Kennels at Tadcaster for six months and were about to move there lock, stock and barrel, taking with us my first pupil, Ian Paton, for whom I had procured 'a noting brief' and who would live with us rent-free. Then, only days before the trial was due to start, Joe Kagan had dropped his bombshell.

My completely uninformed view was that surely he couldn't do that: but, this being a question of company law, a subject I had scraped through in Bar Finals without understanding a word of it, I wondered whom I could consult. Luckily I had already rubbed shoulders with the undoubted leader of the chancery Bar, Richard Scott QC, as he then was. He later became Lord Scott, a Lord of Appeal in Ordinary and a member of the appellate committee of the House of Lords – the ultimate court of appeal before it was converted into the Supreme Court in October 2009.

I had worked with Richard, who was to become Chairman of the Bar before he was appointed to the High Court, because by 1980 I had become involved in Bar politics, representing the interests of the criminal Bar. I rang Richard and explained the situation. 'No problem', he said, 'sounds to me like a classic case of the second exception to the rule in Foss v Harbottle.' He was kind enough not to add 'as you should well know', so I didn't have to reply 'please remind me', which is the barrister's stock response when he hasn't a clue what the other is on about.

Under Richard's tutelage I became, in the course of a couple of hours, one of the world's leading experts on the said second exception. I had not known what the rule was, let alone anything about the first exception to it, but within hours I was on the telephone to George Carman 'reminding' him of the second exception. Basically it boiled down to this: a person controlling a company, as Joe Kagan did with an iron fist, cannot sack a board and replace it with a compliant puppet one, if the effect would be to the detriment of the shareholders of the company. 'So', Richard said, 'all you have to do is find a shareholder who feels aggrieved at what Kagan is doing, and off we go to the Chancery Division of the High Court. Leave the law to me; you boys can deal with the evidence.'

Thus we found ourselves one morning in front of Mr Justice Vinelott, one of the most experienced Chancery judges of his generation. I had been in the Chancery Division only twice before in my life. On both occasions, within a year of my call to the Bar, it was to attend winding-up proceedings: when the judge asked 'do you move Mister Boal?', all I had to do was raise my bottom six inches from the bench, say not a word, bow deeply and resume my seat. So the Chancery Division was to me not only a foreign country, but a very dangerous place, where the very clever inhabitants spoke a strange language and used weapons totally alien to my experience. To make matters worse, when I first spoke to George and explained what lay in store, he suddenly remembered a pressing professional engagement in Manchester on the appointed day, which would have meant that his junior would have to carry the can in London. There must have been something in my voice that made him rearrange his diary though: possibly it was the fee.

One thing I did already know about proceedings in the Chancery Division – it is simply not done to allege dishonesty on the part of anyone concerned. Misunderstanding, yes; mis-remembering, okay; lack of expertise, fine; but lying? No way. I seem to remember a Bateman cartoon of a barrister suggesting to a witness in a Chancery court that he was lying, and the picture to which the caption was 'The barrister who . . .' portrayed utter disbelief on the faces of everybody in court, with wigs flying off in disgust. Here we were going to have to cross-examine Lady Kagan, the chairman of the newly appointed board, putting to her that she was not only committing perjury, but conspiring with her husband to pervert the course of justice by denying it to our clients: simply unheard of in Chancery!

I well remember Vinelott J's face after just a few minutes of George's cross-examination. Having been engrossed in the legal argument between Richard Scott and Robin Potts, another doyen of the Chancery Bar, on the precise application of the rule in Foss v Harbottle, and more importantly the second exception to it (meat and drink to the very learned judge), suddenly he heard 'I suggest that is a blatant lie', swiftly followed by 'I suggest you have been sent here by your husband in an attempt to allow him to escape justice'. Once he had recovered from his initial shock, John Vinelott looked as though he was suddenly starting to enjoy himself, like a child that had been given a day off school. He not only listened intently, but began to join in. Lady Kagan found herself being attacked not only from the Bar, but also from the bench. We left court with an order that the original board's plea of 'not guilty' remained intact, and our brief fees and refreshers intact as well. I should explain that a barrister's brief, when being instructed privately, is normally marked 'X on the brief and Y per day', meaning a fee of X for the preparation and the opening day, and Y for each subsequent day.

Consequently I was able to ring Lizzie and tell her that we were on our way to Yorkshire after all, and one winter's day family Boal set off for Tadcaster, complete with baby and all the paraphernalia that went with him. Lizzie soon made us comfortable and once we had lit a few fires and discovered where the nearest supermarket was, we settled in for what we anticipated would be the rest of the winter.

In those days, trespassing into a robing room on another circuit could be a rather uncomfortable experience, because one was regarded as poaching circuiteers' work. I remember a rather chilly atmosphere when I first walked into the robing room in Leeds until a rather jovial face and a smile hove into view: 'Hello, I'm Harry Ognall. Welcome to Leeds. Where are you staying? Have you got everything you need?' Harry Ognall QC (later Mr Justice Ognall) was extremely hospitable and we became close friends. In due course, when Harry's rising reputation brought him to London more frequently, he used to stay with us, and I negotiated a tenancy for him in our chambers. To be fair to the local Bar in Leeds, though, all were friendly and helpful.

The trial had only just started when Joe Kagan dropped another bombshell. He negotiated a deal with the prosecution whereby he would plead guilty to the charges against him, provided the charges against all the other defendants were dropped. In case anyone thinks that to have been an act of generosity towards the rest of us, I suspect that he, realising that he had no real prospect of acquittal, decided to cut his losses and avoid the embarrassment of us running our 'cut-throat defence', which would have shown him in an even worse light. Kagan was a man who weighed up the odds and made the best of a bad job. He was sentenced to ten months' imprisonment and fined £375,000. An insight into his character may be found in the fact that when his leading counsel, the charismatic Gilbert ('Gilly') Gray went to see him in Armley Prison to discuss the possibility of appealing against his sentence, he apparently said that he did not want to be released just yet, as he was on the point of negotiating a contract to provide prison uniforms. Ever the trader.

Thus the Boal family had to beat a retreat from Yorkshire, so that I could return to London and to my day job, prosecuting as treasury counsel at the Old Bailey. When Lizzie and Thomas followed me, we spent the next few months begging, borrowing and renting, waiting for the builders to move out of our new house so that we could move in. While Lizzie was looking after a new baby in the difficult circumstances of not having her own home in which to do so, I was working hard earning as much as I could to sustain what at the time appeared to be crippling mortgage repayments. Luckily, as junior treasury counsel, there was always work, and one case followed immediately upon the last. In the early eighties I was usually acting as junior to a senior treasury counsel (STC), which meant that, when not actually in court, I would be drafting indictments and drafting opening notes (writing the opening speech for the prosecution). It was a treadmill, but a lucrative one. It was very hard work, but being led did not involve the same stresses as leading. We also had as much of a social life as could be fitted into my work schedule, and in those days dinner parties almost invariably lasted until well after midnight, and involved the consumption of considerable amounts of booze. I was burning the candle at both ends.

Here I will include a reflection on one of the last cases in which I was led as a junior treasury counsel (JTC). I was led by Michael Corkery, who had succeeded John Mathew as First Senior Treasury Counsel. Corks, as we all knew him, was a jovial and effective advocate, who was always willing to inject a little humour into a case if it was appropriate, and he and I worked very well together. On this occasion we were prosecuting a long and serious fraud case, in which the mafia had set up and run a totally fraudulent 'merchant bank' in London. They issued all sorts of documents, purporting to be bills of exchange and negotiable instruments, and indeed anything that a legitimate bank might issue, all backed by absolutely nothing – no assets, no capital, nothing except paper and hot air.

The case was long and complicated, but I want to describe just one incident, as this is, after all, a memoir of my career. The so-called CEO of the bank was a young man called Wagner. His signature was on just about every fraudulent document in the case, and so his wriggle-room was rather confined. He, or someone on his behalf, hit upon an ingenious defence, which can be summarised thus: 'I am not a perpetrator of this fraud; I was a victim. I am of very limited intelligence, and I was taken advantage of by these wicked men, who bought me a suit, put me in an office, and told me to sign any piece of paper they put in front of me; I had no idea what I was signing. I am now told that I have a mental age of about six.' This defence made it possible for his defending counsel, Michael West QC, not to have to challenge much of the prosecution case.

A psychologist, an expert witness called on behalf of Wagner, gave evidence in support of the defendant's claim and said that he had administered various tests to ascertain Wagner's mental ability. One of those tests involved placing a piece of paper in front of the young man, on which was depicted the outline of a face, but bereft of eyes, ears, a nose or a mouth. He then gave Wagner cut-outs of those features, and invited him to place them where they ought to appear on the face. The result was that the defendant (if I remember correctly), put the nose where the mouth ought to be, and vice versa, and put one ear on the forehead, unable to place the other ear. Not surprisingly, during his cross-examination of the psychologist, Corkery suggested that the defendant had not been trying very hard, a suggestion the expert stoutly refuted. I found his explanation to be bordering on the ludicrous, as did almost everybody else in court, and wrote a note to my leader. Michael read it and found himself momentarily unable to compose himself. The judge, a man who also had a sense of humour, invited Michael to continue.

'Would Your Lordship forgive me a moment? Mr Boal has passed me a note.' 'Then share it with us', instructed Judge Gibbens.

After a moment's hesitation, Michael did so.

'Mr Boal's note reads "eye eye, we've got a right one 'ere".'

There was, as they say, laughter in court, shared by everyone except Michael West and his junior. This Michael was red-headed, with a temperament to match, and he exploded.

When his client was convicted, Michael took the case to the Court of Appeal, appealing his client's conviction on the ground that the Crown had ridiculed his client's defence in a totally inappropriate way. As often happened, Michael Corkery found himself to be otherwise engaged when the appeal was called on, and the case for the Crown ('the respondent') was left in the hands of his junior: me. As I went into the court of the Lord Chief Justice, I feared that the judges might not look kindly upon my part in what had occurred. Michael West was not known either for his brevity or for conceding bad points, and as he droned on I could see Geoffrey Lane LCJ thumbing through the transcript to find the offending passage. When I could see that he had reached it, I was much relieved to observe first a smile, then a grin, and finally his hand reaching into his pocket, from which he took a handkerchief with which he covered his face. The appeal was dismissed and my career had not come to a grinding halt after all.

In October 1981, George Carman led me in a case that was unique in my experience, in that it was the only defence I undertook in which I felt, in the end passionately, that a conviction would have represented a grave miscarriage of justice. I use that phrase in its widest sense. Normally when defending one would not stake one's life on the innocence of one's client, and, if that client were convicted, one would simply move on, provided one was satisfied that one had done the job to the best of one's ability. Had Dr Leonard Arthur been convicted of murder or attempted murder and sentenced to imprisonment, I would have been, to adopt a modern phrase that seems the only appropriate one in the circumstances, absolutely gutted.

On 28th June 1980, Mrs Molly Pearson gave birth to a severely disabled Down's Syndrome baby in Derby City Hospital. Baby John was totally rejected by his parents and, after consulting with them in as empathetic a way as possible, the consultant paediatrician, Dr Leonard Arthur, took the agonising decision to prescribe a morphine-type drug called DF 118, and to write on the child's case notes: 'Parents do not wish it to survive. Nursing care only.' The child survived for three days and then died peacefully.

Dr Leonard Arthur was a highly respected consultant, who had seen front-line service in the Korean War, and had been a consultant paediatrician since 1965. He was described by a colleague as 'a kind, gentle, compassionate man who cared for his patients and their families; a great supporter of the weak or poor, he was motivated by firm Christian beliefs'. The many hours I spent with Dr Arthur confirmed for me that description of the man. Nobody ever doubted the sincerity, integrity or *bona fides* of his decision but, unfortunately for him, there was a nurse at the hospital who was a member of the organisation 'Life', whose members believed that human life is sacred, regardless of the circumstances. She reported the matter to the police, and in due course the Director of Public Prosecutions, Sir Thomas (Tony) Hetherington took what he described as 'the most difficult decision of my career', which was to prosecute Dr Arthur for murder.

The DPP could not be criticised for that decision. The offence of murder is a common law offence, in other words there is no statutory definition. For many years it has been defined thus: 'Where a person of sound mind and discretion unlawfully kills any reasonable creature in being and under the Queen's peace with intent to kill or cause grievous bodily harm', then he or she is guilty of murder. The DPP and the lawyers assigned by him would have looked, and probably looked very sympathetically, to see if Dr Arthur had any possible defence to murder based on that definition. They decided he had not. When George Carman asked me to see if I could find a defence, I too felt bound to conclude that I could not. English law knows no defence of 'justifiable homicide'. I have long believed that the law and medicine have been in head-on conflict when it comes to what might be called mercy killing or, to adopt the title of Lord Devlin's book on the Bodkin Adams trial, 'easing the passing'. Responsible and caring doctors have, since time immemorial, taken decisions in agonising circumstances which might have rendered them guilty under the legal definition of murder. I have no doubt whatsoever that my own father eased the passing of patients in what he considered were circumstances in which it was the only humane and compassionate thing to do as a caring medical practitioner.

So what were George and I to do? Advise Leonard Arthur that he should plead guilty, with the inevitable result that he would be sentenced to the only punishment allowed by law, namely life imprisonment? There was no way that we were going to do that. We were instructed by the Medical Protection Society (MPS), who provided us with every possible assistance, and we soon found that the vast majority of the medical profession was not only supportive, but willing to help in any way they could. We were inundated with offers to give evidence by many extremely well-qualified experts, but we had to explain to all of them the fundamental dilemma that we faced – namely that the issue was not whether Leonard Arthur had done the 'right' thing, nor whether what he did was medically or morally justified, but whether we had any defence in law, an entirely different matter. We decided that we had to concentrate our efforts on the issue of causation; that is to say whether what our client did had actually caused John's death, or whether there might have been a *novus actus interveniens*, a medical condition which might have 'intervened' and been the real, or at least a major, contributory cause of death. To that end we had one report which provided more than a glimmer of hope. A very distinguished expert, Professor Emery, wrote an opinion suggesting that, apart from the problems John had as a result of Down's, he had also been born with potentially significant brain and lung damage.

The trial opened on 13th October 1981 at Leicester Crown Court. Leading counsel for the prosecution was Douglas Draycott QC, Leader of the Midland Circuit. He was extremely experienced, and had the reputation of being old school and 'straight down the middle'. I feared from the outset that he and George would mix like oil and water and so it transpired. One of George's attributes was that he was extremely practised in the art of 'robing room advocacy', i.e. putting pressure on his opponent not just in court but also outside the courtroom. The diminutive silk was prone to sidling up to his opponent in the robing room, and engaging him in 'confidential' conversation designed to persuade the other of the error of his ways. When I walked into the robing room in Leicester that morning I found George, with his hand on Douglas's elbow, whispering sweet nothings. From Douglas's reaction, it was obvious what George had been saying, which would have been along the lines of the following (although I am not attempting to reproduce a conversation to which I was not privy): 'Now look here, old boy, you and I are old hands, and I know I can rely on you, counsel to counsel, to do the right thing. Do you really think it is right to go ahead? I can tell you that we have a perfectly viable defence, and a humanitarian decision not to put this honourable man through a trial for murder, at the end of which, I can assure you, he will be acquitted, would be applauded by all and sundry.'

I had overheard similar conversations before, but whereas the likes of Peter Taylor would simply smile and say thank you, but no thank you, I could see that Draycott had given George a more robust answer, probably consisting of two short words. From the outset there was an atmosphere between the two men that amounted almost to distrust. It was an extremely unfortunate start to what was bound to be an emotionally charged trial.

The case for the Crown was simple and formidable, and can be summarised thus: Dr Arthur took the deliberate decision that John Pearson should die, and took active steps to ensure that it happened. The case was encapsulated in the doctor's own words, that the parents did not wish the baby to survive, so 'nursing care only'. This instruction meant that the baby would not be given food or liquid; it would die of dehydration or starvation, and that is what the defendant intended to happen. That, the prosecution contended, was murder.

Very little, if anything, in the evidence for the Crown was challenged, but George, with great skill, extracted from the prosecution witnesses every possible ounce of sympathy and empathy for Dr Arthur's predicament. The crunch came when Professor Usher, the chief Home Office pathologist, gave evidence. He was regarded as pre-eminent in his field, as his appointment would suggest. His evidence was that John had died of bronchopneumonia due to lung stasis caused by dihydrocodeine poisoning and that he had been deliberately deprived of food and medical treatment. If accepted without qualification, that evidence was capable of giving game, set and match to the Crown.

One of the advantages that the defence in a criminal trial always had over the prosecution was that, whereas the prosecution has served on the defence the witness statements of all those it intends to call, and has disclosed any other material in its possession that could be of benefit to the defence, in 1981 the defence had no obligation to disclose to the prosecution whether, and if so what, evidence it proposed to call, or to reveal any material in its possession. That right (to disclose nothing) has now been substantially watered down by such things as alibi notices and defence statements, but in 1981, that right was absolute: with one possible exception.

That exception related to the evidence of experts. It was the convention, not backed by any rule of law, that the reports of experts would be disclosed to the other side. It was based on the assumption that, once the judge had ruled, if necessary, that the witness was an expert in his (scientific) field, then he would give evidence based solely on his expertise, and not tainted by regard to which side was calling him to give evidence. Whereas it was permissible for the defence to lay traps for 'ordinary' witnesses, and to catch them out without giving notice of the entrapment, it was not on to do so in the case of acknowledged experts. Practice had it that there would be an exchange of experts' reports so that, for instance, a prosecution expert could mull over the report of a defence expert and, if appropriate, come to court and say, 'I had thought X, but now I have had an opportunity of reading what Professor Y has written, then I think he may well be right, and I withdraw my opinion that X is the case'.

We had a report from Professor Emery which challenged Professor Usher's opinion in a crucial particular, namely on the cause of death, but George was adamant that we should not disclose it to the prosecution. He wanted to spring it on Professor Usher for the first time in cross-examination. To say that I was unhappy with that decision would be an understatement, but I decided, rightly or wrongly, that, having expressed my concerns to George as firmly and cogently as I could, there was nothing else I could do, short of withdrawing from the case. I concluded that if I were to do so, it would do disproportionate harm to the cause in which I strongly believed, namely that Dr Arthur should be acquitted if humanly possible. Had I withdrawn, it would have been assumed that I no longer believed that we had a case that could, consistent with professional propriety, be presented to the court. In due course, and much to my discomfort, George sprung the trap. Usher, obviously disconcerted by this unusual approach to cross-examination, was caught off-guard and conceded that if someone as eminent as Professor Emery could voice such an opinion, then he himself could not positively contradict it.

George's decision not to disclose Professor Emery's report in advance provoked one of the most unseemly rows I ever saw in a robing room, and caused me to disavow something George said to Douglas Draycott in the latter's presence. It is among the most unpleasant recollections I have.

George's cross-examination would have appeared as masterly as it was devastating to anyone unversed in the custom and etiquette to which I have referred. He began by getting Usher to agree that Emery was at least as great an expert as himself. He then tied him down to the opinion that John's death had been caused by nothing other than what he had described, and got Usher to agree that, if there were any other possible causes of death, then the whole of the Crown's case would be 'inaccurate and misleading'. He then, and only then, put to Usher the passage from Emery's report that suggested that John had been born, quite apart from Down's Syndrome, with underlying brain and lung damage. Draycott was extremely angry; he rose and demanded to know the basis of these suggestions, since he had seen no medical report which could have supported them. There was a break in proceedings, during which there was a furious row in the robing room between Draycott and Carman, in the course of which there was an unholy scramble for the only telephone in the room, since each wanted to report the other to the Bar Council for unprofessional conduct.

In the last chapter I said that I could not quite understand why George had insisted, as I learnt that he did to MPS in this case, that solicitors instruct me as his junior, but I found out one possible reason in the robing room that day. To my astonishment, in view of the disagreement we had had on the issue before the trial started, I heard George say to Draycott, 'as you know, Graham is treasury counsel, and he assures me that he, when prosecuting, would not have taken objection in the way that you have'. My response, addressing the remark more to Douglas than to George, was something rather feeble like, 'I think George has misinterpreted my opinion', but the whole ugly event left me with a very unpleasant taste in my mouth.

Professor Usher's concession, however, gave us a good ground upon which to submit, at the end of the prosecution case, that the Crown had failed to prove to the necessary standard that it was Dr Arthur's intervention that had caused death. The trial judge, Mr Justice Donald Farquharson, therefore withdrew the charge of murder from the jury's consideration, and substituted a count of attempted murder. What was our defence to attempted murder? In law we probably had none. But we still had the protection of a British jury, that prized institution that, in a few cases over the years, has said, in effect, damn the law, we are not going to convict in this case because we think it would be unjust to do so. We couldn't call Leonard Arthur to give evidence on his own behalf because he was an honest man, and if asked, as the first (and probably only) question in cross-examination, 'when you did what you did, did you intend that John Pearson should die?', he would have answered 'yes'. The judge would then have been bound to direct the jury that the answer amounted to an admission of the offence with which the doctor now stood charged.

So instead of calling him, we called a number of eminent medical luminaries, whose evidence might have been construed, through a lot of technical detail, to boil down to 'this caring doctor was placed in a very invidious position, and chose to do what we consider was right'. We had had a positive phalanx of potential witnesses from whom to choose. We chose, to my recollection, about four of the most eminent leaders of the medical profession, among them Sir Douglas Black, then President of the Royal College of Physicians, who spoke thus: 'I say that it is ethical, in the case of a child suffering from Down's Syndrome, and with a parental wish that it should not survive, to terminate life, providing other considerations are taken into account, such as the status and ability of the parents to cope in a way that the child could otherwise have had a happy life.' I remember hearing that word 'ethical' and fearing the retort from prosecution or judge 'ethical maybe; but lawful?'.

No one ever knows whether one piece of evidence proves more persuasive to a jury than another, but an event from my own life caused us to call the last witness for the defence. Thomas Henry Boal had been born in April 1980, six weeks premature, in Devon rather than in London as planned. In those days babies born so prematurely were in real danger of not surviving, but Thomas had been put into an incubator at Barnstaple General Hospital under the care of a young paediatrician called Howard Bluett, and Lizzie and I both think that he and his dedicated nurses probably saved Thomas's life. At a consultation with George I reminded him that our jury would consist of 'ordinary people' and said that as well as all these eminent experts, I thought we should call a paediatrician from an 'ordinary hospital' who had looked after the children of 'ordinary people'. I said that I had just such a person in mind. As soon as I got home I rang Howard Bluett. His immediate reaction on being asked to meet us in George's chambers was that he would be on the first train to London in the morning.

To my mind, Howard's evidence was devastating. In effect he stated that he dealt with all sorts of people from all walks of life, many very like Mr and Mrs Pearson, and had to make similar agonising decisions as the one that confronted Leonard Arthur. We did not dare ask Dr Bluett, or indeed any of the medical witnesses we called, the question 'have you done the same as Dr Arthur did?', for fear that the judge might feel obliged to caution him that he need not answer any question that he thought might incriminate him. We did not need to ask the direct question though, since the entire tenor of Howard Bluett's evidence amounted to an implied assertion that he had acted as our client had, and would do so again. I could not imagine a jury convicting after that.

Douglas Draycott's closing speech was very much a 'more in sorrow than in anger' one, whilst George's was another forensic masterpiece. He tugged at the heartstrings without being over-sentimental; he mixed scolding the prosecution for bringing the case in the first place with gratitude to witnesses for their assistance; he painted a portrait of the man in the dock without that man having uttered a word, except to plead 'not guilty'; and he came as close to describing what his client had done to mercy killing (a concept unknown to English law) as was possible. His final words were these: 'He could, like Pontius Pilate, have washed his hands of the matter. He did not, because good doctors do not turn away. Are we to condemn him as a criminal because he helped two people (the mother and child) at the time of their greatest need? Are we to condemn a doctor because he cared?'

We awaited Donald Farquharson's summing-up with a mixture of anticipation and apprehension. Would he say of George's speech that, however moving it might have been, it had not included a single sentence that would have provided a defence in law to the charge the accused faced? I had known the judge when he was still at the Bar. He was a consummate professional, a superb lawyer and a very fair-minded man; I also knew him to be a man who had very real human emotions, and a man on whom I felt we could rely to cut us any slack that was conceivably available. And so it proved. He allowed our defence submissions to be considered by the jury in a way that I felt made it plain to them that, were he sitting in their jury box, he would not want to convict. After deliberating for only two hours, the jury returned their verdict of 'not guilty'.

At some stage during the trial, before the charge of murder was reduced to one of attempted murder, I was sitting with the Arthurs when Mrs Arthur, a charming woman, asked me what would happen if the jury convicted. My heart sank, because I had to give her a straight answer: that the judge would be obliged to pass the mandatory sentence of life imprisonment, though I did go on to explain about judicial recommendations and the Parole Board. I realised then that husband and wife had not discussed the subject at all, which brought home to me in spades redoubled the stress that the doctor must have been under all this time. The awful sequel to the trial was that Dr Leonard Arthur died of a brain tumour on Christmas Day 1983. No one could ever convince me that the cancer was not brought on by the stress that man had suffered for so many months.

The case also gave me a rare insight into George Carman the man. He and I stayed in a hotel outside Leicester for the duration of the trial, and our wives joined us for part of the time. Lizzie had become friendly with Frances, George's third wife, and it was fairly obvious that living with George was quite challenging. Living with a barrister can be challenging for any woman; most of us are prima donnas, and the phrase 'my mistress the law' only too often describes a barrister's relationship with his professional life. I was certainly guilty of a defective work-life balance, but nothing compared with that of George Carman.

Professionally speaking, George was also getting restive. He was aware that he was not popular in the legal establishment, and I think it had been made plain to him that he would not be appointed to the High Court bench. Whether he realised how fundamentally unsuited to the job he would have been I do not know. He had, however, been to Hong Kong, and he felt that the life out there suited him. The expatriate lifestyle of hard drinking, heavy gambling and unconventional relationships was one that appealed to him. He felt that he was being unfairly judged by the establishment in England because he was a working- or lower-middle-class boy from Blackpool. He believed, whether on good authority or not, that he had an offer of being made a judge in Hong Kong if he made it known that he would welcome it. A great deal of our conversation in Leicester, in the rare moments when we were not discussing the case, was taken up with George vacillating between taking up the appointment or not. Frances viewed the prospect with horror, and Lizzie and I had considerable sympathy with her. Living with George in England was difficult enough; living with George in that environment would probably have proved disastrous. Shortly before the end of the trial, however, something happened which made George realise that the appointment to the Hong Kong bench was no longer on the cards. What it was I never knew, but George's lifestyle was such that he was constantly exposing himself to the kind of embarrassing publicity that would have caused someone to 'have a word in his ear'. Regrettably, his marriage to Frances, whom Lizzie and I both liked a lot, did not survive in any event. George was a man who understood women even less than the rest of us did. He was an inveterate gambler, was arrested more than once for drunkenness and, according to his son Dominic, was violent towards all three of his wives.

My last case with George involved the death of a man known as 'God's banker'. At 7.30am on Friday 18th June 1982, a postal clerk who was crossing Blackfriars Bridge in London noticed the body of a man hanging from scaffolding under the bridge. The man's clothing was stuffed with bricks, and his pockets contained the equivalent of US $15,000 in cash, in three different currencies. The man was identified as Roberto Calvi.

Calvi had been born in Milan in 1920, the son of the manager of the Banca Commerciale Italiana. Roberto himself joined the bank after World War II, but in 1947 he moved to Banco Ambrosiano, Italy's second largest. By 1971 he was general manager, and in 1975 he was appointed chairman. Banco Ambrosiano was always regarded with some suspicion, having close links to people in the Vatican who were themselves the subject of suspicion; it was also being linked with the illegal *Propaganda Due* (or P2) masonic lodge, known as 'the black friars'. Calvi was a member of that lodge, but it was only later that people began to wonder whether the 'black friars' name and the finding of Calvi's body hanging under Blackfriars Bridge was more than mere coincidence. Calvi had been tried in Italy in 1981 for the illegal export of many billion lire and given a suspended sentence.

On 10th June 1982, Calvi went missing from his apartment in Rome and fled the country on a false passport in the name of Gian Roberto Calvini, and, as I said, was found hanged in London eight days later. In the meanwhile, Banco Ambrosiano had collapsed, following the discovery of debts between US $700 million and US $1.5 billion. A considerable amount of this sum had been siphoned off through the Vatican Bank, which owned ten per cent of Banco Ambrosiano and was their main shareholder.

Not all of these facts were known at the time of the first inquest in London into the death of Roberto Calvi, and what we were later to describe as 'a superficial investigation' led to a verdict of suicide. The Calvi family were outraged at this, convinced as they were that Roberto had been murdered, so George Carman and I were instructed to challenge the verdict in the Divisional Court. As more and more facts emerged, and the rather simplistic suggestion that Calvi had so much to hide that he had obviously taken his own life was more carefully analysed and investigated, it became clear that, even if there was no positive evidence that Calvi had been murdered, the verdict of that first jury – encouraged by a rather cavalier summing-up by the coroner – was neither safe nor satisfactory. George, whose normal ebullient advocacy had to be tempered when addressing battle-hardened judges, rather than a jury, found himself knocking at an open door. The original verdict was quashed and a new inquest ordered.

Unfortunately for me, I had a treasury counsel prosecution commitment at the time of the second inquest, and my place as George's junior was taken by Julian Bevan. This time the jury returned an open verdict, but whether that was due to Julian's contribution being greater than mine would have been I will never know. The Calvi family, unhappy with an open verdict too, pursued their campaign, and in 1991 commissioned a New York-based investigation company to dig deeper. Eventually their enquiries led to the exhumation of Calvi's body, and in due course to five men being accused of his murder in Italy. No one has ever been convicted of the crime, but the accumulated evidence clearly suggests that Calvi's death was due to homicide rather than suicide.

That was the last case I did with George Carman, and our social relationship was such that, save at the occasional Bar function, I never saw him again. Indeed he did not contact me, either on the occasion of my being appointed First Senior Treasury Counsel, or when I was made a judge.

Nothing I have written in this chapter should be read as detracting from my description of George as a flawed forensic genius. His work-life balance was skewed to an extent rarely equalled by others. He is quoted as having said 'the law is addictive', and I have no doubt that he was an addict. As I now appreciate, he exhibited all the characteristics of an alcoholic: not just his drinking, but his recklessness, and his driven determination to succeed, despite any self-doubt that lay well hidden below the surface. However many forensic victories he chalked up, however much money he made, however much he was fêted and admired, it was never enough. But as an advocate he was, at his best, peerless, and it was a privilege to watch him in action at such close quarters on so many occasions.

Chapter 10

THE SEEDS OF DOUBT

The majority of my work in the 1980s was prosecuting as treasury counsel; junior treasury counsel until 1985, and senior treasury counsel thereafter. As JTC I would often, but not always, be led, and as STC I would always be leading. But two cases I conducted, leading for the defence in both, perhaps served as warning signs that stress was really beginning to take its toll, leading to episodes of depression.

Before I look at those cases, I should mention a significant occurrence in 1982, the catalyst for which was Diana, our devoted senior clerk at 3 KBW, announcing that she intended to retire. We did not have a junior clerk whom we felt would be able to take over, and the thought of trying to recruit a replacement for Diana filled most of us with horror. This coincided with a feeling that was growing in the Temple that big was beautiful, the justification for that view being that a set of chambers that could offer maximum choice to solicitors, provided all tenants were of the necessary quality, would ultimately prevail over boutique sets like ours. The result of these two things was a sort of Garrick 'billiard-room conspiracy'. One evening, Julian Bevan and I met two members of another set of chambers in private, under the guise of playing a members' snooker match between the two sets, to see if a merger between us was feasible. The other set was another purely criminal one, and we all knew each other very well, as we were frequently in cases together. The head of chambers was Dan Hollis QC, and Julian and I suspected that the big-is-beautiful bug had infected them too. Each team took to this surreptitious meeting a list of the tenants in our set, and as we compared them, it soon became apparent that, to use a bridge analogy, our two hands fitted perfectly – gaps in one set were filled by the other and vice versa. There were no voids and very few singletons.

Another huge potential bonus for the tenants of 3 KBW was that this merged set would have as its senior clerk one of the most respected, if not *the* most respected, of all the clerks of criminal sets in the Temple. His name was Michael Greenaway. A great piece of luck had fallen into our laps, as did one more. It would normally have been very difficult to find premises to house over forty barristers and their clerks under the same roof, but we found out that serendipitously the top two floors of Queen Elizabeth Building would be becoming vacant in the foreseeable future.

When the four of us took the results of our discussions back to our respective chambers, the majority of our colleagues saw the sense in the proposal to merge; some voiced misgivings but in the end everyone agreed to the plan. Thus from 28th June 1982 (incidentally Lizzie's and my fourth wedding anniversary), the chambers of Mr Daniel Hollis QC (formerly of 3 Temple Gardens) merged with the chambers of Mr William Howard QC (formerly of 3 KBW), where there would be seven QCs and forty-two juniors. As soon as word got round, as it did quicker than wildfire, that this hugely powerful vessel was about to set sail, it was nicknamed 'the Megaset', and our competitors used to refer to it as 'a huge trawler about to denude the sea for all other fishermen'. In the result, I think it must be said that the vessel proved to be a huge success that enhanced the careers of almost all who sailed in her. For solicitors, having the choice of so many able barristers on every rung of the ladder proved very attractive, since the return system was a vital ingredient of the whole set-up.

The first of the two cases I want to discuss here was the one in which I felt the first acute symptoms of imposter syndrome. I was instructed to represent a solicitor, and former Lord Mayor of Portsmouth, charged with fraud. Normally such a defendant would have been defended by an experienced silk but, probably because Mr Richard Sotnick was paying for his own defence and did not want to incur the expenditure of a silk and junior, I was instructed to conduct the case. It was heard at Winchester Crown Court, and the trial judge was Mr Justice William (Bill) Mars-Jones, who was regarded as one of the toughest of his kind. It was clear from day one that the judge had taken against my client and it became apparent that I was going to be given no quarter from the bench.

William Mars-J had been born in 1915, the son of a shopkeeper-cum-postmaster in a part of Wales in which the Welsh language was still commonly used. He was state-educated, unlike most of his brethren on the High Court bench. He had managed to get to Cambridge, where he had taken a keen interest in the Footlights; he was musical, and would sometimes play his guitar 'under the stairs' (the members-only holy-of-holies) at the Garrick Club. Outside court he was friendly and jovial and a great mimic and raconteur. In 1945, having served in the war, he had stood as a Labour Party candidate. He was a passionate supporter of the Bar and its traditions, who probably shared the view, very common in his generation of barristers, that solicitors were members of the junior branch of the profession. In view of all this, it might not be totally surprising to conclude that he and the Jewish solicitor, a former Tory Lord Mayor and still very active in local politics, who had made quite a lot of money out of property transactions and who may have given the impression of arrogance, were not exactly birds of a feather.

Mars-Jones's reputation as a judge was that of a fair-minded, common-sense tribunal, albeit a free-thinking and slightly maverick one. I had, of course, encountered him in the Obscene Publications Squad trial in 1978 and I had seen no reason to complain of his attitude in that trial. However, in his biography *Kid Gloves, A Voyage Round My Father*, his son, Adam, a novelist and literary critic, paints a picture of a man who was 'unable ever to admit that he might be wrong', and a father who displayed great intolerance when Adam admitted to him that he was gay. Perhaps it is also worth remembering that by the time he presided over this trial he was nearly seventy, had been on the High Court bench since 1969, and it was rumoured that he was a disappointed man, having not been promoted to the Court of Appeal. I have dwelt a little on the background of both defendant and judge in order to set the scene for the trial, and perhaps to offer some explanation for what happened.

Richard Sotnick was tried with three other defendants in a trial that lasted thirty-one days at Winchester Crown Court. The facts of the case were complicated and, for these purposes, not very relevant except in the broadest outline. Sotnick had acted for a property developer named Savage, who was also in the dock, together with two fellow directors of one or other of his property companies; originally all four defendants were charged with what amounted to conspiracies to defraud. Sotnick was additionally charged with a substantive offence of 'attempting to procure the execution of a valuable security by deception'. The case for the Crown was conducted by an eminently fair QC on the Western Circuit called John Spokes, leading Christopher Wilson-Smith, who had been a friend of mine since we took our Bar Finals together. Nothing that I have to say hereafter should be taken as reflecting adversely on either of them; they prosecuted the case competently and fairly.

As was perfectly permissible, Sotnick and his wife were each directors of a company called Dawnpoint Ltd, set up to advance money to clients or to buy property on their behalf when they were unable to obtain assistance from banks or other sources. Very shortly, the prosecution case was that, when there was a slump in the building industry, and the Savage group of companies was having difficulty in repaying its debts, unlawful and dishonest devices were used to divert money to places where it should not have been sent; those devices included, alleged the Crown, the wrongful execution by Sotnick of a 'deed of release', which would have benefited his company Dawnpoint to the tune of £2,600. There is no need to go into the detail of the complicated transactions which gave rise to that deed of release being sought.

The major problem I faced on behalf of Mr Sotnick, apart from the general impression of a solicitor who had got far too close to a dishonest client, was the evidence of a Mrs Bruce, who was a qualified legal executive in Sotnick's firm, whose evidence, if accepted, was pretty damning. I had to cross-examine Mrs Bruce, an outwardly perfectly decent woman, and suggest that she was, to put it at its lowest, not being entirely frank. From the moment I started my cross-examination, which was probably far too long, and may even have been incompetent, any veneer of neutrality from the bench disappeared. I felt as though I was being constantly, and unreasonably, interrupted, and that every time I might have appeared to be making headway, the judge intervened to come to the assistance of the witness. That, at any rate, was how it appeared to me.

I pass immediately to the summing-up. Defence speeches ended on a Tuesday or Wednesday. I had, of course, addressed the jury on both the counts my client then faced, namely a count of conspiracy with Savage and the count on which he was subsequently convicted. I had twice submitted to the judge that there was no case to answer on the count of conspiracy, once at the end of the prosecution case, and again at the conclusion of all the evidence. Twice that submission was rejected by the judge. Understandably the judge needed some time to prepare his summing-up in what had been a complicated case. He started his summing-up the next Monday and, into the second day, without any warning, suddenly announced that he was withdrawing the count of conspiracy from the jury. If either of my submissions of 'no case to answer' had been allowed before my speech, then my address to the jury would have been very different; even if the decision to withdraw the count had been announced before the beginning of the summing-up, accompanied by an invitation to me to address the jury on this new basis, then that might have remedied the situation.

The judge had ordered that a transcript be made, for his use only, of John Spokes's final speech to the jury. No such transcript was ordered for defence speeches. The judge summed-up the prosecution case by quoting verbatim from long extracts of John's speech. His review of my speech was, at best, not very comprehensive. The upshot was that Sotnick was convicted and fined £10,000. We immediately appealed on the ground that neither I nor, more importantly, my client, had been given a fair crack of the whip by the trial judge.

Because Sotnick was not sentenced to imprisonment, it took many months for the appeal to be heard, which it was in December 1984. The Court consisted of May LJ, and McCowan and Kennedy JJ: not by any means a team of softies or judges noted for their pro-defence sympathies. I found, a little to my surprise, that almost from the outset I was receiving a very sympathetic hearing, and that was reflected in Lord Justice May's judgement, allowing the appeal and quashing the conviction.

The Court of Appeal is always very slow to allow appeals based, not on errors in law, but on a suggestion of bias or unfairness on the part of a trial judge. That would be particularly so when, as in this case, the suggestion amounts to a head-on attack on the impartiality of a High Court judge, and one as senior and experienced as Mars-Jones. The language used in the judgement is necessarily moderate, but there was no escaping the criticism. I quote from the judgement of May LJ:

> 'Mr Boal has submitted . . . that when one looks at the summing-up in the round . . . a fair balance between the Crown on the one hand and the appellant on the other was not kept . . . the jury were not reminded, as they should have been, of a number of points which had been made on Sotnick's behalf . . . we are driven to the conclusion that Mr Sotnick's conviction was unsafe or unsatisfactory.'

There were other criticisms of the summing-up which are too technical to deal with here, but the words I have quoted represent a pretty swingeing criticism of a very senior judge, albeit couched in very diplomatic terms. I was not met, at any stage of my submissions to the court, with what might be described as the usual response to criticisms of a summing–up, such as, 'well, the judge told the jury that it was their view of the evidence that matters, not his', or 'we are sure that the jury had well in mind all the points you made in your speech, even if the judge did not repeat them all'. There was no attempt to 'excuse' the conduct of the trial judge.

So, you might say, all's well that ends well; in some ways I would agree. But this was the first occasion upon which I had left a case in doubt as to whether I had performed to the best of my ability. I kept asking myself questions. Was there something in my conduct of the case that had caused the judge's hostile approach; what else should I have done at the time, before the jury retired to consider their verdicts, to challenge the partiality of the summing-up; perhaps I should have tried to insist that I be allowed to make another final speech, after the judge suddenly withdrew the count of conspiracy in his summing-up. All this introspection amounted to my wondering whether a more competent and effective barrister could have prevented this man being convicted. In other words,

I suffered a bad attack of imposter syndrome. Something else had knocked my self-confidence badly in the interim before the hearing of the Sotnick appeal and the favourable Court of Appeal judgement. This was as a result of the next case that I conducted on behalf of the defence. Not only was it a very unusual one, it was tried by a rather unusual judge.

Judge Marcus Anwyl-Davies QC was an Old Harrovian, who had served with distinction in World War II. He was a very active freemason, who had rather old-fashioned views on a number of subjects. He had once, for example, sent a message to a female reporter that he would not allow her into court if she did not change from trousers into a skirt. I had encountered him on many previous occasions because he was the resident judge at St Albans, where I had practised a lot in my early years. Once, in the very earliest years of my judicial career, sitting as an assistant recorder, I had occupied his room while he was away and found on his desk two things which might have surprised me except for my earlier experiences of him: one was writing paper with his home address but also 'From His Honour Judge Anwyl-Davies QC' on it; and secondly a number of pencils, on each of which, occupying the entire length of each pencil, was embossed the same description. I remember thinking that because 'QC' was nearest the sharpened end, he would lose his letters patent as soon as he had to use a pencil sharpener. After his retirement he lived until his death in California, and I wonder quite what the Californians made of him.

The case itself was unusual because a limited company was being prosecuted for a criminal offence that amounted to harassment. The defendant property company, AMK (Property Management) Ltd, whom I represented, was owned by Arab interests in the Middle East. The building was an enormous block of flats in Park Lane, and a lot of the tenants were Jewish. The company wanted to increase the value of the flats, and thereby charge greater rents, by a refurbishment operation: this was necessarily going to cause very significant disruption and disturbance to the tenants, many of whom felt that the real intention that lay behind the project was to make life such a misery for them that they would surrender their leases. I have to say that my clients were ruthless businessmen who showed little interest in trying to mitigate the disruption. The tenants complained to Westminster City Council, who brought the prosecution.

I don't think I would have had any reason to complain if my clients had been convicted on the evidence. What made the trial something of a nightmare was the conduct of the trial judge. Anwyl-Davies displayed what I subsequently successfully submitted to the Court of Appeal could only be described as hostility to the defence, which meant to the defendant directors *in absentia* (because, the defendant being a corporate body, there was no person sitting in the dock), and to me, as the only person present at whom he could vent his spleen. It was a singularly unpleasant experience, and one that at the time certainly made me doubt my own ability. The summing-up was more like a repetition of the prosecution case, possibly with greater emphasis, and the jury understandably convicted.

I don't have a transcript of the judgement of the Court of Appeal available to me, but my clear recollection is that, almost from the start of my submissions, I was pushing at an open door. The appeal court judges ruled that the trial judge had misdirected the jury in law, and also agreed that the summing-up was so unbalanced that they allowed the appeal on both grounds and quashed the conviction. Between the trial and the appeal, however, I was beset by the same doubts and fears as I had encountered in relation to my defence of Richard Sotnick. Was it my fault? Could I have performed better and achieved a different result? Was I up to the job? Had I finally been found out as not being as good as my reputation might have suggested?

With the benefit of hindsight, I should have just shrugged my shoulders – certainly after both appeals had been successfully concluded – and put my experiences down to the bad luck of having to defend twice within a short period of time in front of two rather 'unusual' judges. At the time, though, I felt as though I had been found wanting. Luckily I was able to return to my day job, prosecuting as treasury counsel: a job to which I now feel, again with the benefit of hindsight, I was temperamentally much better suited.

Why do I feel that I was a better prosecutor than defender? I think I have to examine that question by looking at the fundamental difference between prosecuting and defending. To quote my old friend Johnny Nutting again, 'the Crown wins no victories and suffers no defeats'. That does not mean that prosecuting counsel soft-peddles when firmness, resolve, and tough questioning is called for, but it does mean that though firm, a prosecutor must always be fair. By contrast, fairness is not something that defending counsel always has to have in his toolbox – because defending counsel is there to get his client off. I think I felt happier being, as one was most of the time when prosecuting, on the side of the angels. By using that phrase I do not mean to imply that one's witnesses were necessarily angelic; I mean that in reality one usually had right on one's side. With all the checks and balances that the system provides in place, the reality is that the vast majority of defendants are not only guilty of the offence with which they are charged, but deserve, on the evidence, to be convicted. I genuinely believe that the chance of people who are wholly innocent being convicted is very slim indeed, but we will examine the concept of 'miscarriage of justice' in a particular context in a later chapter.

In 1985 I was appointed Senior Treasury Counsel, and although the responsibility of leading for the prosecution in serious cases was sometimes quite intense, nevertheless I did not suffer as much stress as I sometimes did when defending. I did expose myself, quite voluntarily, to added work and responsibility by indulging in Bar politics, which is the subject-matter of the next chapter.

I must, however, add to my self-analysis about prosecuting and defending that there can be no better feeling for a criminal barrister than to defend in a case in which the evidence against his client is overwhelming, but nevertheless to hear from the mouth of the foreman of the jury the magic words 'not guilty'. I want to remember an example of that, which occurred in the 1980s.

I was defending a professional criminal, who on this occasion was found with his co-conspirators in a basement, with his hand on the handle of a printing press that was churning out forged Spanish 1000-peseta notes. At the time, as some will remember, Harold Wilson's government had set a £50 travel limit; and for those too young to know, the Spanish currency before the euro was the peseta, and though 1000 pesetas was not worth as much as the number of zeros might imply, nevertheless it was not an insignificant sum. The note itself was green and had, in its top right corner, the word *Mille* (Spanish for one thousand). My client's defence can be summed up in this sentence: I am an ill-educated Cockney boy, not very good at reading, and I thought I was printing luncheon vouchers. Again for the uninitiated, in the 1980s luncheon vouchers represented a very tax-efficient method by which employers gave their employees free lunches: luncheon vouchers were green. The highlight of the trial was when my villain was being cross-examined and invited to compare a genuine luncheon voucher with one of the notes he had printed. He suddenly retorted, pointing to the top right of the forged note, 'look at this; it says "meal"'. Looking at the faces of the jury at that moment one had a feeling that we were 'in with a run', and so it transpired. Not guilty!

Chapter 11

BAR POLITICS

The criminal Bar's 'trade union' is the Criminal Bar Association (CBA), and I became involved with this quite early in my career. The CBA of course worked closely with the main body, the Bar Council (BC), and I found myself increasingly representing the CBA on various committees of the BC. In particular, I was for many years the chairman of the criminal sub-committee of the Fees and Legal Aid Committee of the BC, which involved my impersonating someone like Arthur Scargill in meetings with officials from the Lord Chancellor's Department (LCD) and the Treasury. Indeed, on more than one occasion, we threatened strike action, and some of our more militant members were often trying to encourage us to turn our threats into reality. I was never quite sure that I was cut out to stand on a picket line.

I was lucky enough to go to the Bar in the mid-sixties, just when legal aid was beginning to yield sufficient fees on which a barrister could live reasonably comfortably. Incidentally, I left the Bar and went on the bench in the mid-nineties, which was when the constraints on legal aid fees were beginning to bite: so rather more by luck than good judgement I enjoyed the thirty halcyon years when practising at the criminal Bar, even if one was wholly reliant on publicly funded fees, was a reasonably lucrative occupation. Nevertheless there were moments when criminal practitioners felt they were not getting the rub of the green, and then we had to go into battle with those who held the purse-strings. One of those moments was in the mid-eighties.

I was fortunate to work with a lot of very eminent barristers who, despite earning large amounts on their own behalf, gave up their valuable time and effort to represent the interests of those who were faring considerably less well. Among many others I pick out Richard Scott (of Foss v Harbottle fame, and later a Law Lord), Robert Johnson (who became a notable High Court judge in the Family Division) and Robert (Bob) Alexander who, having been one of the leading members (and top earner) at the commercial Bar, went on to be Chairman of the National Westminster Bank as Lord Alexander of Weedon.

In 1985 the criminal Bar felt that the LCD and Treasury were not increasing criminal fees at a fair enough rate, and the Bar Council, led by Bob Alexander, took up the cudgels on behalf of its poorer relations. I worked very closely with him and Robert Johnson during this time, and our endeavours culminated in the Bar suing the Lord Chancellor in the High Court, in the case known as Alexander v Hailsham (Lord Hailsham being Lord Chancellor at the time). The result was that the LCD caved in at the door of the court and conceded sufficiently for us to feel we had made some headway.

Bob Alexander QC (known as 'the welded rail' for his seamless advocacy) had led me and Robert Johnson QC in the preparation of the case. We were assisted hugely by the accountancy firm of Coopers & Lybrand (as it then was), and a team of accountants led by a senior partner who became a close friend, Donald Chilvers. Donald and his team did amazing things on our behalf, and put together an economic argument which finally won the day for us.

Two aspects of their submissions stand out in my recollection. The first was that the criminal justice system was a profit-making operation, because the amount collected in fines in every court, up and down the country, was more than the expenditure incurred in running the courts, including paying legal aid fees. The second was that taking a nuclear missile out of its silo on Greenham Common and driving it round the perimeter of the camp cost more than running the entire criminal justice system for a year.

My work with the Bar Council provided me with many interesting experiences and opportunities I would not otherwise have enjoyed. Those opportunities included two visits to Moscow. The Russian government, for reasons I could never quite fathom, expressed interest in learning about our system of criminal justice, and in particular the jury system. Apparently they wanted to know whether our jury system was one they might want to adopt. A deputation went to Moscow, comprising Roy Beldam LJ, who was Chairman of the Law Commission (the body that looks into law reform); John Clitheroe, a partner in Kingsley Napley, whom I knew well, representing the Law Society and thus the solicitors' profession; and me, representing the Criminal Bar Association (CBA). As soon as we arrived in Moscow we were summoned to attend the office of their equivalent of lord chief justice. He told us that they had a problem. The current rate of acquittal in their courts was running at three per cent, which he said was unacceptably high, and he wondered whether the introduction of juries might solve the problem. The meeting did not last long because, when we told him that the current rate of acquittal in our Crown Courts was over forty per cent, he and his advisers thought that there was little point in continuing the conversation.

In fact I made two visits to Moscow, and on one of them I had a most interesting conversation with a defence lawyer. I tracked him down to a nondescript office in a back street and, having somehow managed to give the slip to our official government guide, I had a fascinating half-hour with him. I asked him: 'What would you do if you had a client who had signed a written confession to a very serious crime like treason, but who told you that he had only done so because he had been tortured in the basement of the Lubyanka, and he was in fact not guilty?' His candid answer was that he would take a protracted holiday. His parting words were, 'you don't know how fortunate you are; your system is the envy of the world'. I left Russia even more convinced than before that we are lucky to be living in the society that we do.

There came a time when I was both prosecuting as Senior Treasury Counsel and running the CBA at the same time. I was vice-chairman of the CBA, but the chairman, Michael Kalisher QC, was in Hong Kong appearing in an extremely long case, so I was left in charge of the shop at a time when quite a lot was going on. In retrospect, I should have said that I could not be STC and vice-chairman at the same time. On the other hand, I always felt that it was a great privilege to represent the profession I loved, and which gave me so much; I wanted to do the best I could for those within the profession who were not as fortunate as I had been. By now, however, I truly was burning the candle at both ends, feeling permanently stressed, and of course taking my own self-prescribed 'medicine', mainly distilled in Scotland. It was at about this time that I first consulted a psychiatrist.

Chapter 12

SENIOR TREASURY COUNSEL

I had been appointed Senior Treasury Counsel (STC) in 1985, and served as such until 1993. It was at the end of that stint that I succumbed and went into The Priory. I had risen from being the most junior STC (I think of six), and ended as First Senior Treasury Counsel (1STC) for two years. Thus I followed in the footsteps of many great advocates, including John Mathew, though I was never 'God'.

Although I have already explained the job of the TCs, it may be worth repeating that they are not only responsible for conducting the most serious cases at the Central Criminal Court (the Old Bailey) on behalf of the Attorney General (AG) and the Director of Public Prosecutions (DPP), but also for advising them, and occasionally the government, on any matter within the criminal ambit. I will deal with two such cases in which I advised, and which in the end resulted in no prosecution, despite considerable public dismay.

The usual diet for STCs was prosecuting in murder cases, very few of which are worth mentioning in this context. That is not to say that they were not very serious, and I wouldn't want anything I write to be taken as diminishing the very human tragedy that each of those cases represented for everyone involved. Other cases I prosecuted involved alleged offences of terrorism.

Perhaps the first case I prosecuted that attracted widespread publicity was that involving a terrorist organisation commonly known as Abu Nidal. To give it its full title, the Abu Nidal Organisation (ANO) was the common name of the Palestinian nationalist militant group Fatah, and was named after its founder Abu Nidal. It was known as one of the most uncompromising militant Palestinian groups of all time, attacking high-profile targets in twenty countries, including the United States, France, Israel and the UK.

Rasmi Awad, a Jordanian doctor, allegedly practising in Madrid, was caught, in a brilliantly executed sting, taking delivery of a package that he understood to contain grenades. Our security services believed that these were intended to be used at Heathrow, in an attack similar to those at airports in Vienna and Rome that had killed nineteen people and injured over a hundred others. Awad thought he was meeting an Abu Nidal courier, but in fact the man he met in central London was a Libyan undercover agent opposed to the regime of Colonel Gaddafi, who had been recruited by our security services. He said he had picked up a parcel containing four anti-personnel live hand grenades from a man wearing a Libyan Arab Airlines uniform at Heathrow and, after police had substituted the grenades with replicas, he delivered them to Awad under the watchful eye of Special Branch, who photographed the handover. Awad was then arrested.

What made the trial unique was that the undercover agent, known in court as 'Mister I', gave evidence wearing a fake beard, moustache and dark glasses. The disguise was, of course, known to the judge (Mr Justice Simon Brown as he then was), who approved this course of action, and to the defence. Mister I said that he had been recruited to be a weapons courier by 'a man high in the regime' in Libya. Had the judge not allowed the witness to give evidence in disguise, then we had agreed beforehand that the Crown would have had to offer no evidence against a very dangerous terrorist. This case was one of a number I prosecuted during which I was made privy to material that could never be disclosed in public. Indeed, in another case I was forced to offer no evidence against two IRA terrorists, because the disclosure of material in the possession of the prosecution would have put the lives of extremely brave undercover officers in peril. These were not easy decisions.

Another case I prosecuted in the second half of the 1980s was that of a man known as the Putney Rapist. Everald Irons was one of the most prolific and dangerous serial rapists of the period, and for a considerable time he created an atmosphere of great fear among young women in south-west London. In the months after December 1985, when the first incident occurred, there were at least eighteen rapes and indecent assaults in the Putney and Wandsworth area, which police began to believe bore the hallmarks of having been committed by the same man. Descriptions of the assailant fitted, the lurid details suggested a modus operandi, and a pattern emerged which caused the police to launch a manhunt for a very devious and dangerous man. The police investigation was meticulously conducted, and piece by piece the jigsaw puzzle began to take shape. Many of these pieces involved hours of scrupulous work by forensic scientists, including comparisons of clothes fibres found on the victims which were found to match clothing belonging to Irons, seized after his arrest. At the end of a longish trial, Irons was convicted on a number of counts of rape and sentenced to eighteen years' imprisonment. His appeal was dismissed.

Understandably the trial attracted quite a lot of publicity, including one article that nearly caused the jury to be discharged and the trial to be aborted. On 13th July 1988, the *Daily Mail* published an article entitled 'Wife cracks under cross-examination in Putney Rapist trial', then went on to read, 'shifting from foot to foot, the WPC admitted lying to give her husband an alibi'. There followed an, albeit fairly accurate, account of my cross-examination of Anne Irons, the defendant's wife.

Irons was married to a woman police officer and both gave the outward impression of being devout Baptists: Anne Irons wore a gold cross round her neck in the witness box. For reasons I was never able to fathom, Mrs Irons had decided to give her husband a false alibi for the night of one of the rapes and, had her evidence been believed, it would have driven a coach and horses through the prosecution case. We, the police officers and I, knew she must be lying, but proving it was not easy. In the end her own police diary undermined her evidence and, after the lie had been exposed, she did, to quote the article, 'break down in the witness box and admit to falsifying evidence to protect her husband'.

The morning the article appeared, Anthony Arlidge QC, representing Irons, applied to the judge to have the jury discharged, on the ground that a newspaper had in effect convicted his client. That application was refused, but the judge administered a strong warning to the jury to ignore the reported views of journalists. The judge then summoned the editor of the *Daily Mail* to attend court to defend himself against a charge of contempt of court, and to 'bring a toothbrush' – meaning that the judge was considering a custodial penalty. The next day the editor arrived with no less a representative than John Mathew QC, who ate a very large helping of humble pie; as a consequence, the newspaper was fined but the editor was able to leave court a free man.

In the mid-eighties, with the Falklands War behind her, Margaret Thatcher embarked on implementing policies which came to bear her name as Thatcherism. I was earning well, but needing to do so to sustain my huge mortgage, and already paying school fees for Thomas which I described as '£100 per learning of each letter of the alphabet'. We were living the life enjoyed by forty-something successful inhabitants of increasingly trendy Notting Hill, which meant dinner parties extending into the small hours and, at least for me, substantial amounts of booze. The serving of port until well after midnight was par for the course. I was under considerable pressure at work because, as well as the day job in court, I was increasingly being instructed to advise the Attorney General and the DPP on whether proceedings ought to be instituted.

One such set of instructions involved a scandal which became for some the epitome of 'the unacceptable face of capitalism'. Lloyd's of London was the leading insurance market in the world and, with house prices rising and the income of many middle-class families rising at the same time, some people had quite a lot of spare cash. It became very popular to put large amounts of money into Lloyd's, encouraged by underwriters and agents who were only too anxious to spread the myth that it would be money for old rope, because the chances of losing your investment were minimal. In the end, hundreds, if not thousands, of people invested money they could not afford: often they mortgaged or even remortgaged their houses in the belief that they would never be called on to settle claims, but instead would make a steady, safe and considerable annual dividend. I, too, was one of those tempted to 'put my house on it'.

Luckily, just as I was about to sign on the dotted line, a big brief was delivered to my desk. This was to advise the Serious Fraud Office (SFO) on the prosecution of Peter Cameron-Webb, Peter Dixon and others involved in the PCW reinsurance syndicate at Lloyd's. For the previous few years, rumours had been circulating that PCW was operating a scam which meant that while 'the outsiders' (that is to say the 'names' outside Lloyd's who had pledged their money to meet claims) would be the ones called upon to cough up in the event of a major crisis like asbestosis or a hurricane, whereas 'the insiders' (the underwriters and their associates) had their money safely tucked away in 'risks' that were in reality gold-plated and provided no risk at all.

As I started to read the brief I began to worry that it was because of my stupidity that I was finding it impossible to understand what I was grappling with. In desperation I rang and asked for help, which arrived in the shape of an utterly straight underwriter who came to my chambers. His response to my request for an explanation of reinsurance was to ask me if I had ever placed a bet on a horse: and, if so, had I understood the concept of a bookmaker laying off a bet? I assured him that I had lost too much money to bookmakers not to understand that concept, to which he replied: 'Right, you've got it; that's reinsurance.' The scales fell from my eyes and I soon began to grasp the concept of the scam. Put very simply, the insiders kept the good bets and laid off the risky ones to the outsiders – the ordinary punters outside Lloyd's who had staked their houses on making, and not losing, money. The good risks were assigned to 'baby syndicates', comprised of insiders only, whilst the potentially bad risks were assigned to the outsiders. Baby syndicates always made a healthy profit.

One of the most valuable lessons Roger Frisby taught me about prosecuting fraudsters was 'follow the money'. If the money starts in the correct account, but ends up purchasing a yacht in the South of France bearing the name of the mistress of the supposed custodian of the funds, then juries will reach the right conclusions. Sure as anything, when we traced the money from the baby syndicates, it landed up in huge amounts in assets (indeed such as yachts) in the names of those in PCW, especially Cameron-Webb and Dixon. Others in the PCW ambit were implicated, but it was clear that it was the two principals who should be prosecuted first, before further consideration was given to whether others, and if so who, should sit in the dock with them. PCW was not the only potential target, and charges were brought against other Lloyd's underwriters, notably Ian Posgate, known as 'Goldfinger' because of the amounts he was earning for himself and some of his names.

The evidence against Cameron-Webb and Dixon was, in my view, overwhelming, so I drew up charges and advised that they should be prosecuted. It was obvious that names had been defrauded, probably to the tune of about £40 million. As soon as the two got wind of what was likely to happen they fled the jurisdiction, Dixon to Spain and then ultimately the USA, Cameron-Webb straight there. They chose their destinations with care, having studied, or been advised upon, the extradition treaties between the USA and the UK. Put very simply, the case against the two fugitives from justice was one of conspiracy to steal or defraud, and the treaty we had with the USA precluded extradition for a conspiracy charge: hence there was no way, short of their returning to our jurisdiction, that we could bring them to justice.

There was a bizarre twist to this story in 1989. On 2nd April I received an urgent communication from the SFO, telling me that Cameron-Webb had travelled, under the name Webb, on a flight from Miami destined for Helsinki. But the plane had been diverted to Prestwick, where he had been arrested by the Scottish police. I was told he was being brought to London, and that I was to appear at Guildhall Magistrates' Court the next morning. All the details were reported in the press that day, the 3rd. Regrettably, the whole thing was an elaborate hoax. Cameron-Webb was still tucked up in Miami, and it was only in retrospect that we realised that the story had originated on 1st April. *The Daily Telegraph*, for one, ate a large helping of humble pie in the 4th April edition.

On 18th November 1987 at approximately 7.30pm a fire started at King's Cross tube station. About fifteen minutes later the fire erupted in a flashover into the underground ticket hall, killing thirty-one people and injuring a hundred. Several hundred people were also trapped underground, on sub-surface platforms for the Northern, Piccadilly and Victoria lines, but were evacuated, thanks to the presence of mind of London Underground staff, on trains running on the Victoria line.

Margaret Thatcher immediately ordered a public inquiry into the tragedy, to be conducted by Desmond Fennell QC assisted by a panel of four expert advisers. They sat between February and June 1988 and concluded, to summarise the complex findings, that the fire had started when a lit match was dropped on an escalator and then fallen onto long accumulated detritus, including a build-up of lubricant grease under the tracks of the then wooden escalator. Quite why such a fire had resulted in the fatal flashover was the subject of much expert debate. The inquiry also concluded that the fire had not been started deliberately, as there was no evidence of an accelerant. Smoking on underground trains had been banned in 1984, and the ban was extended to all underground stations in 1985, but there was evidence that smokers still lit up on their way up to the surface while on the escalators. London Underground and London Regional Transport were heavily criticised in the Fennell Report, and its findings led to several resignations. Wooden escalators were gradually replaced by metal ones throughout the system and the whole safety regime significantly tightened up.

I was instructed to advise on whether criminal proceedings were justified. In the frame were LU and LRT as potential corporate defendants, together with a number of senior employees with responsibilities for safety at the station, and on the network generally. I began with the finding that the fire had not been started deliberately, so went on to consider potential offences involving health and safety at work, together with the possibility of prosecuting the corporate entities with corporate manslaughter by gross negligence. Corporate manslaughter is a concept fraught with all sorts of difficulties. Even if it appears obvious that a disaster has been caused by negligence, even gross negligence, the next question is 'by whom?'; and the one after that, if it is proposed to put a company in the dock, was 'did that person represent "the mind and will" of the proposed corporate defendant?'. Only if the answer to that latter question is in the affirmative can a charge be sustained against the corporate body. To cut a long story short, I concluded that there was no realistic possibility of any charge succeeding against any potential defendant, individual or corporate, and I so advised the DPP, who accepted my advice. Understandably, the families of some of the casualties were perplexed, and in some cases outraged, by the decision not to prosecute. However, that was as nothing compared with the outcry that followed the decision in the next case upon which I was instructed to advise.

In the early hours of 20th August 1989 there was a collision between the pleasure steamer *Marchioness* and the dredger *Bowbelle*, which resulted in the deaths of 51 of the 130 or 131 people who had been at a birthday party being held on the pleasure steamer. The *Marchioness* was struck twice by the *Bowbelle* at about 1.46am, and sank so fast that there was little or no time to deploy life-rafts or lifebelts, or to save those trapped below decks. Both vessels had been travelling in the same direction downstream, but which veered or altered course, and at what point, was never entirely clear. What was clear was that the comparatively huge dredger, with a deadweight tonnage of 1,880 tons, with aggregate in the stern, was much faster, with an average speed of over 6mph, and infinitely heavier than the pleasure steamer, with an average speed of under 4mph. It also became immediately obvious that the master of the *Bowbelle*, partially because of the load in the stern, was unable to see what was happening immediately in front of the bows of his ship from the bridge; consequently a look-out had been posted at the bow, but even he had restricted vision of any small boat that was very close in front.

In many ways, this was a disaster that had been waiting to happen for years. Large vessels such as the *Bowbelle* and her sister dredger *Bowtrader* were plying their trade down the middle of the Thames, while pleasure boats, such as *Marchioness* and her sister *Hurlingham* were entertaining noisy partygoers, often plotting courses which spelt potential tragedy. There had been a number of minor incidents and near-misses earlier in the decade.

Marchioness had about 130 people on board, four of whom were crew and bar staff. She was an elderly vessel that had seen service as one of 'the little ships' that had taken part in the 1940 Dunkirk evacuation. Her captain that night was Stephen Faldo, aged twenty-nine, and he and his mate, Andrew McGowan, sailed from Embankment Pier shortly after 1am. The boat was owned by Tidal Cruises Ltd. *Bowbelle* was owned by East Coast Aggregates Ltd and managed by South Coast Shipping Co. Ltd. The *Bowbelle* had a crew of nine: a master, two mates, three engineers and a cook. Her captain that night was Douglas Henderson, aged thirty-one, and he had been master of *Bowbelle* since May that year. He had visited several public houses that day, and had drunk six pints of lager over a period of three-and-a-half hours, before returning to his ship at 6pm for a meal and a short sleep. His forward look-out that night, Terence Blayney, had drunk seven pints over a similar period. It should be said immediately that the subsequent inquiry found that alcohol had played no part in the tragedy. No one knew how much, if anything, Faldo had drunk.

More importantly, no one will ever know precisely what happened in those fatal moments before the *Bowbelle* hit the *Marchioness*, once from behind and then, as a result of the first impact, amidships. The *Marchioness* went down in a matter of minutes and Faldo, who would probably have been the only person who might have been able to explain exactly what had happened, was drowned. What was clear was that, in the words of the MAIB (Marine Accident Investigation Branch) report: 'No one in either vessel was aware of the other's presence until very shortly before the collision. No one on the bridge of *Bowbelle* was aware of *Marchioness* until the collision occurred . . . the immediate cause of the casualty was therefore failure of look-out in each vessel . . . visibility from the wheelhouse of each vessel was seriously restricted . . . clear instructions were not given to the forward look-out in *Bowbelle*.'

It is interesting that the 'A' in the acronym MAIB stands for Accident, because I remember thinking, in reviewing the evidence both in this case and that of the King's Cross fire, that the word 'accident' might be beginning to represent a concept that was no longer acceptable to the public. Events such as these represent great human tragedies; the families of those who lose their lives are understandably, in their grief, looking to see if someone, individual or corporate, is to blame. There is a strong and understandable desire to see someone brought to book for the loss of the loved one. But the fact remains that in a world inhabited by human beings, accidents, properly so described, do happen. The role of those advising prosecuting authorities is to look at the evidence, apply a cool and realistic judgement to the picture that emerges from that evidence, and advise as to whether the facts reveal criminal conduct rather than accidental misfortune. Rightly or wrongly, in both cases I concluded that no prosecution for manslaughter would be justified; I advised the DPP accordingly and he accepted this advice. I left open the possibility that Henderson, the master of the *Bowbelle*, might be prosecuted for the much less serious offence of failing to have an effective look-out on his vessel. He was indeed prosecuted for that offence, but two juries failed to agree on a verdict, so he was acquitted.

The DPP was subjected to widespread criticism for his decisions which were, of course, based on my advice. I will not go into the twists and turns of all the litigation and inquiries that followed. Suffice it to say that this tragedy may well have resulted in the Thames now being a much safer place for all its users.

The cab-rank principle, which I am afraid I will continue to praise as upholding the fundamental principles of the Bar, meant of course that I was not precluded from advising potential defendants, and that led to my, albeit brief, involvement in another of the great tragedies of the late 1980s, the sinking of MS *Herald of Free Enterprise*.

On the morning of 7ᵗʰ March 1987, I was woken by my clerk, Michael, and told that I must be at the head office of the P&O Group in Pall Mall at 10am. When I protested that barristers did not have meetings with their clients in the client's office, I was met with the retort that this was different, because my conference would be with the entire board of the company and their lawyers, and there wasn't a room in chambers that could accommodate that number of people. Besides, it was perfectly clear that Sir Jeffrey Sterling, as he then was, the chairman of P&O, had no intention of coming to the Temple and being photographed entering my chambers. When I asked Michael what this was all about, he told me to turn on the radio. As I shaved I learnt from the BBC that a ferry had capsized just outside the Belgian port of Zeebrugge, and it was feared that there had been considerable loss of life. That was about all I knew when my taxi pulled up in Pall Mall.

As soon as I got into the room I felt as though I had been invited, not so much to tender advice as to approve an approach upon which the board, or certainly its chairman, had already decided. Obviously it would not be appropriate for me to repeat what was said at the meeting but suffice it to say that it did not last long. I wasn't surprised to hear soon afterwards that my services were no longer required. By tendering advice that my client did not wish to accept, I was of course depriving myself of future remunerative employment: but, without suggesting that I should receive plaudits for so doing, I consider that this may be an example of when counsel must give independent advice, based upon his own experience, and not allow himself to be induced into a position of simply rubber-stamping a decision already made by his client. A barrister advises, and the client is free to accept or reject that advice.

In due course, P&O were charged with corporate manslaughter, but, after a lengthy trial and before the jury could consider a verdict,

Mr Justice Michael Turner caused consternation to the prosecution by withdrawing the case from the jury and directing an acquittal. I will not deal with the reasons for this decision here but the one thing that was achieved by the case was to focus attention upon the extremely knotty problems that could arise when a corporate body was charged with a crime, particularly an inchoate one like manslaughter. It was yet another case after which the bereaved felt that the deaths of their loved ones had not been properly recognised by the criminal law. The world then was certainly one in which health and safety regulations played a much lesser part in the lives of all of us than they do now.

From 1985 until 1993, my day job remained prosecuting as Senior Treasury Counsel, and sometimes that led me to strange places. In many ways the strangest was to the Bar of the House of Lords, from where on one occasion I was required to address their Lordships. Normally, the members of the Judicial Committee of the House of Lords (the Law Lords) sat in suits in one of the committee rooms, arranged in a semi-circle, and counsel in robes addressed them; but for some arcane reason this particular application had to be made at the Bar of the House. I was instructed to appear on behalf of the Northern Ireland DPP to apply for costs at the end of some case. Mercifully the details are lost in the mists of my memory, mainly I suspect because I was so terrified at the prospect. Luckily the application was made at the beginning of the day's business, immediately after Prayers, so I found myself addressing an almost empty chamber, populated only by the Law Lords and a couple of snoozing bishops. Nevertheless it was one of those experiences that I was beginning to find extremely stressful, both in prospect and reality, and I suspect that my old friend the whisky bottle had been self-prescribed as a sleeping aid the night before.

I cannot remember exactly when it was that I first consulted Dr Peter Rohde, a brilliant and caring consultant psychiatrist, but it would have been in the mid- to late-eighties, when I first realised that my workload was causing sufficient anxiety and depression to need treatment. I had been referred to Peter by my friend and GP, Dr Alastair Gordon, who was himself alcoholic, and who finally succumbed to his other drug of choice, nicotine. Dr Rohde prescribed anti-depressants and advised me that I was drinking too much. Although he told me that alcohol is a depressant drug, and that it exacerbates rather than relieves the symptoms of depression, I was not ready to hear that message. I continued to self-medicate on my favourite 'medicines', which had either been distilled north of the border or had grown on vines in France. Certainly I was not diagnosed as being an alcoholic at that stage. Indeed, when I was admitted to the Charter Nightingale Hospital in Lisson Grove to be treated for depression, nobody objected to my having a bottle of Scotch in my locker, to be taken, as it was, every evening before dinner. This was thirty-five-plus years ago, and nobody should be held responsible for what, as I now know, was an incomplete diagnosis. At that stage the connection between alcohol and depression had not been fully recognised.

These were unhappy times for me, and very difficult times for Lizzie too. She was living with a man increasingly tortured by anxiety and depression, while both working and drinking to excess. Bearing in mind that to some extent I was in the public eye and also in a competitive profession in which any sign of weakness could prove disastrous, Lizzie had to suffer the loneliness of being unable to share her concerns with anyone. Our situation was a prime example of alcoholism being a family disease. Even poor Thomas was not immune. When he was brought from prep school to visit me in the Charter Nightingale, he asked his mother, 'Is Dad in some kind of nut-house?', as he somehow became aware of the nature of a psychiatric hospital, some floors of which were secure units for patients who had been sectioned. The writing may have been on the wall, but I certainly wasn't reading it.

Chapter 13

GUINNESS WAS GOOD FOR ME

One twentieth century slogan that everyone seemed to know was 'Guinness is good for you'. It brought great visibility, and hence commercial success, to the brewing company, based in Dublin, and recognition to what had previously been regarded as a rather dour stout. I probably first drank a pint of Guinness in the sixties when it was very un-trendy, and tended to be served warm in a few, but not many, pubs in England. I certainly used to drink rather too much of it on the occasions when I travelled to Dublin's Lansdowne Road to watch England play Ireland at rugby. Unlike those I travelled with, and because of my Ulster roots, I supported Ireland, because even in the depths of the Troubles, Ireland fielded a team comprised of players from both north and south of the border. An American lawyer once asked me whether it was true that Protestant Ulstermen travelled from Belfast to Dublin to watch international matches, shedding their customary orange and donning the green, watched the match surrounded by Catholics from the Republic, drank themselves silly in the pubs of Dublin, and then travelled back north to resume the bloodshed and hatred that was part of daily life for too many years in that benighted province. When I told him that this was a pretty accurate depiction, he simply shrugged his shoulders in disbelief.

By the mid-1980s, the rather sleepy, largely family-owned brewer was ripe for modernisation and takeover. In 1981 Ernest Saunders had been appointed chief executive of Guinness Plc. He had built up his business reputation at Beecham, Great Universal Stores and Nestlé, becoming known for his skills in cost-control but also his ruthlessness: his nickname, apparently, was Deadly Earnest. In early 1986 he convinced the Guinness board that this was the time for expansion, and the target of his ambition became the Edinburgh-based Distillers Company Plc, which was trying to resist a hostile bid from Argyll. The bid for Distillers was made more attractive by boosting the Guinness share price, and this, as a jury subsequently found, was achieved by illegal means. The plan was simple: persuade rich and influential investors to buy huge amounts of Guinness shares by insulating them against potential loss. This involved manipulation of the London stock market to inflate artificially the price of Guinness shares, and thereby assist the £4 billion takeover bid for Distillers.

Those involved, the Guinness Four, who eventually stood trial together, all invested large amounts in order to achieve the inflated share price; they were protected by a guarantee which ensured that they would not lose money and were rewarded through channels that disguised the true nature of the transactions. Those arrangements were not vouchsafed to the main board, who were not implicated in the activity, which was, the Serious Fraud Office contended, fraudulent and contrary to company law. The four men were Ernest Saunders himself, Sir Jack Lyons (as he then was), Anthony Parnes (a City trader, known as 'The Animal' for his ruthless trading tactics), and Gerald Ronson, a highly successful, and perhaps equally ruthless, businessman and property developer.

The share-support device had been revealed when a US stock trader named Ivan Boesky struck a plea bargain with the authorities in that country, and this triggered an investigation by the Department of Trade and Industry (DTI) in the UK. That investigation spread its wings far and wide, and in due course a number of individuals were interviewed. I do not intend to go into any detail about any of the institutions or people who fell under suspicion because, in the end, no one other than the Guinness Four was convicted of any criminal offence. The DTI had draconian powers, designed to insist that those they were investigating answered their questions, and the answers all four defendants, and in particular Lyons, gave proved to be their undoing. Only Ronson told the almost unvarnished truth about what he had done by way of support, saying, more or less 'and what is wrong with that?'. The other three were shown to have been much less candid.

On 15th October 1987, *The Times* published an article entitled 'Lawyers on the winning side', which outlined the expected representation. When Frances Gibb came to deal with Sir Jack Lyons she said that he 'was charged last week, (and) has hired the City firm Stephenson Harwood. His solicitor is Mr Michael Wilson and his counsel Mr Graham Boal QC (sic)' – which of course I wasn't at this stage. I told Michael Wilson as soon as he instructed me that, being STC with other commitments, I could not guarantee my attendance at all stages of the trial, and that he should also instruct a (real) QC to lead and another junior behind me. Michael very properly invited me to propose who that leader should be, and it didn't take me long to recommend Robert Harman QC. Robert had been treasury counsel and had then taken silk, and I thought he had all the right qualities. He had gravitas, impeccable judgement, and a very attractive way with juries, which invited acceptance of his submissions. I was not proved wrong about Robert's performance even though, in the end, he failed to persuade this jury to acquit. Mark Ellison, later himself to become 1STC and then a very successful silk, was the second junior. I thought, if I may be permitted to say so, that we made a fairly formidable team.

Unfortunately the evidence proved insurmountable.

The prosecution team represented an array of talent from two separate disciplines. Because complicated questions of company law were involved, the SFO instructed John Chadwick QC, doyen of the Chancery Bar, to lead for the Crown. Behind him was Barbara Mills QC, former treasury counsel and later DPP; next was Victor Temple, then treasury counsel and subsequently QC, and finally Elizabeth Gloster, the young and glamorous star of the Chancery Bar, later to become Gloster LJ.

When the prosecution team first came into court, we criminal hacks for the defence didn't know quite what to expect. We knew Barbara and Victor very well, but John and Liz (as we all soon came to know her) were almost totally unknown quantities; indeed Liz later confessed that she wasn't sure that she had been in a criminal court since her pupillage, and had certainly never faced a jury. It became quite obvious very early on, however, that 'Chadders' and Liz were taking to this, for them very unusual, experience like ducks to water. They had been accustomed to the rather different and rarefied waters of the Chancery Division, but quickly adjusted to the rather more rough-and-tumble approach of a criminal trial. The case was tried by a very experienced judge, Mr Justice Dennis Henry; he had bathed in both waters over the course of his career.

I don't imagine that you will want to know much about the various twists and turns of the trial, or of the legal issues involved, particularly the rather esoteric questions of company law. All I need say about the evidence is that, whereas Ernest Saunders went into the witness box in an attempt to justify his actions, none of the other three defendants, including Jack Lyons, did so, and all were duly convicted. The other three were sentenced to imprisonment on top of large fines, but Jack escaped an immediate prison sentence because he was older than the others, having been born in 1916, and we were able to call doctors who asserted that a particular cancer from which he was suffering would be severely exacerbated by a custodial sentence. He died in Switzerland in 2008. Ernest Saunders appealed against his sentence of five years, which was reduced to two and a half years on the basis that he was diagnosed as suffering from Alzheimer's disease. He was released after ten months, and is still alive at the time of writing (2021). Ronson and Parnes served short prison sentences. What hurt my client more than the fine of £3 million with £1 million costs on top, was the fact that John Major, by then Prime Minister, removed his knighthood; that was a bitter blow for a man who had risen from very humble beginnings. A series of appeals dragged on for years, without my involvement, until finally in 2002 an appeal to the House of Lords failed.

Two vignettes of this remarkable trial stand out in my recollection. The first may go to explain why Jack Lyons managed to make a huge fortune before his downfall. Born in Leeds, the fifth of six children, he built up an enormous commercial empire, starting with a men's clothing business but eventually including over 1,300 high street retail stores at the lower end of the market. In many ways he was a highly generous and philanthropic man. He donated millions to the arts, particularly to music, received a CBE in 1967, and then a knighthood in 1973, for services to music. He had a concert hall named after him in York. He is reputed to have sold an original 'haystack' painting by Monet to pay his legal expenses, and our fees were certainly not to be sniffed at. But, like many self-made rich men, Jack believed that if you looked after the pennies, then the pounds would look after themselves. Thus, although he hired a suite of rooms near Southwark Crown Court (where the trial took place), to accommodate us throughout, nevertheless he would send his driver out every morning to Marks & Spencer to buy the sandwiches at a reduced price that had gone unsold the day before. I have never since been able to look a tuna sandwich in the eye.

The second recollection, a vivid one, is of my dancing the night away with Liz Gloster in a nightclub the evening after the verdict. One of the great traditions of the Bar, and the criminal Bar in particular, is, or at least was, that once the battle was over we would lay down our weapons and enjoy ourselves together. It must sound odd to a layman to hear a barrister refer to his opponent as 'my learned friend' and in the next breath appear anything other than friendly, but by-and-large we *were* all friends and respected each other as such. There were exceptions, but in that relatively small pond, everyone knew who they were. If I may mix metaphors, one of the great advantages of the criminal Bar being a small barrel was that the rotten apples were soon identified.

The Guinness trial, occurring as it did towards the end of the Thatcher era, again represented in some people's eyes, as had other cases I have already mentioned, the unacceptable face of capitalism. What aggrieved the four defendants who were convicted, perhaps in some ways more than their own convictions, was the belief that they had been picked out for special treatment because they were, as Jack put it, 'north London Jews, and not Old Etonians'. It is perfectly true that other City institutions and establishment individuals were implicated in, if never prosecuted to conviction for, the Guinness scam. It is equally true that there were many other share-support schemes at the time that sailed very close to the wind. My own view is that these four men were not singled out because of their background or ethnicity, but because they overdid it, and then tried to cover up their actions with lies and prevarication. It may also be true that others were very lucky to escape.

Guinness certainly had been good to me. My fee for that trial was extremely generous, and indeed went a long way to financing the purchase of the small cottage we bought on the North Norfolk coast, in the village in which we now live. Indeed some wag from chambers had a plaque made, which he invited me to put outside the door, renaming the cottage 'Lyons Corner House' – a play on my client's name and the chain of restaurants-cum-cafés that used to be seen on the corner of most busy thoroughfares in London. Thomas was about eight when we bought the cottage, and it provided us with some memorable holidays and weekends. It also carried some fairly bleak memories for me, as my episodes of depression were becoming deeper and more regular by the end of the 1980s. I have unpleasant memories of lying on my bed on a Sunday afternoon, not having completed the work I should have done, and dreading having to drive back to London that evening with the anticipation of getting up early the next morning to compensate for what I had failed to do over the weekend.

The storm clouds were beginning to gather, and I must have been pretty good hell to live with. Lizzie was wonderful, but it would have been an extremely difficult and lonely time for her. Neither of us realised the extent of the problem that was beginning to manifest itself, and it is only with the benefit of hindsight that I can now properly assess what was happening to me. Friends have since said that although they were aware that I enjoyed a drink, they were not conscious of there being a problem with alcohol; nor were they aware that I was, obviously quite successfully, managing to keep Churchill's 'black dog' of depression locked secretly away from public view.

Chapter 14

THE POISONED CHALICE

A few days before the end of the Guinness trial, I was contemplating my out-of-date tuna sandwich one lunchtime when the telephone rang. It was the DPP, Allan Green. I had known Allan for years, and we had been fellow treasury counsel before his elevation; indeed we were appointed on the same day. Allan told me that a car would pick me up at 4.15 that afternoon from Southwark Crown Court and take me to the CPS headquarters, where he would be waiting for me. When I asked what this was all about, Allan told me that he could not discuss matters over the telephone. The car picked me up, I was driven to CPS HQ, and Allan got into the car. He told me that we were going to the Attorney General's chambers in Buckingham Gate. As soon as we arrived, the Attorney General, Sir Patrick Mayhew, told me that I was about to be the recipient of what he described as 'a poisoned chalice'.

In 1974 the IRA had launched a bombing campaign in the Midlands, culminating in the detonation of two time-bombs in the centre of Birmingham on 21st November. In 1975 six men, who later became known as The Birmingham Six, were convicted of the bombings. Two subsequent appeals against their convictions failed but now, in 1990, the Home Secretary was about to refer the case back to the Court of Appeal. The AG told me that I would lead for the Crown and could have as many juniors as I felt I needed. Moreover this brief would be unusual, if not unique, in the sense that before any court hearing I would superintend a renewed investigation into every aspect of the case. This review would be in the hands of the Devon and Cornwall Constabulary, under the command of the Chief Constable himself. I know of no other case in which counsel had been instructed, not only to present a case in court, but also to be involved in an investigation prior to the case. The AG also told me that he expected the anticipated case in the Court of Appeal to lead to an inquiry into the criminal justice system as a whole. I left that meeting, or rather staggered out of it, with my brain pretty scrambled.

Back in chambers, my clerk's mind of course immediately focused on the size of the fee, but mine on whom to suggest to assist me in what I realised was going to be no picnic. I subsequently asked if Timothy (Tim) Langdale, another senior treasury counsel, could join me, together with William (Bill) Boyce, a junior in my chambers who was appointed TC very soon after the appeal hearing. That request was granted, and I was also told that we would be joined by the only one of the original 1974 prosecution team still in practice, John Maxwell.

I soon learnt just how unprecedented this assignment would be. We were to superintend the work of a team of police officers whose dual responsibility was to re-investigate the Birmingham pub bombings, re-evaluate the case against The Birmingham Six and, if it proved applicable, prepare a case against any West Midlands police officers who were shown to be party to an attempt to pervert the course of justice in relation to the original prosecution. The conviction and imprisonment of the six men was now the subject of intense media investigation and, it must be said, speculation. I began to understand how daunting the task that awaited me was.

If the enormity of the responsibility had not already impinged upon me, it certainly did so as soon as I travelled to Middlemoor, the headquarters of the Devon and Cornwall Constabulary, to meet the team of officers assigned to 'Aston 2', the name given to the investigation. The first person I met was the immensely impressive Chief Constable, John Evans (subsequently knighted for his achievements). He told me that he had put together a team of officers, but that the first thing he had done was to give each of them the opportunity to opt out if they wished, with an undertaking that if they did, that refusal would not harm their careers. This he did because one important part of the inquiry would involve investigating the behaviour of their colleagues in the West Midlands, and there is nothing that a police officer dreads more than a so-called 'dog-eats-dog' assignment. His team consisted of twenty-six officers – a chief superintendent, a superintendent, two inspectors, six detective sergeants, four police sergeants, six detective constables, three police constables, three woman police constables (as they were still called in 1990) – and five civilian employees. I must say immediately that I have never come across a more dedicated and hard-working team anywhere in my life; it was a huge pleasure and privilege to work with them. The 'visiting team' consisted of Allan Green (the DPP), Christopher Newell (a very senior lawyer in the CPS whom I already knew well; he had instructed prosecuting counsel in the Thorpe trial), Gerald Adams (another CPS lawyer) and Amanda Illing (a CPS clerk), together with us, the four counsel instructed by the AG and DPP.

The first formal meeting of the team provided a memorable moment. Those of us who were required to be there assembled in a conference room at Middlemoor and, because John Evans was meticulous in having a record of everything that took place, the whole thing was filmed. John had just begun his introductory remarks when the door burst open and a flush-faced young lady dashed in, announcing: 'I am Amanda from the CPS!' That immediately broke any ice there may have been, and Amanda Illing took her place: the poor woman had missed her train. I tell that story only to emphasise that Amanda never put a foot wrong from that moment until the end of the hearing in the Court of Appeal. She became my 'go-to girl', and nothing she was asked to do ever seemed impossible. She was twenty-two at the time, and I am delighted to record that she is now, some thirty-odd years later, the chief executive (which is what senior clerks are now called) of a large and very successful set of barristers' chambers. I knew, from the moment I started to work with her, that she would go far.

The inevitable difficulties of the police team working in Devon and the lawyers working in London will be self-apparent, and the delicacy of the inquiry, involving as it did highly sensitive anti-terrorist material, made it necessary for very unusual precautions to be taken. Tim, Bill and I were moved out of our chambers into a basement in the Temple, specially fitted out with discrete, monitored telephone lines to Middlemoor and CPS HQ, together with a fax machine and two large safes. The safes had combination locks with my knowing half the combination and Tim and Bill knowing the other half, so that to open the safe I had to be present with one or other of them. We gradually got used to working in this unprecedented way, although there were moments when the system proved imperfect. We more than once had to get the security services to come and open a safe for us, and there was an extremely embarrassing moment when, for some reason, we had to move from one basement bunker to another. When the men came to move these huge, heavy safes, as one of them was lifted onto a trolley, it suddenly tipped forward, the door flew open, and the entire contents, including files that should never have seen the light of day, fell all over the floor. We did not hold an inquest into which of us had failed to lock the safe the previous evening.

It is unnecessary to go into any detail of our work, except to say that we were all – police, CPS and counsel – absolutely committed to making sure that, as far as was humanly possible in all the circumstances, justice was done. That was our sole aim, and I am convinced that every single one of the forty men and women who were engaged on this enterprise signed up to that principle.

Meetings took place at frequent intervals, usually at Middlemoor, but I remember one occasion when I needed to meet John Evans and a very senior representative of the West Midlands force, together with someone from the security services, and the most convenient venue for all parties was a motorway service station near where the M5 joins the M4. We huddled over our coffee at a corner table, in a scene reminiscent of a John le Carré novel.

This is neither the time nor the place to go into all the ramifications of the inquiry. Suffice it to say that no stone was left unturned, every aspect of the evidence was scrutinised, and every possible interpretation examined. The AG and DPP were informed of our progress at every stage, as we tentatively began to come to our conclusions. After months of work by all those I have mentioned, we reached a certain consensus as to how we would present the case to the Court of Appeal.

To understand the position we took on behalf of the Crown, it is necessary to look at the legal framework against which we had to formulate our submissions. Section Two of the Criminal Appeal Act 1968, which was the statute in operation at the time, stated that, 'the Court of Appeal shall allow an appeal against conviction if they think that the conviction should be set aside on the ground that under all the circumstances of the case it is unsafe or unsatisfactory'. We had to consider every phrase of that test, and then help the court arrive at its conclusion. First, 'if they think' meant that the three judges had to form their own view, and it would only be in the rarest of circumstances that they would, for instance, simply rubber-stamp a conclusion by the Respondent (the prosecution) to concede that the appeal should be allowed. Secondly, the words 'under all the circumstances of the case' meant that, as in this case, the court would often require counsel to deal with the case as a whole, to allow the court to assess the whole picture. Thirdly, the words 'unsafe or unsatisfactory' were not further defined. One of the issues that exercised my mind, and upon which I made submissions to the court, was whether the words 'unsafe' and 'unsatisfactory' meant different things, particularly when separated by the word 'or' rather than 'and' and, if so, what the difference, and the consequence of a difference, might be. Lastly, it is important to note that neither the word 'guilty' nor the word 'innocent' appears in the statutory test.

The six appellants were originally convicted in the trial in 1975 by the unanimous verdict of the jury on twenty-one counts of murder. The prosecution case certainly rested on two main pillars, although there was a wealth of circumstantial evidence that, said the prosecution, supported those main pillars and was capable in itself of representing a formidable case. Space will not permit me to rehearse that circumstantial evidence, but the movements of the defendants immediately after the bombings provided part of it. The first main pillar of the prosecution case was the evidence of a forensic scientist called Dr Skuse. He gave evidence to the effect that swabs from the hands of Power and Hill, two of the six accused, taken within hours of the explosions, demonstrated that each had been in recent contact with nitroglycerine, which constituted the explosive substance in the bombs. The second pillar was the evidence of the police that four of the six defendants, Power, McIlkenny, Walker and Callaghan, had all signed written confessions, and that the other two, Hunter and Hill, had made oral admissions. The defendants alleged at trial that the written confessions had been beaten out of them and the oral admissions fabricated. The jury took under two days of retirement to arrive at their verdicts of guilty. The judge, Mr Justice Bridge, described the evidence in the case as the clearest and most overwhelming that he had ever heard.

The defendants appealed against their convictions on the ground that the trial judge's summing-up had been unfair, but those appeals were dismissed in March 1976. There could be no further appeal unless the Home Secretary referred the case back to the Court of Appeal.

Over the course of the next decade, a campaign was mounted for a review of the convictions. A Granada television programme suggested that the six men might have been the victims of a miscarriage of justice, and a book by Chris Mullin, then a Labour MP, entitled *Error of Judgement: The Truth About The Birmingham Bombings* added to the misgivings. The campaign attracted the support of senior churchmen. I am bound to say that both the television programme and Mr Mullin's book painted only half the picture, and were regarded by many objective observers as one-sided: but some of the issues they raised caused Home Secretary Douglas Hurd to refer the case back to the Court of Appeal in 1987. A strong court of three experienced appellate judges rejected those appeals, with the president of the court, Lord Chief Justice Geoffrey Lane, saying in the course of his judgement, 'the longer this hearing has gone on the more convinced this court has become that the verdict of the jury was correct'. That was a comment for which he was subsequently, very unfairly, castigated, and the Court of Appeal in 1991 acknowledged that, on the information before it, the 1987 court could have come to no other conclusion.

What happened between then and August 1990 to cause the new Home Secretary, David Waddington, to refer the case back yet again to the Court of Appeal, and trigger the events I have been describing and the final appeal in March 1991? Between 1987 and the summer of 1990, two pieces of evidence emerged that undermined those two central pillars of the prosecution's case in 1975. First, further scientific advances made it possible to test the original findings by Dr Skuse that proved, as the Crown had contended, that at least two of the defendants had touched explosives. Without going into the extensive detail that was laid before the court in 1991, the new evidence cast doubt on Dr Skuse's findings to the extent that it was agreed on all sides, if not by Dr Skuse himself, that his findings were now unreliable. We, the respondents to the appeal, decided that this new evidence, commissioned on behalf of the Crown and presented to the appellants and the court by us, was such that the convictions could not be sustained on the basis of that scientific evidence.

The other pillar of the prosecution case in 1975, namely the evidence of the confessions made to the police, was also undermined to a significant extent by new scientific evidence. In March 1990 the Home Office wrote to the Chief Constable of the West Midlands, asking for his comments on questions raised by solicitors acting on behalf of the six convicted men. That Chief Constable then wrote to the Chief Constable of the Devon and Cornwall Constabulary, John Evans, asking him to carry out a further investigation. As a result, all important documents, including the four written confessions, officers' notebooks and other contemporary records, were subjected to a new test known as electrostatic document analysis, or ESDA. When something is written on a piece of paper which is lying on a pile of other pages, an imprint or indentation will normally be found on the sheet of paper immediately below it, and sometimes, dependent on the pressure exerted by the writer, on a third or fourth sheet. ESDA is a scientific process which allows one to read the imprint on the sheet below the one upon which the writing appears. Without going into the detail of the evidence the Crown provided to the defence and to the court in 1991, it became clear that some of the documents could not have been recorded in the way the police had sworn they were.

To lay out here the totality of the evidence that was accumulated during the latter months of 1990 would be inappropriate to this memoir, but by mid-December we, by which I mean the whole team representing the Respondent, had reached a concluded decision.

At a hearing not long before Christmas I informed the court that the Crown would be inviting the court to allow these appeals. It is very important, in view of some of the things that have been said and written since, that it is remembered that it was the Crown that provided the defence and the court with the ammunition that allowed the appeal to take the course it did, and that it was the Crown that specifically invited the court to quash the convictions.

When the names of the three judges (all Lords Justice) who would hear the appeal were announced, Roger Frisby's wise words to the advocate, 'know your judge' sprang to mind. It may come as a surprise to some people that judges, underneath their robes, are ordinary human beings, with the strengths and weaknesses, and even the fallibilities and prejudices, of ordinary mortals. If, as an advocate, you know something of the background and experiences of your judges, then you, the advocate, have an advantage over those who don't. Two of the judges assigned to this appeal were well known to me. It is with no disrespect that I refer to the judges, as we inevitably did at the Bar, in footballing terms as the centre forward, the inside right (the more senior of the two 'wingers') and the inside left. The inside right was Lord Justice Michael Mustill, in front of whom I had appeared more than once, and whom I regarded as one of the cleverest and soundest of his ilk. The inside left was Lord Justice Donald Farquharson, whom my reader will remember from the trial of Dr Leonard Arthur. I knew Donald well, had been led by him while he was still at the Bar, and I respected him enormously. The centre forward, Lord Justice Anthony Lloyd, was completely unknown to me, and our paths had never crossed. Whereas Mustill and Farquharson were extremely experienced in the criminal courts, Lloyd came from an almost exclusively civil background, and was not, unlike the other two, 'steeped in crime'.

Unfortunately, Lloyd LJ and I got off to a bad start. At that first preliminary hearing in December, considerable discussion naturally ensued as to the form the appeal would take in view of the Respondent's invitation to the court to allow the appeals. It was agreed on all sides that, in view of the wording of the Criminal Appeal Act, the court was obliged to reach its own decisions, and not just to rubber-stamp the DPP's decision. That would require counsel for the Respondents to set out in considerable detail the whole of the evidence in the case, and it was made plain that this was what the court wanted us to do. When I suggested that it would be helpful if we served some of the material in advance of the hearing, so that the court would not be starting with a blank canvas, Lord Justice Lloyd replied, 'All right, but I am not going to allow it to ruin my Christmas'. That remark, doubtless intended as a light aside and possibly perfectly permissible in a civil context, was unfortunate in the context of a criminal case that was already, in some quarters, attracting more heat than light: the result of it was keenly awaited, not only by the six men who had been in prison for sixteen years and their supporters, but also by the families of the twenty-one people who had lost their lives in those horrendous terrorist bombings. Neither levity nor a relaxed atmosphere was called for.

The substantive hearing of the appeal, which extended over nine days, took place in early March 1991. Five of the appellants were represented by Michael Mansfield QC and a junior, and one of them, Robert Hunter, by Lord Tony Gifford QC and a junior. I appeared for the Crown with my three juniors, without whose steadfast support, meticulous hard work, and ability I might never have survived the experience. Mansfield and Gifford presented the case for the appellants, almost exclusively using the material with which they had been fed by the Crown, and then I addressed the court. I hoped that my opening remarks made it absolutely clear, not only to their Lordships, but also to everyone else in a crowded court, together with media from all over the world, precisely what our position was. I began:

> '*May I start by making it abundantly plain that we adhere to the two primary submissions that we made (at an earlier hearing), namely, first and foremost, that it is for this court and no one else to determine these appeals; secondly, to assist the court, we submit on behalf of the Respondent that these convictions are no longer both safe and satisfactory.*'

I repeat those words because some commentators have asserted, quite wrongly, that the Crown tried to uphold the convictions and prolong these men's imprisonment.

Our submissions lasted many hours over a period of days. Here I will simply refer to one or two of the issues highlighted by myself and Timothy Langdale, who kindly agreed to deal with the scientific evidence while I tried to rehearse the important aspects of the rest of the evidence, including the vast amount of circumstantial evidence, and to deal with one matter of law which I felt needed to be explored.

That point of law involved the interpretation of those words, to which I have already referred, 'unsafe or unsatisfactory'. In a nutshell, I suggested that the inclusion of the word 'or' must necessarily mean that the words 'unsafe' and 'unsatisfactory' were disjunctive, and therefore must denote different concepts. I invited the court to conclude that although the appeals should be allowed, because in the light of the new evidence the convictions could no longer be regarded as satisfactory, it did not follow that the court had necessarily to conclude that they were also unsafe. It is a submission that Gilbert ('Gilly') Gray QC, one of the greatest wits at the Bar, described as 'the condom submission . . . safe but not entirely satisfactory'.

To cut to the chase, the court did not accept my submission, and in fact decided that 'these convictions are both unsafe and unsatisfactory'. However I take some comfort from the fact that, following the report of the Royal Commission on Criminal Justice, commissioned as a direct result of this case, a new Criminal Appeal Act was passed in 1995, which repealed Section Two of the 1968 Act, and replaced it with the words, 'the Court of Appeal shall allow an appeal against conviction if they feel that the conviction is unsafe'. The word 'unsatisfactory' had disappeared: something of a Pyrrhic victory perhaps.

There was a moment during my submission when I crossed swords with Lord Justice Lloyd directly. During what I accept was an exhaustive review of the evidence as a whole, Lloyd suddenly seemed to lose patience and suggested that I was 'engaged on what seems to be a form of damage limitation'. There followed an unpleasant exchange during which I had to remind the learned judge that I was engaged in no such thing, but was doing what the court itself had asked me to do in the light of the statutory test, namely to put the court in possession of all the material needed in order to reach its decisions. I have good reason to believe that it was not the unanimous view of the court that had been expressed by Lloyd during that rather unfortunate passage of arms, and it may be significant that no similar interventions occurred after that.

At the end of the hearing, the court announced that the appeals would be allowed and the convictions quashed, and that their Lordships would deliver their reasons later. That evening I watched on television with mixed emotions the scenes outside the Old Bailey when the six freed men emerged to a media circus of celebration. The court delivered its judgement on the 27th March 1991. It was a long and carefully reasoned one which concluded that, since a retrial would be impossible after more than seventeen years, and since it was impossible accurately to assess what impact the new evidence might have had on the original jury if the members of that jury had known what had now emerged, then the convictions could not be allowed to stand. In view of some of the commentary that followed, however, and to put the decision in context, I feel

I should quote one short passage from that judgement. Referring back to the statutory test to be applied by an appellate court in Section Two of the Criminal Appeal Act 1968, the court said:

> 'Nothing in Section Two of the Act or anywhere else obliges or entitles us to say whether we think that (an) appellant is innocent. This is a point of great constitutional importance. The task of deciding whether a man is guilty falls on the jury. We are concerned solely with the question of whether the verdict of the jury can stand.'

I cannot leave this case without recording my immense gratitude to all those who so greatly assisted me. I was supported throughout by my juniors, all those representing the CPS, and by both the DPP and Attorney General. It was a great privilege to have been entrusted with this brief and, although at times it proved hugely taxing and stressful, my task was made immeasurably easier by those around me. Perhaps it was only later that I realised the toll it had taken on me.

I was hugely lucky that Sir Patrick (Paddy) Mayhew was Attorney General at the time. He was not only immensely supportive, but he also brought a fund of experience, common sense and wisdom to superintending our efforts. One personal episode may begin to paint a portrait of the man. All prosecutions are brought in the name of the Crown; hence 'R (Regina) v John Jones'. At the moment when the final decisions were about to be made before the court hearing, I found myself standing beside Paddy at the large picture window of his room in Buckingham Gate which overlooked the Palace. As we stared out of the window he said to me: 'Graham, we are about to make a decision which will have profound consequences. Do you think we ought to pop over the road and ask our lay client what she thinks we ought to do?' He was a man who had that great gift of combining gravitas with lightness of touch.

I also want to pay tribute to my old friend Allan (or Sir Allan as he rightly became) Green, the DPP. I had known Allan for many years; before he took up the post he had been treasury counsel, quite a few rungs above me on the ladder. We who continued in post welcomed his appointment, and we were not disappointed. He supported those he instructed to conduct his cases to the hilt, not least in this difficult saga. I was honoured to be instructed by him to conduct this particular case, and throughout it he provided me and my team with the kind of support that enabled us to do our duty, sometimes in difficult circumstances. He was often in court during the hearing and gave encouragement at times when it was sorely needed. I am pleased to say that he remains a close friend.

As for myself, I had managed to prepare for and conduct the case of The Birmingham Six by abstaining from alcohol for a period of weeks or months, but once it was over I found sustaining that abstinence increasingly difficult. Within days of the conclusion of the case I was on a plane (somewhat ironically named The City of Birmingham) with Lizzie, bound for a luxury resort on a secluded island in the West Indies. There I found the temptation of rum and Coke in the sunshine on a boat on clear blue water irresistible, and the red flag which we had to hoist outside our chalet by the seashore to summon service should have been taken as a red card against consumption of alcohol. I failed to heed yet another warning sign. During the following months I was a fully functioning alcoholic depressive who did not know that that was what he was.

Chapter 15

MY ALCOHOLIC JOURNEY

I must preface this chapter with an important warning. I am no expert. I have no medical or counselling qualifications, and I would not want anyone reading this to think that I am giving advice. What follows is a very personal story of one man trying to face a situation in his life that was unique to him, even if that situation is very similar to problems faced by many other people. If this account of my experiences strikes a chord with a reader who then finds it helpful, then one of the objects, indeed the primary object, of writing this book will have been fulfilled. If it is of any assistance to just one person, then I will feel that the whole exercise has been worthwhile. But neither this chapter, nor indeed the whole book, should be viewed as some kind of self-help manual.

In September 1993 I was admitted to the Priory Hospital in Roehampton, suffering from a serious episode of depression. Everyone goes through times when they feel depressed, but clinical depression is an entirely different thing, and I have long believed that it is highly unfortunate that the illness, which is what clinical depression is, should share the same name as the condition that all human beings experience from time to time. The old word 'melancholy' would be a far better description of the illness, and it would distinguish between the two conditions; even better might it be to adopt the title of a wonderful book written by Professor Lewis Wolpert, *Malignant Sadness*. I read somewhere that '(clinical) depression is a country the undepressed cannot visit', which is why well-meaning people often say unhelpful things like 'try to snap out of it; we all get depressed from time to time'. As I have mentioned, I was diagnosed with clinical depression by Dr Rohde some years earlier, and had been on anti-depressant medication ever since.

If anyone wants to understand more about this crippling illness, I would recommend reading *Darkness Visible* by William Styron, which is a short and compelling account of what clinical depression is like through the words of a chronic sufferer. Lizzie tells me that it gave her the first real insight into this paralysing condition. Those who might prefer a description of the illness from an eminent psychiatrist should read *Depressive Illness: The Curse of the Strong* by Dr Tim Cantopher, which dispels any notion that the condition is a sign of weakness: that is usually the implied suggestion behind exhortations to 'snap out of it'. I would strongly advise both sufferers and their nearest and dearest to read both books.

During the period between the Birmingham Six appeal and the end of my two-year stint as 1STC, which was a few months before my admission to hospital, I had done my best to fulfil my function as Number One, but had found it increasingly difficult. Luckily that period was not one during which any very high-profile cases came to court, so my daily diet, apart from the advisory work which went with the job, was the prosecution of 'ordinary' murders. I must emphasise yet again, even at the risk of repetition, that no case of murder is 'ordinary' to a victim, to his or her family, or to the defendant, but I mean ordinary in the sense that the cases I was doing, even if they were reported on page five or perhaps page three of the daily newspapers, were not making headline news on the front pages.

Nevertheless, each of those cases required me to exercise such skills and experience as I had accumulated over the previous twenty-five years and more, and I like to think that I was able to perform to the best of my ability. Over those months, however, I was finding it increasingly difficult to drag myself to court, as I woke up almost every morning plagued by the black dog of depression, coupled with a sometimes overwhelming anxiety, which in my case was its constant companion. More than once I had to pretend that I had the 'flu, because I simply could not make it to the Old Bailey, and the case was either adjourned or my junior carried on in my absence. On one occasion my great friend Johnny Nutting, who succeeded me as Number One, had to take me home because I simply could not go into court. Most weekends in Norfolk were ruined because I would take to my bed, nursing that black dog.

How can I describe my personal black dog? He was the precise opposite of the faithful and comforting black labrador that I would have loved to have had as my companion. My black dog was faithful in the sense that he was my constant companion; indeed he never listened to my asking him to please go away and leave me in peace for a few hours. Of course I was not constantly thinking about my depression, and the best way of keeping the dog in his basket for a time was to concentrate on other things, like my work. But my thoughts were increasingly dominated by all those negative emotions that invade the brain and cause it to malfunction. I have referred earlier to my fear that today was the day I was going to be found out; I knew now that the day was fast approaching when my ability to function professionally might well grind to a halt. I had nightmares and daily panics, imagining the whole of my life crashing down around me, bringing Lizzie's and Thomas's crashing down with it. I foresaw myself unable to meet the mortgage repayments and thus losing our home, having to withdraw Thomas from his school, and for me the ensuing disgrace and humiliation. Lizzie remembers the conversations we had better than I do, but it must have been sheer hell for her, as she not only watched her husband disintegrate before her eyes, but also contemplated a bleak future for herself and her only child, whose welfare was rightly at the forefront of her mind. One of the most distressing and debilitating aspects of my depression was the isolation it produced, and however much Lizzie tried to encourage me and sympathise with me, I was in that country that the undepressed cannot visit. I felt totally alone in my misery. I tried, as best as I could, to keep working, to do my job, not only to put bread on the table, pay off the mortgage and pay the school fees, but to ward off these dark feelings.

Another feature of clinical depression that affects many of those who live with the sufferers, and which afflicted us in spades redoubled, is that they are unable to share the misery that is occurring inside the house with their friends and relatives outside. Lizzie simply couldn't share her fears and worries with anyone, in case word should leak out and adversely affect my career.

As 1STC I quite often had to appear in the Court of Appeal on behalf of the Attorney General when he referred sentences to it that he considered to be unduly lenient. The power to refer such cases was conferred by Section 36 of the Criminal Justice Act 1988, and was entirely novel. Never before had it been possible to appeal against a sentence on the ground that it was too lenient rather than too severe. Until the passing of this legislation, if defending counsel visited the cells after sentence, and was congratulated by his client on 'getting a good result', then the grateful client could be assured that this result could not be altered. I personally was at first opposed to the new power, and did not look forward either to advising the AG that he had good grounds for referring a sentence to the Court of Appeal or to advancing the basis for doing so to the court.

My view changed over the course of time, and I began to realise that my concerns were based on the feeling that it just wasn't cricket. Just as decisions of 'not out' can now be referred to the third umpire in international cricket matches, in order to rectify decisions that are seen on review to have been palpably wrong, so, as I looked at the papers that landed on my desk upon which to advise the AG, I realised that the ability to refer in a strictly limited number of circumstances was enhancing the principles of justice. I began to see some truly inexplicably lenient sentences coming in from all over the country. There were not many of them and, as I began to realise, they were often from 'the usual suspects' – the same judges' names seemed to come up time and again. Some of them must have looked at transcripts coming back from the Court of Appeal and begun to question whether they should adjust their sights. The primary role of the Court of Appeal is to right injustices, and it must be legitimate that victims of crime have the ability to invite the Law Officers to intervene in cases where they – the victims and their families – feel that an injustice has occurred. Another function of the Court of Appeal is to try to arrive at the sort of consistency in sentencing that allows the public to have confidence that the same principles apply throughout the country and, as a result of a few of these referrals, the Lord Chief Justice would issue 'practice directions' to further that end.

Just in case any of my readers has begun to wonder if I was a man who was turning up to court under the influence of alcohol, I should make it absolutely clear that, throughout my drinking years, I never once drank in the morning (except at weekends when I sometimes enjoyed a good lunch), nor did I ever do so before going into court. I was never the kind of alcoholic who carries a bottle of vodka around in his briefcase. I may have suffered hangovers, and indeed I did, but I was never drunk on duty and never consumed alcohol before going into court. That may leave unanswered the next question, as to what kind of alcoholic I was. I did not discover the real answer to that until I was in the Priory. My problem was that I used alcohol to relax and quell the anxiety at the end of the day, but once I started drinking in the evening, which I did every day, I drank far too much and had no ability to control the amount. One or two glasses was never enough. I drank to excess almost every evening and was also prone to binge drinking when I felt confident that I could get away with it. Holidays were often the times when I let rip, and occasionally behaved in an embarrassing way.

One morning, after a particularly bad weekend, Lizzie asked some great friends to come round and I was persuaded to let them drive me to Roehampton. There I was admitted for depression and placed under the care of Dr Desmond Kelly, who was one of the most distinguished psychiatrists in the country. As I was driven to the hospital I remember thinking, I have reached rock bottom and it is all over; but I had not yet learnt the lesson that alcoholics often have to reach their own rock bottom before they can start the upward journey of recovery. As I walked through the front door I was as frightened as a small boy being delivered to boarding school for the first time and an occasion came to mind when Thomas had once begged us to drive him home when we had taken him back to school. Whereas I would probably have given way, Lizzie was strong enough to let him go. I think Thomas would now agree that Lizzie did the right thing, but as I checked into the Priory that September day I felt that I was too weak to be able to deal with whatever followed. Number One was just a frightened little boy.

For the first week or so I was treated solely for depression, using the well-established method of combining the right anti-depressant medication with talking therapy on a one-to-one basis with a psychologist. There came a moment when Dr Kelly asked me how I had been dealing with the depression myself. I talked about pacing myself, taking time off, getting enough sleep, and trying to relax. At this point I didn't allow the mask to slip too far; I wanted him to see a man and not a child. But then came the moment when he asked me what I did to try to relax, and I answered: 'When I get home and, if I can put off any work I have to do by getting up early the next morning to do it, I pour myself a glass of whisky.' Before long, Dr Kelly elicited, by a form of cross-examination of which I would have been proud, that 'a glass of whisky' was something of an underestimate. He skilfully dragged the truth about my drinking out of me. He established, both to his satisfaction and to mine, that I was trying to self-medicate and was 'treating' my depression by dulling the pain with alcohol. He reminded me that alcohol, far from helping to alleviate depression, is itself a depressant drug.

Dr Kelly (now retired) was a world-renowned expert in the relatively recently discovered condition known as dual diagnosis, or the concept of the alcoholic depressive. Before my feet touched the ground I was transferred to Galsworthy House, the addiction unit at the Priory. As soon as I got there I rang Lizzie and told her, 'they've cracked it; I am something called an alcoholic depressive'. Lizzie's immediate reaction was to tell me not to be silly, saying, 'you are not an alcoholic, you drink far too much, but you are not an alcoholic'. That conversation marked the moment when both she and I started on the journey to understanding what alcoholism really is.

What is alcoholism? Here please heed my warning that I am no expert, but what follows was certainly relevant to my situation. Too many people think that alcoholics are only to be found living in cardboard boxes under bridges or in sleeping bags outside shops at night. Too many people believe that whether or not a person is an alcoholic can be judged by how much he drinks. (As before, if I refer to he, rather than he or she, that is only for the sake of brevity and not because more men than women suffer from alcoholism, although that seems to be true.) There are numerous definitions of alcoholism, but the one that I would choose is this: alcoholism is a pattern of alcohol use that involves problems controlling your drinking, being preoccupied with alcohol, continuing to use alcohol even when it causes problems to yourself and those around you, having to drink more to get the same effect, or having withdrawal symptoms. I would humbly suggest that anyone who reads that definition and finds that it, or even parts of it, rings a bell, he should perhaps take a close look in the mirror. A much simpler question, but one which I find helpful, is: 'Does my intake of alcohol cause problems?' Mine certainly had.

Anyone wondering whether a friend or loved one is merely a heavy drinker or is suffering from alcoholism often finds it difficult to draw the line. In my view, the distinction lies in a close examination of the definition of alcoholism given in the last paragraph. For someone like me, who has personal experience of the condition, it is like the classic reference to an elephant: you may find it difficult to describe, but you know it when you see it. The condition certainly has something to do with compulsion and an inability to exercise self-control. As an illustration, if one sees a man who has already had more than enough, unable to leave the table if half a bottle of wine remains without making sure that it is empty before he gets up, then one must begin to wonder if he has a serious problem.

At Galsworthy House I was introduced to its programme of recovery. It was a salutary, and at first terrifying, experience. As I looked around at my fellow inmates, my immediate reaction (and it is a reaction I have found shared by many of those who have started on the same road to recovery) was that I had nothing in common with these people, and that I came from an entirely different world to most of them. Gradually, though, I began to grasp a fundamental truth. Alcoholism is a form of addiction, and an addict is an addict, regardless of his social or ethnic background, his education, his job or indeed anything else. I should of course add, regardless of gender or sexual orientation. I began to learn that lesson on my first morning, when I attended my first session of group therapy.

Group therapy is a remarkably successful treatment for addiction because it is a great 'bullshit deterrent'. If, as I did, you go into the process thinking that you can give an anodyne account of yourself, merely sliding across the surface of your life-story, you are in for a rude shock. The whole rationale of group therapy is that if you try to tell half-truths or glide over uncomfortable realities, then you will find yourself shot down in flames, and even humiliated. The thought 'I am intelligent enough to be able to deal with this lot' is likely to leave you floundering and feeling even smaller than you did when you started. As I sat in a semi-circle of about eight fellow patients, facing a counsellor, I experienced emotions ranging from resentment to fear, hope to despair, and above all wishing that I was anywhere on earth rather than where I was. What on earth was this all about, and what was I doing here? The counsellor, herself a recovering addict, as all the most effective counsellors are, started to go round the group, asking us the same question: 'What is your current drug of choice?' The man on my left was Charlie Mortimer, who wrote the book *Dear Lupin* and has since spoken courageously of his experiences. Charlie, who became a friend, was at that time addicted to a painkiller. As the counsellor went round the group I heard answers including heroin, nicotine, shopping and gambling as well as my own response, 'alcohol'. The man on my other side at first refused to share his problem. After considerable encouragement from the counsellor and the rest of us he eventually blurted out, 'Okay then, I can't stop fucking other men's wives!'. As you can well imagine, that broke the ice and we realised that we had a 'full house'. We were all in the same boat, because the disease or condition is actually addiction: pure and simple.

The next realisation to dawn on me was that, once an addict, you remain an addict for the rest of your life. There is no such person as a recovered addict; you are either a recovering addict, hoping to remain as such for the rest of your life, or you are a using addict, and you will continue your journey down the slippery slope. Once you accept that you are an addict, be it an alcoholic or any other kind, you have arrived at a destination from which there is no return. You have somehow, and it matters not how, arrived at a station named 'addiction' and, as they say on the rail network, this train terminates here. There is no return ticket. If I ever hear someone refer to themselves or to another as a recovered addict or a recovered alcoholic, I know that that person has no real understanding of the condition: recover*ing* is the correct word.

In my own case, it matters not how or when I became an alcoholic, but nevertheless I will just glance into the rear-view mirror for a moment. I said at the outset that I suspected my father may have had a problem with alcohol; I don't know that for certain, and I have no way of investigating whether it was in the family. I do remember, as a child of no more than fourteen, that he mixed some very powerful cocktails and that, after guests left, I would go round the glasses, lapping up the remnants. I was introduced to whisky by my mother in my teens, and certainly kept pace with my fellow students at university. In retrospect I now see that, as soon as I went to the Bar, I was a very willing pupil of Roger Frisby, who died a sad, penniless and drinking alcoholic, not only in chambers, but also in El Vino's, the criminal Bar's favourite watering hole. George Carman was, in my opinion, certainly an alcoholic, and it is without doubt that alcoholism was, and I suspect still is, rife in my profession. None of this is meant to imply that I blame anyone else for the condition in which I found myself.

With the benefit of hindsight, I suspect that I chose my friends and formed relationships with people who I knew enjoyed a drink and, perhaps more importantly, would not criticise me if I over-indulged. Perhaps the best example of that would be my relationship with Angie, with whom I had a passionate but alcohol-fuelled relationship for a number of years in my early thirties. She was, as I slowly came to realise, most definitely alcoholic, and her inability to come to terms with this led to her sad and untimely demise. It may be difficult to accept now, since we know so much more about alcoholism, but back then in the early seventies I had no inkling that I was in a co-dependent relationship, in which what held the two of us together, other than great affection, was our mutual friend, the demon alcohol. Had I fully understood what was happening, and had the courage to act upon it, I might have been able to save Angie's life.

As the days and weeks went by in Galsworthy House I learnt more about my condition, but only slowly did I begin to accept the basic principles of recovery. Too often did thoughts intrude on my mind such as, I can control my drinking; now I understand the problem I can cope with it; and I think that I am really only a heavy drinker. It wasn't until an octogenarian Roman Catholic priest, himself a recovering alcoholic and a brilliant counsellor, metaphorically pinned me against the wall and said, 'Graham, when are you effing well going to stop thinking and start feeling?' that the penny began to drop. He taught me, to use my words not his, that addiction is a sickness of the soul; it is all about how you feel. Having a first-class degree (which I did not have) or any other qualification will avail you nothing unless you can get in touch with your feelings. At that moment my feelings could only properly be described as 'pretty shitty'.

There were lighter moments, indeed much laughter, in those rooms. One of these occurred when Charlie Mortimer arrived late for a group meeting and, having apologised profusely, explained that he had been stuck on the phone in a futile attempt to get some sense out of his mother who (quoting his racing journalist father), 'had clearly had her head in the Martini bucket all morning and was thus totally unplayable'. Another moment which temporarily relieved the gloom I felt came on the day Lizzie drove Thomas to his public school to start his first term. They came to see me on their way, and their arrival coincided with a visit by two of the younger members of my chambers, Richard Horwill and Ian Winter, now highly successful QCs. Both were enthusiastic petrolheads, and were about to embark on a rally. They drove to Roehampton in their vintage car, which had, emblazoned on the side, a sticker in support of Alcoholics Anonymous. Funnily enough, that provided me with some comfort against one of my greatest worries, namely the stigma that still attached to addiction generally and alcoholism in particular. The thought of that stigma, together with the belief that my career was at an end, had kept me awake at nights; as I said earlier, it was the primary reason why Lizzie was unable to share her predicament with anyone.

After my colleagues had left and I had waved goodbye to Lizzie and Thomas, I embarked on the painful journey that leads to steps four and five of the twelve steps of the Alcoholics Anonymous recovery programme. These concern the damage one's drinking has done to other people. I remember sitting in my room in tears, torturing myself with thoughts of what I had done to cause my beloved son to start his adolescent life by visiting me in this place. What had I done to my wife, that she had to drive our son to school on her own, and then return home, also on her own, to contemplate her future?

Over the years that have followed, I have had to revisit those thoughts on many occasions, for example when it looked, for a moment, as though Thomas might be setting off down the same road as his father by abusing drugs at school and university. Luckily, through his own courage, honesty and integrity, Thomas halted any such potential slide and grew into the commendable man that he now is. As for Lizzie, looking back, I now realise that the real effects of my addiction probably lay dormant until ten years after I left the Priory. Alcoholism is not defeated when the alcoholic stops drinking; the 'ism' at the end of the word is just as dangerous as the drinking, and can cause, as in my case, behaviour that can be equally damaging. I accept that my personal 'ism' caused me to be distant, emotionally detached and selfish.

What exactly do I mean by the 'ism' though? Recovery from addiction is all about change; it involves an acceptance that one's life in sobriety must be very different from one's life as a using addict or drinking alcoholic. It is about changing behaviour and changing attitudes. The 'ism' is about what hasn't changed, even if one has stopped using or drinking. It can give rise to the concept of 'the dry drunk' who, despite not consuming alcohol, has not changed his behaviour or attitude to life and to other people.

As an alcoholic in the initial stages of recovery in Galsworthy House, I attended AA meetings every day, and was introduced to the twelve-step programme which has saved millions of lives. I would suggest that it might be useful for the reader to Google those steps, so as to see what I was trying to grasp in those initial weeks and months.

Following my discharge from Galsworthy House, after many weeks of treatment, I had a particular difficulty with conventional AA meetings. Although everything said in those meetings is supposed to remain confidential, human nature being what it is, confidentiality and anonymity cannot always be guaranteed. As I was hoping to resume a career at the Bar, I was terrified of exposure. In the early 1990s there was not the acceptance of mental health issues there is now; alcoholism is indeed a mental health issue. I had nightmares envisaging articles in the red-top newspapers with headlines like Top Prosecution Lawyer is a Drunk, and even references to such cases as the Birmingham Six appeal. Consequently, I tried to follow the teachings of AA and its steps without necessarily attending many meetings. I should say immediately that I do not recommend anyone in the process of recovery to follow that example. One of the mantras of AA is 'ninety meetings in the first ninety days'; another, uttered at every meeting, is 'keep coming back'. I strongly recommend strict adherence to both, even if I failed to practise what I am now preaching.

When I left the Priory I started to try to rebuild my life, a long and often painful process and one in which I am still engaged to this day, almost twenty-eight years into my recovery. I hope to die a recovering alcoholic.

I have not found it easy to write this chapter. Alcoholism is a condition wrought with pain, both for the sufferer, and for those around him inevitably affected by his drinking. Writing this chapter has evoked painful memories. But it has also reminded me how lucky I have been to have found the help and support I needed to survive. Every day I remember that I am lucky to be alive, because, make no mistake, alcoholism is a life-threatening condition. My life as a sober man in recovery is challenging but, almost always, rewarding. Had I gone on drinking I would surely be dead by now. I think we should all say the Serenity Prayer every day: 'God grant me the serenity to accept the things I cannot change. The courage to change the things I can. And the wisdom to know the difference.' If I say it to myself, and then, more importantly, reflect upon its meaning, it helps me to try, not always with success, to change what still needs changing.

How do I try now to make sure that I remain sober? Although I do not attend the AA meetings that I needed to at the beginning, and which many recovering alcoholics regard as essential to their continued sobriety for the rest of their lives, I am a member of a small group, usually five or six in number, who meet on Zoom once a week and hold what I would loosely describe as an informal AA-type meeting. We are at varying stages of recovery, and that helps to put into action what I think of as the rope-ladder theory. Imagine someone trying to climb a rope ladder onto a warship in a rough sea. Without a helping hand it would be very difficult, if not impossible. If, however, someone three or four rungs further up the ladder puts his hand down and helps the person below to climb up, rung by rung, it not only helps, but it gives the person on the lower rung the confidence to try, so often lacking in the alcoholic. Then imagine that having been helped up the ladder, that person in turn extends a helping hand down to someone further down, on the lowest rung. That is how I believe recovering alcoholics can best help each other.

Chapter 16

THE ROAD TO RECOVERY

The fundamental lesson I had learnt in Galsworthy House, reinforced at other AA meetings, was that to maintain my sobriety and mental health I could never have another alcoholic drink as long as I lived. I am pleased, and indeed proud, to say that I have managed to follow that rule for over twenty-seven years, with the single exception of one night in 2005. I am still on the road to recovery. An alcoholic cannot control his drinking. He may believe he can and he may be able to sustain 'controlled drinking' for a few weeks, months, or even years, but in the end alcoholism will get him. If you are an alcoholic you can't fight it; you have to learn how to live with it, and that entails total abstention.

I am often asked how I have managed to achieve this. The answer is that every time I have been tempted, which has happened many times, I remind myself that if I drank again it would inevitably eventually lead to my death – either by a disease of the liver, by falling drunk downstairs or under a bus, or, more likely, to suicide. Every time some well-intentioned friend or acquaintance has tried to persuade me – 'oh surely after all this time a glass of this wonderful vintage claret won't harm you' – I have to answer that I am afraid it would. Once one has that, literally sobering, fact firmly lodged in one's brain, it becomes easier, and it is no more 'strong' to abstain than it is 'strong' for a diabetic to absorb insulin every day. You do it or you die.

Of course abstention altered my social life. In modern western society, alcohol is the lubricant that oils the wheels of social intercourse. I try not to put myself unnecessarily in the path of temptation. Gone are the days when I used to sit 'under the stairs' at the Garrick Club enjoying glass after glass of port while listening to great raconteurs like James Crespi, Brian Masters, Robin Day and even Bill Mars-Jones. As soon as I was living a life of sobriety, it just didn't seem as much fun to sit there nursing a glass of Coca-Cola, which had become my usual beverage, if not my 'drug of choice'. The sad fact is that since 1993, if I ever find myself in the company of those who still imbibe too much, then by about 10pm they have begun to become less enthralling company, even boring and repetitive. I now wake up without a hangover, whereas I suspect that some of them wake up with both sore heads and that awful feeling of remorse, that I remember so well. In the cold light of day, memories are only too vivid of what one said or did the night before. The reality is, as the saying goes, that you can tell a man who boozes by the company he chooses.

Some people in the early stages of recovery choose not to have any alcohol in the house, a measure some need to adopt as a safeguard. Personally I have always had alcohol in the house, because I think it would be desperately unfair to make Lizzie, my family or my friends suffer, more than they already have, because of my condition. Indeed, I think if I had tried to make our home a prohibition zone we would have found ourselves losing friends pretty quickly.

After a couple of months of recuperation I decided to put my toe in the water and try to return to work. By now I was in silk. It had become customary for 1STCs to stay in office for about two years, partly because it was a fairly gruelling job, but also because it was important for TCs to be able to climb the ladder and not be prohibited from taking their turn because someone at the top was refusing to move on. Thus I became Graham Boal QC. Whereas the award of a silk gown represents the pinnacle of success for most barristers, most at the criminal Bar would agree that becoming Senior Treasury Counsel, let alone 1STC, is at least as much of an accolade, if not more so. That was recognised, not long after I vacated the post, by the Lord Chancellor, and now all STCs are automatically awarded silk. I rather regret that. If I ever arrive at the pearly gates, and if Saint Peter asks me what was my greatest professional achievement, I will not say Queen's Counsel or Old Bailey judge: I will answer First Senior Treasury Counsel, and await the look of utter bafflement as he writes that down on his clipboard. It might even be enough for him to refuse me entry, and thus send me to a place where I suspect I would find a number of my friends.

The ever-optimistic Michael Greenaway, my senior clerk, assured me that defence solicitors had been eagerly awaiting the day when they could instruct me again, despite my temporary absence, but I was less sanguine. Senior clerks, like nannies, are there to soothe the brows of their charges or protégés, whose egos require constant polishing. Nevertheless, Michael soon found me a brief to defend in an interesting, and reasonably newsworthy murder case.

Mrs Rene Sampat was charged with murdering Janet Marshall, who was the wife of her driving instructor. The Crown's case, which was ultimately proved to the satisfaction of the jury that convicted her, was that she had formed a fatal attraction for Ancell Marshall and that, in order to further her ambition to have Mr Marshall for herself, she had suborned her own eighteen-year-old son, Roy Aziz, to stab and strangle Mrs Marshall, who stood in her way. At this point, Aziz had been convicted of the murder, whilst Mr Marshall had originally been tried for his wife's murder – a trial at which Rene Sampat had given evidence for the prosecution. But Marshall was acquitted and a subsequent investigation gave rise to Mrs Sampat herself now being charged with the crime.

Those facts, barely stated, made this a rather unusual case, particularly because at the new trial the tables were turned, with Rene Sampat in the dock and Ancell Marshall giving evidence for the prosecution. The case for the defence that I had to advance was that Mr Marshall was indeed guilty of the murder, and that he should have been convicted at his own trial. I was not surprised that, despite my best endeavours, the jury convicted my client. According to a press report, when I addressed the judge in mitigation I described Mrs Sampat as 'a woman who was obsessed to a point which could best be described as mentally abnormal', going on to say 'you may think that this (could be) described as a fatal attraction and a fatal obsession'. I regard that now as a rather hackneyed piece of advocacy: I had obviously seen the film! The judge, His Honour Richard (Dick) Lowry QC, was kind enough to report that I had performed well enough to suggest that my forensic abilities had not totally deserted me.

There was an unusual postscript to this case. Rene Sampat was of course sentenced to life imprisonment, but a few years later, when I was appointed a judge, I received a charming letter of congratulations from her, writing from HMP Bullwood Hall. I think that all members of the criminal Bar would agree that it is quite rare to receive a letter of thanks from a client one has represented, even if one has achieved 'a good result'; even rarer, if not unprecedented, to receive a letter from a former client now serving a sentence of life imprisonment, as the result of a trial at which one has failed to achieve the desired acquittal.

Being in silk meant that I was truly back on the cab rank and, although I defended in a number of cases, I also prosecuted cases that would not have been on the treasury counsel menu. Looking back now on my time in silk, I wonder whether the transition from TC to QC had a psychological effect on me that I did not recognise at the time, and which may have exacerbated my depressive tendencies. The Old Bailey had been not only my place of work, but also my spiritual home, as it were, for over fifteen years: I had spent my working life out of court much more 'in the room' (the accommodation on the third floor where we TCs all worked together) than in chambers. Now I was back in the general swim, going to different courts and robing in robing rooms just like every other member of the Bar. I know that even at the time I felt as though I was in a slightly alien environment; what could certainly be described as being outside my comfort zone. An aspect of this was the experience of appearing in front of 'lesser' judges, and sometimes against advocates of a lesser calibre than before. That must read as the expressions of a man who thought himself in a class apart, and indeed in a rather superior class, but the fact remains that I had been incredibly spoilt by my sixteen years as a TC; in many ways, for so long as one performed adequately, almost a protected species. The judges at the Old Bailey were, almost without exception, of a higher calibre than some (but by no means all) of the circuit judges who presided in other Crown Courts. One's opponents were also, almost universally, of a very high standard, for the obvious reason that they were defending in the most serious cases, and thus the recipients of 'a certificate for two counsel', which meant that the accused was represented by a silk and a junior as I have explained. I repeat: for sixteen years I had been spoilt. But the other side of the coin was that I had been working at quite a stressful level all that time.

To give but one example of how my working life had changed, I will cite a particular case. I was instructed by the Fraud Investigation Group (FIG) of the CPS to lead for the prosecution in a mortgage fraud. The defendants included a solicitor plus mortgage brokers and agents who had conspired to defraud banks by the basic device of inventing fictitious applicants for mortgages. What I knew about mortgages and conveyancing could easily have been written on the back of a postage stamp, so I was extremely lucky to have as my junior Colin McCaul (now an eminent QC), whose experience in civil practice allowed him to instruct me, and through me the court, on the niceties of such dark arts. Colin and I had never met before but we seemed to bond immediately, and the whole case became, not the nightmare that I had anticipated, but a positive experience. We shared the same sense of humour, which is essential in any team of counsel, and especially when engaged in such dry subject-matter as conveyancing. Defending counsel might best be described as 'not quite up to Old Bailey standard'. All in all, the case was an altogether different experience for me.

I began to wonder whether I wanted to spend the rest of my working life trailing around widely scattered Crown Courts. I was also aware that I was heading for the sell-by shelf. Every generation of barristers is overtaken by the next, and I could feel the young Turks breathing down my neck. Practices were creeping in of which I disapproved. Throughout my career it had been frowned on to tout for work; now it seemed accepted practice for sets of chambers to lay on events, usually portrayed as being for further education purposes, but which in reality were an excuse to invite as many solicitors as possible to a party and pour champagne down their throats.

One of the final straws came one day when Michael rang me at lunchtime in the Bar Mess at the Old Bailey and said, 'you have a con' – conference or consultation – 'at Brixton Prison at four-thirty this afternoon'. I asked what he was talking about, as I had no papers for a con. Michael's reply was that I didn't need any papers, as I would be attending 'a beauty parade'.

It transpired that a very high-profile defendant, whose case would be long, lucrative and attract a great deal of publicity, had decided to interview four silks before deciding which one to employ. This was a practice that was totally alien, and utterly obnoxious, to me. Counsel should be chosen by the solicitor on the simple criterion of who would do the job best, and not by impressing a criminal by his charm. I refused to go. Michael said quietly, 'I'm very sorry, sir, but that's the way it's going', and I knew that that was his gentle way of telling me that I might have passed my sell-by date.

Not long after that I happened to have lunch with my friend Michael McKenzie. Michael had been the Clerk of the Court at the Old Bailey, and was the last one to hold that office who had been called to the Bar – more's the pity. Since then he had been elevated to the post of Registrar of Criminal Appeals. In both those roles he, although a civil servant and part of the administration, came into daily contact with members of the Bar and understood how to deal with us. He had been a close friend of mine for many years, and acted as clerk of the court during the Birmingham Six hearings.

Neither Mike nor I can remember what prompted us to arrange that lunch in 1995; nor can we remember the conversation in any detail. What I do remember, only too well, was that Mike for some reason asked me how I saw my future. Mike cannot remember, or even perhaps chooses not to remember, whether he was conveying some sort of coded message from on high. In those days barristers did not apply to become judges, whereas nowadays they have to fill in a long form, including an assessment of their own abilities. In 1995 things were rather different, and sometimes barristers were invited to put their hats in the ring.

I had started my judicial career as long ago as 1982, when I was appointed as an assistant recorder, as it was then known. That was the lowest form of animal life in the judicial hierarchy, but meant that one sat from time to time, usually for about twenty days a year, in a Crown Court, and tried minor cases with a jury. I well remember my first trial. The defendant was charged with 'being a man, committed an act of gross indecency with another man'. As I sat in my room contemplating with fear and dread the papers in the case, I reflected how sensible the listing office at that court had been to give me such a straightforward baptism. The case involved what happened between two persons in a public lavatory (known as cottaging), and all went without incident until I decided to intervene.

The evidence of the police officers who had arrested the defendant, and had said in evidence that they had witnessed the events which, taken at face value, constituted the offence, had not been challenged by defending counsel: so I took the opportunity, in the absence of the jury, to ask counsel what his client's defence was. I thought I detected a slight smile on his face when he replied: 'My client's defence is that my client is not a man.' I thanked him profusely as my mind started to race. What on earth was going to happen next?

When the time came for the court to rise that afternoon, an application for bail was made, which I refused, and my bottom had already left the bench when the dock officer piped up. 'Excuse me, Your Honour, but is the defendant to be taken to Brixton (the male prison) or Holloway (the female prison)?' I asked for counsel's assistance, and suggested that the best course would be to invite a doctor to make that decision. Defending counsel then argued, '. . . but that will pre-determine the only issue in the case, which you, rather than the jury, will then pre-empt, based on the evidence given by that doctor'. I replied, rather pathetically: 'Well, a doctor will be summoned and I need not know the result of the examination, which will be communicated by the doctor to the dock officer, who will make the necessary decision.' With that I fled from the bench. Luckily the next morning the defendant changed his plea to one of guilty. I tremble to think what would happen in a similar situation these days.

Despite that rather unnerving start, I found that over the next dozen or so years, as I graduated from assistant recorder to recorder, sitting for about four weeks a year as such, I increasingly enjoyed the experience, and even began to wonder whether I was better suited to the bench than the Bar. On 4th September 1995 I sat as Mr Recorder Boal QC in Court Two at the Central Criminal Court; the first time I had sat at the Old Bailey. Obviously my performance on the bench over the years had not met with total disapproval.

At the lunch with Mike McKenzie, I probably said that I was seriously mulling over whether I relished the idea of hawking my barristerial talents around until retirement. What I did say, however, probably rather hubristically, was that the only judicial appointment I would consider would be as a permanent judge at the Old Bailey. Prior to a change of approach in the nineties, 'a job' at the Old Bailey would have been, for a former 1STC, mine for the asking. Many of my predecessors had found their way onto the bench there, almost as though it went with the rations. Times had changed, however, and the first message I got, after Mike had reported back to those on high, was that appointments were not made directly to the Bailey any longer, and that I would have to sit as an ordinary circuit judge elsewhere whilst my abilities were assessed. That rebuff was sweetened by the rider that they had no doubt that I would prove my worth and be promoted in due course to the Bailey.

My instant reaction was no, thank you, and there the matter rested until the intervention of Mr Justice John Blofeld (brother of Henry, the cricket commentator). On 12th January 1996, John, whom I had got to know quite well when he was still at the Bar, wrote to me to tell me that the Senior Presiding Judge, Robin Auld LJ, was offering me appointment as a permanent judge at the Central Criminal Court, but that, because of 'listing difficulties' I would have to sit, for a period of three weeks, as a circuit judge at another Crown Court. I was sworn in on 5th March, and sat at Middlesex Crown Court for three weeks from the next day. This wonderful exercise in British compromise had allowed the establishment to maintain the new rule that no one would be appointed directly to the Old Bailey. After a short holiday, I sat for the first time as an Old Bailey judge on 19th April 1996.

Chapter 17

ON THE BENCH

Sitting as a judge at the Old Bailey felt like coming home. I would be doing the same job but from a different seat. For years I had been involved in the administration of criminal justice at that court, so despite being viewed from a different aspect, everything was familiar.

The Old Bailey was, and I believe still is, very different from any other Crown Court. It oozes tradition, and possesses unique features that distinguish it from all others. I was lucky enough to be assigned to Court Four, which was in the original building opened by King Edward V11 in 1907. It was wood-panelled and, as with all the courts in the 'old' part of the building, all the seats and chairs were of green leather, embossed with the coat-of-arms of the City of London. That was because the building – together with the new courts opened in 1972 – is owned by the City of London Corporation, and the Lord Mayor and aldermen jealously preserve their superintendence over the court and its traditions. The Lord Mayor for the time being opens every session of the court, while the two Sheriffs of the City of London each have a flat in the building. In my time, every working day one of the sheriffs would host the judges' lunch, at which their invited guests would join us; we attended fully robed, eating our lunch in wig and gown. Although some of my brethren were not very keen on these events, I found them to be rather a bonus. Not only did they go to disprove the theory that there is no such thing as a free lunch, but to me they were a better alternative to what happens at other courts, where one either had to bring one's own sandwiches or sit in a judges' mess with other judges, most of whom wanted to discuss their cases. At the Old Bailey one would always be within reach of a guest, nearly all of whom would prove to be of some interest, and with whom, once one had disposed of the 'are you trying an interesting case?' question, one could have a conversation not confined to the day job.

Every day, at about 12 noon, a 'red band' (City of London attendant) would come into court clutching a piece of paper, which would be handed to the usher, then to the clerk, and then up to the judge. If the paper was blue, then our host was the lay sheriff; if pink, the aldermanic sheriff. On the paper were the names and CVs of today's guests, so that one could mug up on one's neighbour at lunch. One day I realised that I would be sitting opposite George Carey, then Archbishop of Canterbury. My immediate thought was to wonder what on earth we were going to talk about, other than the obvious topics. Then my eye was attracted by the last line of his CV: 'a great Arsenal supporter'. Being a lifelong Gunner myself, as soon as he had said grace my opening gambit was to ask if he thought we should sell Patrick Vieira. The rest of the meal passed in a flash, and not long afterwards Lizzie and I were asked to a private family dinner at Lambeth Palace.

That anecdote reminds me of another piece of sage advice from Roger Frisby: 'If you are appearing for the defence at the Bailey, and you are hoping to slip in a question of marginal admissibility, always do it when the judge is reading that pink or blue missive.' A good apprenticeship at the Bar does not only include matters of law.

The other great advantage of sitting at the Bailey rather than anywhere else was that one retained one's own staff, often for years on end. In my case my usher, for the whole of my tenure, was Gladys Green. Later I discovered that not only had I chosen her, since I had seen her at work over many years, but that she, when she learnt of my appointment, had asked if she could be assigned to my court. Gladys was the embodiment of loyalty, and I relied on her as though she were my right arm. My shorthand writer was Cynthia, who had opened the bowling for the West Indies ladies' international cricket team, and had a physique to match. Gladys and Cynthia between them ruled Court Four with a rod of iron and suffered no nonsense from anyone. Many a time Cynthia would interrupt either the evidence or my summing-up with the command 'slow down' and, if it were my summing-up, adding 'My Lord' for the sake of appearances. 'My Lord' is how Old Bailey judges are addressed (as distinct from 'Your Honour' in other Crown Courts, unless presided over by a High Court judge), and I am told that young barristers, who might not have appeared at the Old Bailey before, were sternly reminded of that by Gladys before the court sat.

We would also have the same court clerk for the duration of any case, however long it lasted, a service not afforded to judges in other courts. I was always loyally served by them, and I particularly remember Karen Gedge, who graced (in every sense) my court for many of my longer trials. All in all, I was afforded every possible assistance at every turn: I was totally spoilt during my working day, as I was frequently reminded when I got home. If I had had a pound for every time since 1996 I have heard Lizzie say 'you are not in court now', I would be a rich man indeed.

I sometimes feel that the public overlooks the fact that judges are, underneath the wig and gown, usually otherwise quite normal human beings. I hark back to Roger Frisby's advice to the advocate of 'know your judge'. Judges come in different shapes and sizes, have different bees in their bonnets, and sometimes allow their own foibles to become apparent. To give but one example, I would cite a case in which the first jury disagreed, and thus there was a second trial in front of a different judge. The first trial was presided over by Judge Bernard Gillis QC, who was generally regarded as an old-fashioned judge. His particular eccentricity was that he insisted on the English language not being abused, saying that 'the Bar is the repository of the English language'. The case involved a serious affray, which resulted in a man being killed. In his summing-up, Gillis described the case as 'an incident of serious public disorder outside a public house after statutory licensing hours'. The second trial was presided over by the then Recorder of London, Sir James Miskin QC, who was of a different ilk. He began his summing-up by saying to the jury, 'this case is about a punch-up outside a pub after chucking-out time'.

I sometimes wonder whether the layman thinks that judges come, fully processed, from some sort of factory, devoid of all personal experience and with immunity from all the prejudices and eccentricities inherent in the human condition. The myth that each one is male, public school and Oxbridge-educated and lacking in any experience of real life, may still be harboured by some people. Although that may have been more true when I was called to the Bar in the mid-sixties, it is now a parody of the truth. Whether the judiciary is sufficiently representative of the society it serves is a topic to which I will return in another context. Judges are individual human beings, and some are better than others.

What sort of a judge was I? I am the last person who could answer that question. I would imagine that every judge would like to be thought of as being 'firm but fair'; I would hope that I came somewhere near that description. What I did try to bring to the court was an atmosphere in which everyone knew that they were expected to observe all the etiquette appropriate to the solemnity of the occasion, but to be as relaxed as possible, and not to leave a sense of humour outside the door of the court. I am a firm believer in the power of humour to lighten, and thus make more bearable, some of the more solemn occasions in life, and I often felt that a moment of levity, provided it was not inappropriate, could lower the temperature and cause people to behave more reasonably.

I have no intention of listing all the cases I tried, but if I mention just a few, they may shed some light on the working life of this particular Old Bailey judge. I will not look at the cases in chronological order, and before I deal with any of them, this might be the appropriate moment to review the general issue of how judges arrive at the sentences they impose.

Appropriate sentencing is an art rather than an exact science. Having said that, there have been increasing efforts over the last few years to ensure that there is a degree of consistency, which itself ensures that sentences do not appear to depend upon some kind of postcode lottery, or upon the whims and prejudices of individual judges. Although each case must depend upon its own unique facts and upon the individual circumstances of offenders, consistency is achieved in a number of ways. First, all judges have volumes of sentencing manuals, constantly updated, and available to counsel, who can refer to them when addressing the judge on sentence. When I retired, the primary manual had already run to three volumes. Secondly, the Court of Appeal can always review sentences, now at the instance of both prosecution and defence, and that court occasionally reviews a number of cases that throw up the same issues in 'consolidated appeals', thereafter issuing Practice Directions. Finally, almost all offences, except those of homicide, are created by statute, and those statutes always state the maximum punishment available upon conviction. One frequently reads in the press of a suspect being charged with an offence 'which carries a sentence of X years' imprisonment'; that means the maximum sentence available to the court in a case which involves the most aggravating features imaginable.

In recent years we have seen increasing pressure for minimum, as well as maximum, sentences to be fixed by law. I would oppose any such innovation. Not only is it unnecessary, since unduly lenient sentences can be rectified by the Court of Appeal but, more importantly, it could create great potential injustice. To give but one example of this contention, I would refer to the case of Heather Pratten, which I will review in due course. If there were a minimum sentence for manslaughter, which would necessarily state a term of imprisonment, I would not have been able to pass the sentence that I decided reflected the justice of the case.

In my day, the diet was mainly murder, with a sprinkling of very serious sex cases and the occasional serious fraud. Terrorism had not reared its ugly head to the extent that it now forms a considerable part of the court's work, although I did try one case in which it was alleged that a significant terrorist attack had been thwarted by our security services.

An important issue there was the relevance of large amounts of material found in the defendant's flat, which the prosecution alleged pointed to his involvement in a conspiracy to commit terrorist outrages. A lot turned on the defendant's use of the word 'jihad', and both prosecution and defence called experts who gave various definitions of it. To prepare myself, I had read the Koran, albeit in an English translation, so as to have some notion of the issues involved. I listened attentively as the academics debated whether, in the context of this case, the use of the word jihad implied that the author was championing *armed* struggle, or merely struggle in the sense of struggling against the challenges that life throws up. The interesting thing for me was that the more I learnt about Islam, the more convinced I became that the similarities between the three monotheistic religions – Judaism, Islam and Christianity – far outweighed their differences; although extremist supporters of any one of the religions would deploy those differences to justify acts of violence, all three were in essence philosophies which, if followed in a spirit of tolerance, would lead to human beings living spiritually richer lives.

I tried three cases which might be described as gang murders. Jason Grant was part of a gang of nightclub bouncers: they had raided the home of an Asian man who was involved in a dispute about a particular bar. In what turned out to be a case of mistaken identity, Grant stabbed the victim thirteen times and then (which is what attracted the attention of the media) licked the blood of the deceased while shouting 'I love claret!', claret being slang for blood. Grant was convicted of murder, and thus received the mandatory sentence of life imprisonment, and I sentenced three other members of the gang to between two and eight years.

In the early years of the twenty-first century the civil war in Sri Lanka had spilled over onto the roads of Alperton in west London, culminating in a man of Tamil extraction being gunned down at the end of a brutal twenty-four-hour campaign to exact revenge for a killing in his own country. Hours earlier, the gang of which the actual killer was a member had bungled a drive-by shooting, and at the trial of five of the gangsters, the jury and I heard of what sounded like a motorised version of a Wild West film. The gang drove around the streets of Alperton, firing from their cars, and eventually laid siege to the house of one member of the opposition faction, storming inside and shooting a man in the chest. My abiding memory of that trial was of the number of Sri Lankan housewives who came to court to give evidence, without a word of English, who had not been outside their own front doors for years. I knew that virtual ghettos existed in this country, but the fact that one such existed within a few miles of where I lived came as something of a shock.

By far the most memorable gang trial over which I presided was that of R v Luisa Bolivar and Others. Luisa Bolivar was a thirty-seven-year-old Colombian mafia boss and a leading light in a ring of international drug smugglers; she was known as

La Patrona (the lady boss). She had ordered the assassination of a sixteen-year-old boy, Jorge Castillo – known as *Huevo* ('Little Egg') because of his shaven head – as retribution for his having had the impertinence to snatch a gold chain from the neck of her lover, Juan Carlos Fernandez, known as Scarface. Bolivar hired two hitmen, Hector Cedeno and Hernando Guevara-Jaramillo, to perform the premeditated execution, which was carried out by luring Castillo into a car. While Guevara-Jaramillo drove, Cedeno was sitting in the back, behind Castillo who was in the front passenger seat. Cedeno leant forward and throttled Castillo with a black boot-lace. It took about twenty minutes for Huevo to die, after which his body was dumped in an industrial bin near a children's playground in south London. If that précis sounds like the trailer for a Hollywood thriller, then added details, such as La Patrona being asked if she would like a severed finger or ear to prove that the contract had been fulfilled, might remind one of the Godfather films. The hitmen were paid £2000 for their day's work. Fernandez fled the country and Bolivar was arrested at Heathrow airport with £20,000 in her underwear.

The trial lasted nearly four months. It was notable for having been the first one in this country in which the prosecution relied to a substantial extent on the evidence of cell site tracing of calls made on mobile phones, a technology that was in its infancy at the time, to plot the movements of the defendants and of the victim up to his death. The three defendants were convicted by the unanimous verdicts of the jury and, in sentencing them to life imprisonment, I told them that they had been convicted 'on compelling evidence of a cruel, cold-blooded contract killing'. A feature of that compelling evidence was that the Colombian community in this country, including the least attractive elements of it, was so repulsed by what had happened that the police were assisted by an unusual amount of intelligence from its underworld. Bolivar's half-brother, himself a self-confessed drug dealer, informed on his own half-sister and gave evidence against her. A fourth man in the car at the time of the murder, who had been paid £200 to keep quiet, also gave evidence, thus breaking *omerta*.

A very unpleasant feature of the trial itself was that Bolivar was represented by a rogue barrister, whom I will refer to as 'C'. Although a junior, he led in a case that demanded representation by silks, and his behaviour throughout the trial was such that it created, in a trial already fraught with tension, an extremely unhelpful atmosphere. I subsequently learnt that he had been declared bankrupt and was under investigation for both drug and sexual offences. His tactic, in the face of almost insurmountable evidence against his client, was to try to goad the trial judge into indiscretions: a temptation I at times found difficult to resist. At one stage I felt constrained to say to C that even if he could not bring himself to show any respect to me, would he please show some respect for the coat of arms under which I sat. C's unprofessional conduct reached its zenith when I received a telephone call from a High Court judge who was trying a case of conspiracy to murder at Stafford Crown Court. When Kay J and I compared notes over the telephone, we were able to confirm what each of us had suspected – namely that C was conducting two cases at the same time without the permission of, or indeed the knowledge of, either trial judge. Our suspicions had been raised because C was absenting himself from each of our courts on days upon which his attendance was required and leaving whichever case in the hands of inexperienced juniors. The explanations C gave to both Kay J and myself for his absence were disingenuous to the point of being untrue.

This episode was probably the worst example of professional misconduct that I witnessed in the whole of my career at the Bar and on the bench: C was suspended from practice as a result. Bolivar subsequently appealed to the Court of Appeal, as did the convicted defendant at Stafford Crown Court, on the ground that her counsel's conduct had rendered her conviction unsafe. The

Court held that both trial judges had done their best to ensure that the defendants received a fair trial, which they had indeed received, and Bolivar's conviction was upheld. It was a trial I will never forget.

In the context of violent cases, I have often been asked if I have ever been in fear for my own or my family's safety. Twice when prosecuting I was warned by the police of a threat which they took seriously; once when the defendant was a member of the terrorist organisation Abu Nidal, and the other when the case involved the IRA. I do not propose to go into the details, nor do I think it would be right to describe the measures the authorities took to protect me – other than to say that on one occasion my wife very nearly drove over an officer who was searching for a bomb under our car.

Perhaps surprisingly, when I was on the bench I was not aware of any threats, other than the occasional expletive uttered in the heat of the moment by a convicted prisoner whom I had just sentenced. I believe that there are two reasons why relatively few attempts are made to attack prosecutors or judges. First, I think that most criminals realise that one is only doing one's job, and that if it were not to be done by this person it would be done by another. I am told that defendants, witnesses and jurors often do not even know the name of the judge in the court in which they are appearing.

The second reason is the anonymity afforded by our robes. A man or woman is rendered scarcely recognisable by the court wig. Many times I have walked up and down the escalators at St Paul's tube station, past witnesses, jurors and defendants on bail whom I recognised, without the faintest glimmer of recognition from them. I suppose one explanation for that might be that some people simply do not believe that judges travel by tube! On one occasion, when there was a delay on the Central line, Gladys came to tell me at about 11am that two of the jurors were deeply apologetic that they had only just arrived; when I asked her to reassure them that

I understood because I too had been held up on the same line, the whole jury expressed astonishment that I had come in by public transport. Perhaps they thought I was driven in every morning in a Rolls-Royce accompanied by outriders.

As I describe some of the more notable murder cases I tried, perhaps it is the right moment to explain the sentencing procedure. The mandatory sentence for murder, prescribed by statute, is one of life imprisonment, and that is the sentence pronounced in court. After pronouncing that sentence, the judge goes on, either in open court or upon reflection later and in writing, to announce what is sometimes described as 'the tariff', i.e. the minimum term to be served before release can be considered by the Parole Board. The media sometimes reports that 'X was sentenced to thirty years for murder'. That is inaccurate shorthand for what should properly be reported as 'the judge sentenced X to life imprisonment, and fixed the minimum term at thirty years'. In my day, the normal tariff for a run-of-the-mill domestic murder (if any such offence can be described in that way) was about twelve to fourteen years, with figures above that being reserved for particularly horrendous offences that merited condign punishment. Another common misapprehension is that a prisoner is automatically released at the end of that minimum term: that is certainly not the case.

I served on the Parole Board for a number of years, and I found it a most interesting and rewarding experience. I was appointed to the panel of judges who review the sentences of those serving life sentences, known as lifers. A board always consisted of a judge (never, of course, the judge who had passed sentence), a psychiatrist, and a lay member, who was invariably someone steeped in the ethos and practices of the criminal justice system, typically a retired probation officer. The hearings necessarily took place in prisons, and our job was to decide whether a prisoner could safely be moved to open conditions, with a view to ultimate release, or, if already in an open prison, whether it was now safe to release him or her on licence. Prisoners serving life sentences had their cases reviewed annually once the tariff period had expired, so we often saw men (and very occasionally women) who were being reviewed many years after that minimum period had expired. There was never any question of throwing away the key; every lifer's case was reviewed once a year.

The onus was always on the prisoner to demonstrate that he no longer posed a threat to society. We were always provided with reports from psychologists, psychiatrists, probation officers and prison staff; and the main criterion, designed to give maximum protection to the public, was 'if in doubt don't release'. The thing that I found comforting, and even a little surprising, was that I do not remember any occasion when we reached a decision that was other than unanimous. The three of us, albeit coming from different disciplines and exercising different skills, were able to distil the evidence and the arguments presented on the prisoners' behalf by counsel and solicitors, and arrive at a conclusion to which we could all subscribe.

Back in my day job, I do recall two instances when I made recommendations to the Parole Board that they should consider my view that life should mean life. The first was extremely unusual in that, having passed seven life sentences on a young man of seventeen, I went on to recommend that very serious consideration should be given as to whether it would ever be safe to release him. Adewale Odubawo began a sequence of horrific attacks on women when he was just fourteen, including four rapes and two attempted rapes. I described his offences as 'degrading, humiliating, sordid and terrifying attacks', and went on to say that I regarded it as my duty to 'protect women in this country against your predatory and depraved instincts'. I concluded my sentencing remarks in this way: 'I regard you as very dangerous indeed; so dangerous that it is impossible to predict whether, and if so when, it will be safe to let you out on the streets again.'

Ian Haywood had already served part of a life sentence for murdering a woman with a machete, hacking at his teenage victim thirty-five times, some years before he appeared in front of me. He had been released on licence for just over a year before he attacked a seventeen-year-old and her boyfriend, described as a courting couple, at an isolated West Sussex beauty spot. In sentencing Haywood to five life sentences for the horrifying attack on the couple, I said that I regarded him as such an obvious danger to the public that I felt obliged to recommend that he should never be released.

Those cases obviously attracted the attention of the media. Other, less obviously newsworthy, sometimes did. One such was when I sentenced a teenage carjacker to six years' imprisonment. Lanray Busari terrified two drivers into handing over their cars by brandishing a handgun-shaped cigarette lighter, holding it to their heads, and threatening to kill them if they did not comply with his demands. The imitation weapon was so realistic that I noted in my sentencing remarks, 'it must be so glaringly obvious that such objects might be used in the way you chose to use yours that, in my view, the sooner such objects are taken off the market the better'. Some elements of the press used these words to start a campaign.

Some cases attracted the attention of the press more for the identity of the victim than for the crime itself. One such was that of Victor Guppy, who shot his former partner Louise Schuller, who was a highly ranked competitive cyclist. Guppy brought Ms Schuller's promising career to an abrupt end when he shot her on the doorstep of her east London home, in order to stop her enjoying her pastime with her new boyfriend. In sentencing Guppy to seven years for causing grievous bodily harm and possession of a firearm I observed, 'it is plain your intention was to disable her and prevent her pursuing her pastime of competitive cycling'. Ms Schuller had to undergo a series of operations and a lot of physiotherapy and, at the time of the trial, eighteen months after the offence, had only just learnt to walk without a stick.

Just in case the reader is beginning to wonder whether I was always prone to passing condign sentences, consigning the accused to very long terms of imprisonment, I will refer to two other cases.

Colin Bland pleaded guilty to the manslaughter of his friend Roy Ayling as a result of an alcohol-fuelled brawl after a night of heavy drinking. After some scuffling and pushing, Ayling fell backwards and struck his head, fracturing his skull; he never regained consciousness and died two days later. The case was a tragic example of the potential consequences of relatively minor violence. Normally I would have regarded the offence as one that merited an immediate sentence of imprisonment, but Ayling's mother made a statement saying this: 'Even though this is a hard time for our family, I think this was a tragic accident, and I think that Roy would not want him to go to prison for a long sentence. It would mean that two lives would have been wasted.' In putting Bland on probation rather than sending him to prison, I referred to this being 'a terrible tragedy for two families', and I echoed Mrs Ayling's opinion that Bland would have the death of his friend on his conscience for the rest of his life. I saw no point whatsoever in sending this man of otherwise impeccable character to prison.

The case of Heather Pratten, to which I have already referred, attracted much more attention. Mrs Pratten was a sixty-three-year-old woman who had gone through the agonising experience of watching her son's inevitable deterioration while suffering from Huntington's disease, for which there was no cure. She had nursed her husband and another son when they too had suffered from this awful genetically transmitted hereditary brain condition. The son in this case, Nigel Goodman, knew that his decline would be extremely unpleasant, and had decided that he wanted to end his life before the worst symptoms kicked in; he had repeatedly threatened to shoot himself and had become increasingly dependent on alcohol. On his forty-second birthday, his mother collected Nigel from hospital and, as soon as they got to his flat, he unwrapped some heroin and begged her not to let him leave the flat alive. After trying unsuccessfully to inject himself, he swallowed the whole amount, after which mother and son lay together for a considerable time and cuddled. Mrs Pratten deliberately delayed calling an ambulance because she feared her son might be resuscitated. A note was found in the flat, signed by Nigel, which read 'I am suffering and I want to die'.

The prosecution charged Heather Pratten with murder, with the inbuilt alternative of manslaughter, and in law they certainly had a case. Just as in the case of Leonard Arthur, the facts of this one provided ample evidence that in law the offence of homicide had been committed – but as I sat in my room reading the case papers prior to the court sitting, I formed the very strong view that justice demanded that I should intervene. I asked counsel on both sides to come to my room and, in the presence of a shorthand writer, expressed my views in strong terms. I asked prosecuting counsel to tell the CPS that in my view justice would be served if a count of aiding and abetting suicide were added to the indictment and that a plea of guilty to that charge should be accepted by the Crown. I made it clear to defending counsel that if his client pleaded guilty to that charge, then that plea would be accepted by the court.

In the end that is what happened and I passed a sentence of conditional discharge. I addressed Mrs Pratten thus: 'I believe that you too, in a wholly different way, have suffered enough. Human life is precious, many regard it as sacred. It follows that only in the rarest and most exceptional cases can those who contribute to the death of another be sentenced to other than immediate imprisonment. But your case is indeed exceptional; your story is one that would move the hardest of hearts.' Hard cases make bad law, and I made it plain that this lady's case should never be regarded as a precedent.

All the cases I have described so far involved death or very serious violence, but that was not the exclusive diet of this Old

Bailey judge. The only other case, apart from Heather Pratten's, in which I tried to intervene to prevent what I thought might lead to a potential injustice, was indeed a strange one, and one in which my intervention proved to be to no avail. In June 2000, a man fell over a hundred feet to his death in the Earl's Court Exhibition Centre. He was a rigger who had been dismantling mobile platforms inside the roof of the vast hall when he fell through fragile false ceiling tiles installed as part of a refurbishment project. The Health and Safety Executive (HSE) brought a prosecution against both Earl's Court Ltd, the owners of the building, and Unusual Rigging Ltd for breaching section 3(1) of the Health and Safety at Work Act 1974, which required employers to ensure that workers are not exposed to risks to their health and safety.

As I read the case papers in my room, I began to feel more and more uneasy about this prosecution. It was clear that for some reason David Mott, who was an experienced rigger, had left the comparative safety of the catwalk and had ventured out onto what was in effect a false ceiling which he should have known could not bear his weight. He did so without attaching his safety harness to anything which could ensure that he did not fall. An explanation for this reckless behaviour was to be found in the fact that a blood sample taken post-mortem from the deceased revealed that he had recently consumed a significant amount of cocaine. On the basis that, as conceded by the prosecution, the defendant companies had done all that might reasonably be expected of them to ensure the safety of their employees, I therefore formed the view that this was a misconceived prosecution, as what had happened could reasonably be described as a most unfortunate accident.

I asked all counsel to come to my room, where I expressed this view and invited prosecution counsel to consider offering no evidence. To my surprise all three counsel told me that the same thoughts had occurred to them, but that the only interpretation of the legislation, together with a consideration of the decided authorities on the issue, pointed to the indisputable conclusion that the defendants had no defence in law to the charge. This was, to all intents and purposes, an almost absolute offence. Having had the assurance of both defence counsel that they could not, in all conscience, mount any defence to the charge, I of course was powerless. The defendants pleaded guilty and, having reviewed the authorities on sentencing in a case of this kind, I passed the minimum sentence I felt possible, fining the companies a total of £100,000. This case did not enhance my confidence in the good sense of some of the manifestations of the health and safety regulations to which we were becoming increasingly accustomed. On the other hand, the attitude of all three counsel enhanced my belief that the Bar could be relied upon to give judges their principled assistance, consistent with serving the interests of their clients.

The only fraud case I tried was necessarily a serious, long and complicated one, since it was only those that fulfilled these criteria that came to the Old Bailey, rather than being tried at other Crown Courts. Stephen Hinchliffe, as the jury found after a trial lasting many weeks, was indeed a substantial fraudster. He was a man of considerable intelligence and with considerable business acumen. After training as an accountant he began to build what was described as 'an empire', by buying up failing retail businesses under the umbrella of the Facia Group of companies; before its collapse in 1996, Facia owned up to 850 retail outlets, and Hinchliffe became a well-known businessman in his home city of Sheffield. He was not shy about his wealth, driving expensive cars, travelling in his own helicopter, and enjoying a lavish lifestyle in a substantial mansion. All, however, was not what it outwardly seemed, and Hinchliffe's 'empire' was built on convoluted deals, backed up by what became a mountain of debt. It all came crashing down, and the catalyst for the collapse was a debt of £3 million that Hinchliffe had incurred to the United Mizrahi Bank, Israel's largest bank. As the evidence demonstrated in due course, that loan was obtained due to a corrupt relationship Hinchliffe enjoyed with John Doherty, the chief lending officer of the bank's London branch. Hinchliffe had been forced to look for loans from sources that would not necessarily be the first choices of many legitimate businessmen because his strategy had been built upon buying underperforming brand names, but delaying payments to suppliers and channelling money into his own private company.

The case was complicated and involved large amounts of documentary exhibits and schedules based upon them. I am often asked how juries can be expected to understand and assimilate such evidence, and my answer is always the same: that if the case is competently and responsibly prosecuted and defended by experienced counsel, and provided the judge plays his part as well, then juries can, and do, find their way to sensible and justifiable verdicts. In this case the jury and I were given every possible assistance by Timothy Langdale QC for the prosecution and Ken Macdonald QC (who subsequently became DPP and then Lord Macdonald) for the defence, together with their able juniors.

The jury found that Hinchliffe paid £813,750 in 'gifts' to Doherty, to obtain £13 million of unsecured loans, and both were convicted of offences arising from their corrupt and fraudulent activity; two other men were also convicted of playing more minor roles in the fraud. I sentenced both Hinchliffe and Doherty to five years' imprisonment, which was at the top end of sentences for fraud at the time. Hinchliffe appealed against his sentence, which was reduced in the Court of Appeal to four years, but having served two years of this sentence he was released and then sentenced to a further period of eighteen months' imprisonment by another judge for further fraudulent activities.

At the end of the twentieth century, people-smuggling was not as widespread as it now is in the third decade of the twenty-first; but I tried one case which demonstrated the evil nature of treating human beings as commodities, the value of which lay in how much could be extorted from the cargo itself for smuggling it into the country. The four defendants, Chen, Li, Tang and Wang, were members of a gang controlled in China by an organisation known as 'Snakeheads'. They smuggled people into the UK in exchange for extravagant sums of money. Some victims paid up to $30,000 to be brought into Britain where, instead of being helped to make a new life as they had been promised, they were held prisoner. Their relatives in China were then asked for $15,000 by way of ransom and 'fined' $300 a day if they failed to pay within three days. Victims told of being chained to radiators while being held prisoner. Eventually one man jumped from a window over a shop, was found by police, and his evidence led them to China's Fujian province, where the families of the victims were interviewed. Upon conviction I sentenced Chen, described as the British boss, to fourteen years; Li, the chief enforcer and bully boy, to thirteen years; Tang, a guard and 'willing tormentor', to eleven years; and Wang, an interpreter, to seven years. In passing sentence, I described them as having participated in 'a wicked trade . . . involving organised extortion on an international scale'. Police subsequently estimated that five hundred or more immigrants had been exploited by this gang over a period of two years.

The last case I consider worthy of mention concerned police corruption. A so-called businessman, whom I will refer to as 'B', who was almost certainly a criminal money launderer, was said to owe £600,000 to a suspected drugs dealer called Robert Kean. Fed up with the non-payment of the money, Kean turned to DC Martin Morgan, with whom he already had a corrupt relationship, to help him recover the debt. To cut a long and complicated story short, a plan was hatched whereby B would be kidnapped and forced to pay up, or otherwise meet a sticky end. B was arrested and taken into protective custody and a sophisticated sting operation was devised by the Complaints Investigation Branch (CIB) at Scotland Yard, designed to trap corrupt police officers who were in cahoots with career criminals. The upshot was that a police officer posed as B and CIB let it be known that he would be in a hotel in Guildford, where he would ostensibly be prey to the criminals' plan to kidnap him and extort the money. The sting involved covert surveillance, bugs being placed in the hotel (the management of which was oblivious to what was going on), tracker devices placed on cars and all manner of other techniques. What the straight officers observed was three bent officers – Martin Morgan, Declan Costello, and a third who was subsequently acquitted ('G') – in conspiracy with at least two criminals, Kean, and another suspected drug dealer, Carl Wood, and about to pounce on their target in the hotel. In the end CIB was forced to spring the trap earlier than intended because they learnt that Wood was about to go abroad. Morgan, Costello and G, together with Kean, Wood and two of their associates, were arrested, and all seven were charged with conspiracy to falsely imprison B. The three corrupt police officers were also charged with conspiracy to pervert the course of justice.

All five of those I have named appeared before me, but before any jury could be empanelled to try the case, the police officers, through their counsel, took a number of points, all designed to persuade me that there should be no trial. Upon their clients' instructions, counsel, who were not to be criticised in any way for doing their professional duty, took every conceivable point to advance their submission that a trial would be 'an abuse of the process'. This involved challenging the evidence of the CIB officers, alleging *mala fides* (literally, bad faith, so an intent to deceive), and disputing any suggestion that they were acting in conspiracy with the criminals. As to their indisputable contact with those criminals, they trod the well-worn path so often adopted by corrupt officers, by suggesting that they were trying to cultivate informants. I ruled against all the defence submissions, but allowed counsel to test my ruling in the Court of Appeal before embarking upon a substantive trial. The Court of Appeal upheld my decisions.

One by one the defendants then accepted the inevitable, namely that to repeat their dishonest defences in front of a jury would be very unlikely to succeed, and would only negate the possibility of shortening their sentences. They knew that if they pleaded guilty, I would reduce those sentences by about one-third. One after the other they did plead guilty. I sentenced Morgan and Kean each to seven years' imprisonment. I gave Wood four years and Costello thirty months. In the Court of Appeal, Morgan had his sentence reduced by one year and Kean had his reduced by eighteen months.

In my sentencing remarks, I observed that the facts of the case had revealed a situation in which the poachers and gamekeepers had become indistinguishable. In sentencing Morgan I told him: 'Your conduct was calculated to bring the rank of constable into disrepute. There is no more despicable spectacle than that of a bent police officer, and that is what you are.' I found the whole process of sentencing rogue police officers highly unpalatable, but I wanted the public to know that no one despised a bent officer more than a straight one did, so after the defendants had been taken to the cells I addressed counsel, and invited the representatives of the press who were in court to report what I said. 'As those who spend their working lives in these courts know only too well, the task of investigating the nefarious activities of other police officers is one that is never relished by those charged with that duty.' I went on to commend the CIB officers who had investigated this case, and concluded my remarks by adding this: 'If the public is justifiably concerned when it hears of malpractice within the police force, it should also take comfort from the fact that there is a body of conscientious officers who are determined to root out corruption and malpractice; and equally that they do so fairly and without fear or favour.'

Those last four words came from the oath that I, and all other judges, took on appointment: 'I swear to . . . do right to all manner of people after the laws and usages of this realm, without fear or favour, affection or ill will.' I can say with a degree of confidence that throughout my time on the bench I did my level best to be true to that oath. Whether I succeeded will be for others to say.

Judges in the higher criminal courts work day in and day out with juries, for whom I have always had the greatest respect. My experience is that they apply the benefit of their combined intelligence, experience of the world, and plain common sense, with a diligence and integrity which might surprise some people. A good judge should rely upon those twelve men and women to come to conclusions that can be relied upon. Thus the judge should never try to impose his will upon a jury; when he says, as he must, 'it is your view of the evidence that counts, and not mine', he should mean it. Of course that does not mean, as Lord Devlin explained when trying Dr Bodkin Adams, that the judge cannot express a view on the cogency or otherwise of pieces of evidence, or indeed the evidence as a whole, but he must be careful not to overstep the mark by trying to bulldoze a jury into a particular verdict. If he does so try, and the case results in a conviction, the Court of Appeal may, as we have seen on two occasions in this memoir, quash the conviction. But before that a jury may itself decide to intervene.

That proposition may be best illustrated by a true story. An Old Bailey judge of the old school, known for his propensity to sum up in favour of the prosecution, did so in a case to such an extent that when the foreman of the jury, a well-known actor, returned a verdict of not guilty, the judge was obviously furious. Some months later the judge and the thespian found themselves drinking at the bar of a London club. The judge asked how what he regarded as a perverse verdict had been arrived at. The actor replied: 'I'll tell you. As soon as I had been elected foreman, I asked my fellow jurors three questions. First, are we agreed that the judge wants us to convict? A unanimous vote in favour of the proposition. Second, are we agreed that the judge is an unfair shit? Again, all twelve of us were in agreement. Finally, are we agreed that we should register our disapproval by acquitting? That is how it happened.'

I want to end this chapter with a reflection upon the relationship between bench and Bar. It always was one of trust, and I hope it still is today. I have repeated, probably ad nauseam, my belief that the cab rank principle is one of the principal reasons why the bench, and the public at large, can have faith in the integrity of the Bar. I have to say that I now view from afar, but with increasing dismay, a tendency for barristers to offer themselves as representing certain constituencies. The whole concept of some members of the Bar holding themselves out as 'human rights lawyers' is something I find insulting. The clear implication that those of us who simply represented ourselves as barristers in private practice, sitting on the rank and available for hire by anybody, were not, or are not, equally concerned with the human rights of every citizen, is one I heartily resent.

Chapter 18

OFF THE BENCH

During the years I sat as an Old Bailey judge I don't recall suffering a serious episode of depression. I strongly suspect that was partly due to the fact that I did not find that role nearly as stressful as practice at the Bar but, much more significantly, I did not touch a single alcoholic drink throughout those years on the bench. Having been in recovery from alcoholism for three years when I was appointed, and over ten years when I retired, I believed that I could live 'a normal life' without alcohol; even if the demon would never be slain, at least I had him at bay. Perhaps later events were to prove me wrong.

As well as being less stressful, life as a judge was less time-consuming than my last hectic years at the Bar. From at least the mid-eighties, my mistress the law had been very demanding indeed, not only of my ability to sustain high stress levels but also of my time. Nevertheless, I always tried to follow other interests when I could.

Ever since my father had introduced me to the game of golf on a playing field in Eastbourne when I was about ten, I had always played, in the sense that I would on occasions attempt to take on a golf course, almost always with very little success. (The only sport at which I had ever shown any ability was tennis, but I had long since given that up.) In 1997 I arranged a match between four judges and four members of the Royal West Norfolk Golf Club at Brancaster, to which I had recently been elected. This led to my forming the Old Bailey Judges Golfing Society (OBJGS), mainly so that I, and those of my fellow judges who played the game, could keep in touch with our former colleagues at the Bar. Our first match was against a team of former and current treasury counsel. Fairly quickly we developed quite a following and we now have a membership of over forty and play about eight matches a year against kindred spirits. In case it seems unlikely that there would be that many past and present Old Bailey judges who play golf, I should explain that the criteria for membership of OBJGS are elastic, and are determined by the President for Eternity, who happens to be me. As to the standard of golf, I need only say that we adapted the motto of the SAS, 'Who dares wins', to fit our attitude to the game: ours is, 'Who cares who wins'. Over the last twenty-odd years, OBJGS has provided me with a great deal of entertainment, and kept me in touch with a number of members of my erstwhile profession. I should add that we now have a ladies' section too.

Indirectly, golf also introduced me to the charity sector. One day in the late nineties, a Professor of Oncology called Tim Oliver, a specialist in male cancers, organised a golfing day at Brancaster in aid of his fledgling charity, the Orchid Cancer Appeal. I took part, and at the end of the day casually observed to the professor that if there was any way in which I might help, I would be interested in doing so. Within a week he appeared in my room at the Old Bailey, with the remarkable Colin Osborne, a former patient and founder of the charity, and announced that I was to be chairman of the board of trustees. My protestations, that I knew nothing about medicine and had never sat on, let alone chaired, a board of directors or trustees, were brushed aside, and I found myself assembling a board consisting of people with the right kind of experience. Thanks to the efforts of Colin and Tim, the charity really grew over the next few years, and by the time I handed over the chairmanship in 2004 it was a thriving concern, and continues to flourish. With the help of experts in their respective fields such as Robin Broadhurst, to whom I handed the reins in 2004, Robert Fellowes, Mike Walsh and Richard Fallowfield, to all of whom I owe a great debt of gratitude, I was able to appear as though I understood what was going on, despite any scientific discussions being in a foreign language of which I knew not a word.

Helping to fund-raise for Orchid, I surprised myself by summoning up the courage to participate in a sky-dive, which raised £25,000. Dropping out of a small plane into the Oxfordshire sky, I found myself on the lap of a soldier in whose hands, and under whose parachute, my future on this planet depended. As we hurtled through the air, and before he pulled the cord that opened the parachute, he shouted into my ear in his Geordie accent, 'so what do you do for a living?' and I was stupid enough to tell him. His response? 'If I pull this other cord, you'll be detached from me and out on your own!' In September 2001 I helped organise another charity golf day for Orchid at Brancaster, which raised over £80,000.

Just as I had time to interest myself in activities outside court, so I was able to think about my future and that of my family. I had always anticipated retiring soon after my sixty-fifth birthday. One of my great heroes, Henry Pownall, who had been both treasury counsel and an Old Bailey judge, had carried on until he was over seventy and died within two years of his retirement. Very shortly before he died he said to me: 'Don't be an idiot and do what I have done; there is more to life than this job. Retire in time to allow yourself the opportunity to do other things.' Taking that advice to heart, Lizzie and I decided to downsize in London, and to look for somewhere in Norfolk to which we would be happy to retire in due course. Having failed to find something suitable, a friend called

Peter Hopkins, who ran a business specialising in finding houses in North Norfolk, pointed to an empty field and asked whether we would contemplate building on it. The plot was in Thornham, the same village as our small holiday cottage, and it looked over the marsh and onto the North Sea. Between 1999 and 2000 the house in which we now live was built. It fulfilled all our hopes and expectations.

I was able to indulge another passion much more frequently when I was on the bench rather than at the Bar. Cricket was a sport that had always appealed to me and I had wisely invested in life membership of the MCC when it was first offered, meaning that I could sit in the pavilion at Lord's, the holy-of-holies; there I would find a number of judges also sitting on the coveted white benches. Incidentally, it was a great pleasure for me when I discovered that my publisher for this book is Andrew Johnston, son of the revered 'Johnners', who, together with 'Blowers' (Henry Blofeld) provided me with many an hour of cricket entertainment on the radio. I am told that one of the duties I imposed upon those who worked with me in court during Test matches was that I was to be informed via post-it notes of the latest score.

Now to a less happy memory. In April 1999, I made the speech that I mention in the introduction to this book, and which proved to be a major setback in my life. One of the unwritten obligations of being an Old Bailey judge was that, as a kind of *quid pro quo* for the hospitality of the sheriffs at lunchtime, one would accept invitations to make after-dinner speeches at livery dinners in the City. Over the course of time I built up something of a reputation in that regard, and I found a kind of masochistic pleasure in submitting myself to the ordeal of trying to amuse an audience of black- or white-tie diners. People were kind enough to say that I was quite good at it. The largest audience I ever faced was in July 1998, at the annual dinner of the London Criminal Courts Solicitors' Association, held at the Grosvenor House Hotel in Park

Lane and attended by hundreds of people. The event was known at the Bar as 'the touts' ball', because it was the occasion upon which solicitors invited their favourite barristers to be their guests. The after-dinner speech, usually made by a senior barrister or a judge with a reputation for extra-judicial public speaking, was known as a graveyard for some who had thought themselves proficient at this very difficult art. Flattered though I was to be asked to perform, I was terrified as well by the thought of following in the footsteps of such masters as John Mortimer.

Probably buoyed up by the fact that I had escaped relatively unscathed from that ordeal, when I was asked to speak at the annual dinner of the Criminal Bar Association (CBA) in Inner Temple Hall on Friday 23rd April 1999, I accepted that invitation too. The annual dinner of what had been my trade union was one I looked forward to every year because it was purely an in-house event for members, and there was always an atmosphere of conviviality and a lack of formality. As usual, the chairman announced that Chatham House rules applied ('what is said here, stays here') and I felt that I was among friends.

Over the years I had developed an increasing antipathy towards political correctness. I am a great believer in trying to create level playing-fields to promote equal opportunity. But when a playing-field is sloping in one direction, to the advantage of some and to the detriment of others, it is usually a mistake to try to tilt that playing-field back beyond level, so that it now slopes in the other direction. The intention should always be to create a completely level surface upon which everybody has the opportunity to succeed. In other words, I have never been a great fan of positive discrimination as a way of challenging negative discrimination. Part of my repertoire as an after-dinner speaker was therefore to satirise the worst aspects of political correctness which, probably because I was used to addressing predominantly middle-aged audiences, usually went down well.

In 1997 Tony Blair won the general election by a large majority and appointed Derry Irvine as his Lord Chancellor. By the time I made my speech at the CBA dinner I had detected what I thought were definite signs that appointments to silk and to the bench were being influenced by politically correct considerations. I decided to give voice to these concerns but made the terrible mistake of doing so by including what I intended to be an amusing parody. To say it backfired would be a huge understatement. When my words were reported in the *Guardian* and on the BBC I was branded a sexist, racist, homophobic bigot. To make matters worse, the *Daily Mail* contained a sympathetic article headed 'The jocular judge who blundered into a quip too far', and included this description: 'Graham Boal's ready wit, clubbable nature and sense of the absurd have long made him a popular figure on the legal party circuit.' The next few days were extremely uncomfortable, with criticism pouring in from many quarters, and including a serious written reprimand from the Lord Chancellor. I have no doubt that, had I made that speech twenty years later, I would have been dismissed. I suspect that even at this distance of time, were I to be invited to address an audience at most universities, I would be no-platformed or 'cancelled'.

I very much regret the whole incident, and recognise that my attempt at combining humour with a serious point was totally misguided. As I did at the time, I apologise again here to those to whom I caused offence. But I do not resile from the serious point I was trying so clumsily to make. Indeed, as political correctness has morphed into 'wokedom', I see the dangers of the attitude I was criticising are infinitely greater now than they were in 1999. Writing now (in 2021), I do see some encouraging signs that attitudes may be changing. Recent newspaper articles with headlines such as, 'Positive discrimination is racism by another name' and 'Quotas for diversity betray Dr King's dream', make the argument in moderate and persuasive language that I was myself trying to present, albeit in a cack-handed and inappropriate way.

For a long time after that speech, if a case I was trying was reported in the press, the report would always end with 'Judge Boal is the judge who . . .'. One day, sitting at the breakfast table with Lizzie and Thomas, I read a report which did not end with those words and remarked on it. Thomas retorted: 'It's all very well for you, but I'll have to read it again in your obituary!'

Overall, my time as an Old Bailey judge was, both on and off the bench, one of the happiest times of my life. I felt, rightly or wrongly, that I was a round peg in a round hole, and I believed that I did the job tolerably well. As I said earlier, it is for others to judge whether I am justified in that belief. I have also pointed out that judges, being human, come in all shapes and sizes, each with different character and personality traits. I can think of no better demonstration of that than to relate the true story of correspondence between two High Court judges who were about to share lodgings on circuit. I will refer to them as Mr Justice T and Mr Justice S, but many of those who share my advanced age may well recognise their true identities.

Mr Justice T, who was well-known for his punctilious aloofness and pomposity, wrote to Mr Justice S, who was an amiable soul, in these terms. 'Dear S, I understand that we are due to share lodgings at Stafford next term. I will of course be the senior judge, and I have certain rules about conduct in lodgings. I am given to understand that you are an inveterate smoker. I will not tolerate smoking in lodgings so, while we are together, would you kindly desist or do it in the garden.' S's reply was succinct. 'Dear T, I am given to understand that you are a serial adulterer. While we are together in lodgings, would you kindly desist or do it in the garden.'

I was lucky enough to meet judges from other jurisdictions too. One of the most colourful and charming of these was Judge Gene Sullivan, a senior judge in the USA, who organised a series of debates between members of the legal profession on either side of the Atlantic. I was lucky enough to be amongst those chosen to represent the UK on several occasions. The debates took place alternately in London and Washington, and topics included majority jury verdicts, rights of audience, the death penalty, and whether judges should be appointed or elected.

The debates were not only extremely enjoyable and generously hosted by Gene Sullivan, but gave me a valuable insight into another jurisdiction. In particular it left me with a profound belief that we had, and I hope still have, a system that is indeed rightly labelled 'the envy of the world'. Without casting any aspersions on the US judiciary, I came away mightily relieved, not only for myself but also for our country, that I was sitting as a judge because I was deemed worthy of appointment, rather than because I had been elected upon a party political ticket.

Recent events, concerning the Brexit debate amongst other things, have caused some people to doubt the independence of our judiciary. The media has been far too quick to suggest that some decisions of the higher courts, and particularly the Supreme Court, have been motivated by the political persuasion of the judges. I would reject those suggestions out of hand. We are extremely lucky to live in a country in which we can have confidence in the independence of our judiciary. If we compare our system of appointment to all ranks of the judiciary with what happens on the other side of the Atlantic, we should be grateful that no prime minister could, or I hope would, attempt to pack the highest court in the land with judges whom he or she believes share his or her political inclinations. We live in a country governed by the rule of law, and that is something that must be preserved at all costs.

Chapter 19

MY PERSONAL TSUNAMI

In December 2003 my marriage broke down. I was totally unprepared for such a devastating personal catastrophe. I had thought that we were in clover, as I was ten years into recovery; we had only recently built what was, to me, a dream house in Norfolk, a representation of my life's work in bricks and mortar; and I was thoroughly enjoying the less stressful nature of my work as a judge. The circumstances which led to the breakdown are of course private, but what I will say is that my years of alcoholism and depression must have been, at the very least, a major contributory cause.

One of the results of our separation was that we had to sell our house in London. Shortly before I left, I vividly remember walking down the road to where a tobacconist and an off-licence were side-by-side. I had given up smoking (at the third or fourth attempt) some years previously, but as I walked I said to myself that I must have something to help me cope; was it to be a cigarette or a drink? Thank goodness, I went into the tobacconist and bought two packets of twenty. I think I realised, consciously or subconsciously, that cigarettes might kill me, but alcohol definitely would.

In due course I was admitted to what was then called the Charter Nightingale Hospital in Lisson Grove, where I was treated for reactive depression. I was there for some weeks, and was looked after by two saintly professionals. Dr Elza Eapen, my psychiatrist, is someone to whom I genuinely believe I owe my life. Peter Smith, my psychologist, is a man I now recall with great affection, though not when he first came into my room. Observing his T-shirt and trainers, and that he was carrying a copy of the *Guardian* to boot, I'm afraid I told him to eff off. Luckily he didn't.

During the next three years, I sank lower and lower into depression. I must confess that this led to the moment, which I now greatly regret, when I found my state of mind so intolerable that I attempted to take my own life. It was a serious attempt, not a cry for help; it was made, as I now appreciate, when 'the balance of my mind was disturbed' to use the old words of the coroner's court. I had taken every pill I could lay my hands on; I obtained double prescriptions of sleeping pills, one from my NHS GP in Norfolk, and the other from my private GP in London. I swilled them down with a huge glass of whisky, the only time I have drunk alcohol in twenty-eight years. Thank goodness my attempt did not succeed. I now know that our son Thomas was right in describing it as a very selfish act. Taking one's own life may seem, if one is in utter despair, to be a way out of one's misery, but I have seen the devastation it leaves behind. Utter despair is a state of mind that is very difficult to describe. All I can say is that, at the moment I decided to do it, I felt that there was not even a flicker of light at the end of the tunnel, that there was nothing to live for, and that others would be better off if I no longer existed. I believe that the balance of my mind was indeed disturbed.

Some time after that attempt, and following more therapy, I discussed with Dr Eapen whether or not I could – or should – return to work. Her judgement was that I was not yet fit to go back, but that she hoped I would be before the end of that year, 2005. I then raised another question with her; would I be able to bring the required objectivity to the cases I would be trying?

The daily diet at the Old Bailey is murder, and the majority of homicide cases are domestic; in other words the killing by one partner of the other, or the killing of a third party as a result of extramarital relationships. The defence, more often than not, is not a denial of the act of killing, but an attempt to have the offence of murder reduced to that of manslaughter by reason either of provocation or of diminished responsibility. Provocation, very closely defined in law, amounted to saying, 'I was driven to do it by the behaviour of the deceased'. Diminished responsibility amounted to 'I was mentally ill when I did it'. The question which concerned me was this: if I were required, as I would be, to try a case involving the break-up of a marriage or relationship, and the killing either of a spouse, a partner or of a third party, could I bring the necessary objectivity to bear in view of my own experience? I doubted it, and so did Elza.

With that in mind, I went to see Sir Hayden Phillips, Permanent Secretary to the Lord Chancellor. I had known Hayden ever since we had sat on opposite sides of the table during negotiations with the Treasury during the fees war. I had always found him approachable and affable, even though he could play hardball if required. On this occasion I found him to be his usual friendly self and extremely sympathetic. As head of his department, he had extended to me every possible indulgence over the previous eighteen months; indeed, the practice was to allow judges a maximum of six months' sick leave, but he had given me three times that amount. He was kind enough to say that that was because they thought highly of me as a judge, and had hoped that I would be in a position to return. When I explained what Dr Eapen and I had resolved, however, he immediately saw that returning to the Old Bailey would not be possible. He offered me the possibility of going to another, lesser, court, where I would not try murder cases or cases of great gravity, if I recovered within the next few months, but we both agreed that that was not the answer.

I retired on 15ᵗʰ July 2005, and five days later there was a valedictory ceremony at the Old Bailey, at which the Recorder of London and the then First Senior Treasury Counsel (Richard Horwill, who had brought his car to the Priory in 1993) both said some very kind and complimentary things. I did not attend, but Thomas did, and I have a transcript of the proceedings. I remember weeping when I read it. I also retired from the Parole Board. I never sat in court, or in any other judicial capacity, again. Ironically, on almost the same day as my retirement, a letter came appointing me as one of the senior circuit judges who sit from time to time in the Court of Appeal Criminal Division.

There was, however, an extremely happy ending to this very sad part of my story. In November 2006, Lizzie came home, and we have lived together as man and wife ever since. In the early years it was not easy, but we now both agree that we are happier than we ever were before. There are bumps in the road, of course, but I suspect that is the case in any marriage.

I look back on the three years of our separation as by far the unhappiest time in my life. I don't remember a great deal about how I spent my time. I think I watched a lot of television and, when I felt able to, I read. I was on quite heavy doses of anti-depressant drugs for most of the time, which affected my concentration. There were long periods of solitude and loneliness, interspersed with the occasional game of golf and kind friends doing their best to help me deal with my unhappiness. One game of golf gave rise to a sub-title that I once thought of giving to this book. That day a great friend (whom I had first met when he too was a Priory patient, being treated for depression) persuaded me to play golf with him at Brancaster. I say 'golf' but, whereas he was a good golfer, that day I could hardly hit the ball I was so deep in the depths of despair. On the thirteenth tee, he said to me: 'Do you remember the mantra with which we were both discharged from hospital?' When I replied that I did not, he reminded me that it was 'It Changes'. I wrote this down on a golf card, and it hangs in my loo to this day. We spent the rest of the round discussing that most useful expression.

I didn't perform well in any way during those three years. I said and did things of which I am not proud; I was angry and resentful. But the one thing of which I am proud is that, save on that night when I washed down every pill I could find with copious amounts of whisky, I did not touch a drop of alcohol and, by the time Lizzie came back, I had kicked my nicotine dependence as well.

The early years of our reconciliation were very difficult for both of us. Slowly we were able to put our lives back together; but that did not mean simply acting as we had before. The most important change was that we began to communicate really honestly. During the drinking years I permanently wore a mask, to conceal the pain I felt inside. The hallmark of alcoholism and depression is isolation, and I didn't want to let anyone in: I didn't want anyone, not even Lizzie, to see the frightened little boy inside the shell of a man. As I looked back at what preceded our separation, I realised that even the sober husband was not communicating with the woman he loved; the mask, albeit a slightly different one, was usually in place and it was humour. I have always used humour as a weapon with which to combat adversity, as well as a camouflage for my true feelings.

In retrospect, I have begun increasingly to realise that what happened during those three terrible years may well have been a blessing, albeit a very heavily disguised one at the time. Originally my plan was to go on working until I had earned approaching a full judicial pension and then to retire gracefully. The job I was doing at the time suited me, or so I thought, down to the ground, and I had no ambition for promotion – though there was a possibility that I might throw my hat into the ring again, should the Recordership of London become vacant within the next few years. Had I entered the lists, I very much doubt that I would have been selected, mainly because of the speech in 1999; but in the very unlikely event that

I had been, then it would have spelt total disaster for me. The Recorder of London has to devote large amounts of his time to the affairs of the City of London, has to attend countless livery dinners, make lots of speeches, and also to be genuinely interested in the aldermanic and lay governance of that ancient and slightly unusual institution. I was neither wedded to it, nor well suited to such a role, and it is likely that my marriage would have broken down irretrievably in such circumstances. My marriage and my family are the most valuable assets I possess, and I count myself a very lucky man indeed to have what I now have – a wife and family of which I am extremely proud.

Chapter 20

RETIREMENT

A number of people I know, particularly men, have told me that they find retirement difficult. I have to admit that I took to it like a duck to water. Whether that is simply because I am, by nature and inclination, very lazy, I am not quite sure. I think it is also because I no longer wake up with that churning in my stomach that I remember so well from my days at the Bar. Instead, I now wake up thanking my lucky stars that I am living a life of sobriety and, almost always, looking forward to the day ahead. That does not mean that I do not have to deal with occasional minor episodes of depression, but I know that I am now far better equipped to cope with them than I was in the past. I am lucky enough to live in a place I love with the woman I love, and that in itself is a huge privilege. I am seldom bored, and seem to find quite enough to keep me both occupied and interested.

I play golf, not obsessively but when I want to, and I read a lot; mainly political biography and modern history. That is when I am not writing a book, of course! I enjoy our garden, even though I am hopelessly ignorant about what is growing in it. I mow the lawn on a ride-on mower, and I enjoy listening to conversations between Lizzie, who is a natural and well-informed gardener, and David Mahon, who comes once a week to do what Lizzie is physically unable to do. Our house was built on a greenfield site of over an acre, and David and his father Tom created the garden from nothing. David has become indispensable, as has his wife Teresa, and we often ask ourselves what would we do without them. I have learnt to empty the dishwasher and I take out the bins. I am pretty undomesticated but I hope I am a little better than I was; cooking is still not my forte. I do not pretend to be master of the house.

If I have 'a drug of choice' (to use the language of addiction) now, it is probably watching sport on television. As Lizzie would be the first to attest, I spend far too much time watching football, golf and, above all, cricket. I am still a dedicated 'Gooner', having been an Arsenal fan through thick and thin. I watch professional golf with a mixture of admiration and envy. But my real obsession is cricket, and in retirement I am able to follow it much more closely than I ever did before. One of the very few happy memories I have of those miserable years between 2003 and 2006 is of England's Ashes triumph in 2005.

My further involvement in the charity world came from a chance (or maybe not) placement at a lunch to celebrate the birthday of a distinguished member of OBJGS, Richard Hayward, who rose to the rank of President of the Bar Golfing Society – only slightly below that of the President for Eternity of the OBJGS in the pecking order. I sat next to a lady who knew, or discovered at that lunch, that I was a recovering alcoholic. She told me she was a trustee of a small addiction charity called Seventy4, and asked if I would be prepared to join the board. I agreed and in due course became chairman. I soon realised that Seventy4 was too small, and too poorly endowed, to succeed as an independent entity, so I started casting around for a compatible larger charity with which to merge, or by which to be taken over.

I hit on WDP (formerly known as the Westminster Drug Project), and found myself having a very convivial lunch with Yasmin

Batliwala, its chair, and James Saunders, effectively her vice-chair. I had come across James before as he was, and still is, a respected criminal solicitor. Although Yasmin and I came from backgrounds that were very different in almost every way, we found that we got on like the metaphorical house on fire. More importantly, we found that we held between us two hands that might well fit. We at Seventy4 could only bring as our dowry to the marriage the fact that we owned the building in Dartmouth Street, virtually in the shadow of Westminster Abbey, from which we operated, but it was a substantial asset. In the end our organisations did merge and I became a trustee of WDP. The alliance has proved to be a very happy one.

For my part, I feel that my work for WDP may be giving something back, in gratitude for all the support I have had over the many years of recovering from alcoholism. I am deeply conscious of the fact that I was in a very privileged position, being able to undergo treatment for both alcoholism and depression in the private sector. I hope, in some small way, to be able to facilitate the recovery of those far less fortunate. For those who do not know where to go to find advice, support and help for problems with alcohol or drugs, may I suggest that they could do far worse than to look up WDP and then send an email or make a telephone call. My experience of the organisation is that all those who work for it are caring and dedicated professionals, who do a wonderful job. I regard it as a real privilege to be a trustee and on the board of directors.

Our village is situated on the north coast of Norfolk, and one of the greatest honours ever accorded to me was being invited to be chairman of Thornham Cricket Club. Not in any way due to me, it is a vibrant club, which has gone from strength to strength in recent years. One of the evenings I have most enjoyed was when Graham Gooch (a former captain of Essex and England), who is now our patron, accepted my invitation to speak at an event to raise money for the club to purchase an electronic scoreboard. We are also honoured to have Peter Parfitt, of Middlesex and England, as president of our supporters' club, the Thornham Taverners. As a result of my tendency to delegate and let others do the heavy lifting, all the hard work is done by the three people without whom the club would not be the success it is: Billy King-Harman, Stephanie Mocatta, and Ron Williamson who, as our club secretary, sees to all the day-to-day running of the club. All of the above were present when Graham came to 'open' the new scoreboard, which reproduced the exact moment when he was out after scoring 333 runs for England versus India at Lord's in 1990. Other club supporters, too numerous to mention, contribute greatly to its success.

I love my golf as I have said, even though my handicap is twenty-two and rising. The OBJGS, which keeps me in touch with former colleagues, continues to thrive, and one of our most successful annual fixtures is still against RWNGC. I play weather-permitting golf at Brancaster, roughly twice a week. Lizzie is a member of the ladies' section, and our marriage has even survived a number of rounds of 'gruesomes'. We also play quite a lot of bridge with friends who live on, or have weekend homes on, this extraordinary golden triangle of the North Norfolk coast. I sometimes try my hand at teaching people who have never played the game before how to get into it. I am not a good player, but I have played bridge for a long time, and therefore have the basics, which are often so difficult for the newcomer to master.

Thornham itself is a vibrant and flourishing community and a wonderful place to live. Let no one say that living in the country is boring until they have sampled it for themselves! Both Lizzie and I try to contribute and do our bit in various ways within our local area, as well as enjoying all that it has to offer in terms of entertainment. I love Norfolk in all seasons, but of course the ability to take holidays when one wishes, and for as long as one can afford, is another great joy of retirement. Only too often while I was at the Bar, and to a lesser extent when I was on the bench, I had to take holidays when it was convenient to my professional diary, and sometimes even had to cancel arrangements if a trial overran. Not any more.

The greatest joy of my retirement is, however, my family. I think I have made it clear already that I am married to a wonderful woman, but if I bang on too much about her she will exercise her veto and insist that I edit it out. Our only son, Thomas, is a man of whom we are rightly extremely proud. Currently he is Head of Operations of What3Words, and I insist that the uninitiated now go immediately to a computer, iPad or smartphone to look it up and log on. Incidentally, I cannot do any of the amazing things everybody else seems to be able to do on their phones; my Nokia is at least ten years old, and Thomas justifiably thinks that I should never be let loose on anything like Facebook. I hope the publication of this book does not justify his fears. Thomas is married to every parent's dream daughter-in-law; she is a psychologist, who no doubt exercises her expertise to make sure that her husband is better behaved than her father-in-law. They have two delightful children, Matilda and Xander, and it is to them, together with the service-users of WDP, that this book is dedicated.

I count myself a very lucky man indeed.

Postscript

Why have I written this book? Has it been merely an ego-trip, or an example of the recklessness that so often afflicts alcoholics, either drinking ones or recovering ones? Did I simply succumb to the flattery of being invited to do it?

I have been asking myself these questions over the last few months as I have been sitting at my laptop, tapping out these words with two fingers. Now, at the end, I must try to answer them honestly. As I said in the introduction, I had never contemplated the possibility of writing a book for public consumption. I had written a much shorter version, entitled *It Changes,* courtesy of LifeBook Ltd, simply for my grandchildren to read, probably after my death; but I had always maintained that mine was not a story worth publishing to a wider audience. When I was first approached by literary agent Heather Holden-Brown, through my great friend Patrick Clarkson QC, I resisted, but Heather somehow persuaded me to have a crack at it. Of course I have enjoyed recounting some of the many interesting experiences I have had during forty years of involvement with the criminal justice system, but I may also have fallen for the temptation to gloss over my inadequacies whilst exaggerating some of my successes.

One of the reasons I embarked upon writing at all was that the suggestion coincided with the Covid lockdown in the spring of 2020. I had been wondering how I might usefully occupy my time, and Heather's invitation arrived at precisely the right moment. I quickly found myself becoming involved in piecing together the ingredients for this memoir, a task in which I was greatly helped by those I mention in the acknowledgements. As the memories came flooding back, some good and some not so good, I began to enjoy the discipline of trying to put those recollections into some coherent form. I have experienced joy and contentment, but I have also had to relive many less pleasant experiences, and the emotions that went with them. I have certainly had to face some of my demons. All in all, I have found it a cathartic experience.

I can honestly say that two primary reasons prompted my endeavours, which are far more important than simply blowing my own trumpet. The first is that I was lucky enough to enjoy the halcyon days of the criminal Bar, and I greatly fear that those days may have gone. I hope they have not gone for good, and that the criminal justice system can be restored to its rightful place in our democratic society. As the reader will have observed, the criminal justice system in which I practised was the envy of the world – a view I heard from many sources abroad, not least from the polar opposites of Moscow and Washington. Judges and practitioners in both those jurisdictions were as one in saying that they envied us, that we were very lucky, and that ours was the best system in the world. Is that still so? I have asked two practitioners for their views, from their different perspectives.

This is what a senior silk, still practising at the criminal Bar, has to say:

'It is a truth, universally acknowledged, that successive governments, Labour, Coalition and Tory, have eviscerated the criminal justice system by deliberately depriving it of money, thereby reducing what was once the envy of the world to a pale and limping carcass, which is unfit for purpose. The politicians and their mouthpieces clearly calculated that

there were no votes to be lost by cutting deep into the bone of a budget "spent on criminals". They ignored the innocent, who might be incorrectly swept into the system. They passed over the fact that even criminals deserve a working system, with short queues, properly funded courts and properly paid lawyers. They pretended that properly operational justice was not necessary for a properly operational democracy and a fair society. They brought the criminal justice system to its knees. Some of them have said that they are now sorry for what they have done, although there is little evidence of that. Nowhere is there the enthusiasm for putting right that which they were so enthusiastic about getting wrong. Just find a lawyer who you trust – no, I'm not being ironic – who works in the criminal justice system, and ask him or her to tell you the unvarnished truth about what it is like. Then, what are you going to do about it? It's your criminal justice system, your society, your democracy, your MP and your government. Are you going to be bothered?'

So what is the view of a more junior member of the criminal Bar? This is what a barrister who was called to the Bar in 2004 has written:

'The pleas of my profession for investment in the criminal justice system have largely fallen on deaf ears. We are overworked, despondent, and there is a steady flow of us leaving the criminal Bar. This will be an exodus if nothing is done, and I will be part of it. Not so long ago, I was in a court in the London commuter belt, trying to find a new date for a trial that was meant to have started that day. The trial couldn't go ahead because the lift didn't work. It had been broken for eight months, but the court service could not say when it would be fixed. The defendant was in a wheelchair

and unable to access any courtroom in the building without the lift. We looked into whether we could do the trial at one of the other local courts; neither had working wheelchair access. I went back into court to tell the judge the unhappy news. Most of the fold-down chairs in counsel's row were covered in red tape (the type you get at the scene of an accident). I tried to remember how long they had been like that; one year, or two, or was it more? Or was I getting it muddled up with all the other Crown Courts I go to, where the furniture and facilities have fallen apart, never to be fixed? The final straw came when I was told that I couldn't have a tissue; they were reserved for witnesses "because of cost saving". My sense of justice should have been appalled; that a man in his seventies, accused of serious offences, and his anxious accuser, were left in limbo, not knowing when their respective ordeals would be over. The state of the court, and the fact that I lost a week's income because of the decay, should also have ignited some kind of emotion, but I didn't really feel anything at all. Like so many in my profession, I have become weary and resigned. I am so accustomed to delays, cancelled trials, lost income, closed courtrooms, and inadequate facilities, that I have little fight left in me. Our criminal justice system is propped up by a trinity of hard-working practitioners, the judiciary, and endlessly helpful court staff. We are proud of our uniquely British rule of law, that we work so hard, and for so little, to protect, but sometimes enough is enough.'

I suppose I could say 'I rest my case', but despite what you may have seen on screen or read in novels, that is a phrase I never once heard in forty years in court, so I will refrain. I will just add this. One day, our political masters may wake up to the damage that their short-termism has done. Governments always have a tendency to observe the not-on-our-watch approach to policy; so long as disaster can be averted whilst they are in power, then it is over to the next lot.

Failure to fund the criminal justice system properly may not result in visible damage to our way of life for some time, but sooner or later the citizens of this country will come bitterly to regret the demise of one of its greatest assets. The cost will not only be miscarriages of justice, which will be the inevitable result of not paying for competent representation, but it will mean that we all pay in economic terms. Crime will increase, criminals will not get their just deserts, and victims will suffer; all of that will, in the end, cost us dear. So, as the senior QC says, if you go to political hustings, if you are moved to write to the newspapers, if you feel you have any political clout anywhere, then please raise this issue. If the failure by government to act causes junior barristers to leave the Bar and take their energy and talents elsewhere, then society as a whole will be the loser.

There is a terrible temptation for old men to say 'things aren't what they were in my day', but objective evidence that the criminal justice system, and the criminal Bar with it, is in serious decline is irrefutable. The whole edifice is so seriously underfunded that it is difficult to see how we can still maintain that our system is what was once described as a Rolls-Royce: it appears to me to more closely resemble a clapped-out old banger. If the publication of this book does anything to raise awareness of what I see as a potentially very serious crisis, then my first objective will have been achieved.

The other, and indeed the main reason I have written this memoir, will by now have become obvious. As you will see from the book jacket, under the lectern is written 'a memoir of crime, justice and overcoming personal demons'. It is certainly one man's account of many criminal cases; I hope it is an account of justice being done; but it also contains recollections, many painful, of a struggle to cope with addiction and depression. I believe that there have been many in my profession who have faced the same demons, and many who do so today. I know of some who have not had the good fortune to overcome them. I also know that what I am talking about is not in any way confined to my profession. Many people, from differing backgrounds and lifestyles, face similar problems.

If government needs to direct more financial assistance to the criminal justice system, then the same certainly applies to alcohol treatment services, and indeed to all those hard-pressed services attempting to deal with the likely huge increase in rates of addiction due to the Covid crisis. Rates of alcohol abuse, and addiction generally, have increased at an alarming rate and, just as with the criminal justice system, failure properly to resource treatment now will cost the community dear in the future; and that is to say nothing about the human misery that failure to act will produce.

What must never be forgotten is that alcoholism has been rightly described as 'the family disease'; that description can also be applied, not only to every form of addiction, but also to clinical depression. Whereas attention is focused upon the sufferer, the immediate, and sometimes the extended, family can suffer just as much, often in silence and without support. Organisations such as Al-Anon can offer that support, which is badly needed to cope with the lonely and isolated life so often endured by those whose lives are damaged by the behaviour of the addict or depressive. What those of us who are recovering from these conditions must never forget is that our illness adversely affected, and maybe still affects, those we love in ways we too often never acknowledge. I would like to think that this memoir may be of some assistance to all those suffering in silence.

In addition, perhaps my story may provide a bit of hope to someone, somewhere. I was privileged and lucky enough to find enormous support and to undergo expert treatment for my condition. Support and treatment are increasingly available within organisations such as WDP to those less privileged than myself. My fervent hope is that some of those who are currently suffering in silence find the courage to reach out and ask for help. It is not a sign of weakness to do so; it is precisely the opposite. Dr Tim Cantopher has described depressive illness as 'the curse of the strong'; similarly, alcoholism, and indeed all addiction, is a mental illness, which should not be stigmatised any more than physical illness should be. I believe that society is at last beginning to realise this.

If someone reads this book and recognises in themselves – or in a colleague or loved one – the symptoms I have described, leading to that person seeking assistance from one of the many support systems available, then the writing of this memoir will have been worthwhile.

Glossary of Abbreviations and Acronyms

AA	Alcoholics Anonymous
AG	Attorney General
ANO	Abu Nidal Organisation
BC	Bar Council
CBA	Criminal Bar Association
CEO	Chief Executive Officer
CIB	Complaints Investigation Branch (of Scotland Yard)
CPS	Crown Prosecution Service
CRO	Criminal Record Office
CSM	Company Sergeant Major
DC	Detective Constable
DCI	Detective Chief Inspector
DI	Detective Inspector
DPP	Director of Public Prosecutions
DTI	Department of Trade and Industry
DS	Detective Sergeant
ESDA	Electrostatic Document Analysis
FIG	Fraud Investigation Group (of CPS)
IRA ASU	Irish Republican Army Active Service Unit
JTC	Junior Treasury Counsel
KBW	King's Bench Walk
KC	King's Counsel (a 'silk')
KTL	Kagan Textiles Limited
LCD	Lord Chancellor's Department
LJ	Lord Justice
LRT	London Regional Transport
LTDA	London Taxi Drivers' Association
LU	London Underground

MAIB	Marine Accident Investigation Branch
MPS	Medical Protection Society
NSY	New Scotland Yard
OBJGS	Old Bailey Judges Golfing Society
OPS	Obscene Publications Squad
PCW	Peter Cameron-Webb (a Lloyd's reinsurance syndicate)
QC	Queen's Counsel (a 'silk')
RSM	Regimental Sergeant Major
RWNGC	Royal West Norfolk Golf Club
SFO	Serious Fraud Office
SMP	Solicitor to the Metropolitan Police
STC	Senior Treasury Counsel
1STC	First Senior Treasury Counsel
TC	Treasury Counsel
WDC	Woman Detective Constable
WDP	Westminster Drug Project